From Red Ink to Roses

The Turbulent Transformation of a Big Ten Program

Rick Telander

SIMON & SCHUSTER

NEW YORK   LONDON   TORONTO   SYDNEY   TOKYO   SINGAPORE

SIMON & SCHUSTER
Rockefeller Center
1230 Avenue of the Americas
New York, New York 10020

Designed by Hyun Joo Kim
Manufactured in the United States of America

10   9   8   7   6   5   4   3   2

Library of Congress Cataloging-in-Publication Data

Telander, Rick.
    From red ink to roses : the turbulent transformation of a Big Ten program /
Rick Telander.
        p.   cm.
    1. University of Wisconsin—Madison—Football—History.   2. College sports
—United States.   3. Intercollegiate Conference of Faculty Representatives.
I. Title.
GV958.U587T45   1994
796.323′63′0977583—dc20   94-25558
                                                                          CIP

ISBN: 0-671-74853-X

PHOTO CREDITS

*Rick Telander, 1, 3, 4, 5, 7, 9, 10, 11, 12, 13, 15, 16, 18, 19, 20, 21, 22, 23, 24, 25, 26,
27, 28, 29, 34, 35; courtesy of the University of Wisconsin Athletic Department, 2, 6,
30, 31, 32, 33; courtesy of Tony Lowery, 8; Peter Rudy, 14; David Wahlberg, 17; Scott
Seid/Wisconsin State Journal, 36.*

"I find the three major administrative problems on a campus are: sex for the students, athletics for the alumni, and parking for the faculty."

—Clark Kerr, President of the University of California at Berkeley, 1958

"The powerlessness of our educational leaders to originate, and their failure to adopt, effective measures for evolving order out of the athletic and gymnastic chaos over which they nominally preside constitutes one of the marvels of our time."

—Report of the United States
Commissioner of Education, 1898

"The weakness of the American university as it exists today lies in its lack of intellectual sincerity. It stands nominally for high intellectual ideals. Its effort at intellectual leadership is diluted with many other efforts in fields wholly foreign to this primary purpose. Intercollegiate athletics form only one of these."

—Carnegie Report on college athletics,
1929

"Whatever may be the limitations which trammel inquiry elsewhere, we believe that the great State University of Wisconsin should ever encourage that continual and fearless sifting and winnowing by which alone the truth can be found."

—Written by the Board of Regents,
1894; inscribed on the Memorial
Plaque, Class of 1919

"The serving of oleomargarine or margarine to students . . . of any state institutions as a substitute for table butter is prohibited . . ."

—Wisconsin state law

Preface

Why the University of Wisconsin?

Why did I spend a year observing an athletic department at a state university historically more noted for its academic achievements than for its prowess afield? Why did I pick this time period (December 1990 to January 1992) to make my observations? And who cares what those observations might be, anyway?

All fair questions. I'll answer them as well as I can.

I chose the University of Wisconsin partly because it's near my house. Well, not exactly near, but only 141 miles away from where I live in a suburb north of Chicago; 282 miles round-trip. (Trust me with these figures; I made over seventy trips to Madison in 375 days, sometimes zipping up and back in the same day. How many traffic tickets did I receive in the process? Zero, thank you.) It was a big-time university I could get to, and I wanted a big-time university to observe.

I could have chosen Northwestern University, also an NCAA Division I sports school, also within driving range, but Northwestern is my alma mater, and I didn't want to stumble over bones of my former irresponsible self while researching a serious work of nonfiction. I also could have chosen Notre Dame, but that school is not overly receptive to intruders. Moreover, the books on Notre Dame sports—well, football—could fill a wing in the Library of Congress. My insight was not needed.

The University of Wisconsin was virgin territory, near enough to me to be accessible, yet far enough away, both physically and emotionally, to be provincial, endearing, mysterious. Books on the UW sports teams, as far as I could tell, consisted entirely of the rah-rah type found at any university. Moreover, I found the administration at UW to be open and basically courteous to outside information-gatherers. And though I had visited the campus only two times prior to 1990, I knew well of Madison's reputation as a party town—that didn't hurt, either.

So UW qualified on several levels as subject material. But why write about *any* athletic department?

I am a sportswriter and the realm of sport is my world, the planet where I reside during most of my waking hours. It is where, for better or worse, I find my truths and pleasures and betrayals. I have written books on the ability of sport to help people transcend their lives (*Heaven Is a Playground*), and on its ability to be hypocritical and deflating (*The Hundred-Yard Lie*), and I wasn't sure I had the knowledge or the desire to write another book on the topic. I was a little burnt out. Still, I wondered if maybe I shouldn't see if someone, some institution, some . . . athletic department . . . couldn't do this sports thing differently. I had written about the stark grace of kids on the playgrounds of Brooklyn, the searing pain of football players on the fields of Oklahoma and Washington and South Carolina; why not take a look at the actions of an entire sports operation at an educational institution in the middle of the country, to see once and for all how the big machine works, and if its goals coincide with those of the people for whom it ostensibly exists, the athletes themselves? Recent tumult in the world of college sport, culminating in the formation in 1989 of the Knight Foundation Commission on Intercollegiate Athletics and its two-year study of the corruption in big-time sport, only piqued my interest. The commission's report stated that, among other things, "big-time athletics programs have taken on all of the trappings of a major entertainment enterprise," and that "the sad truth is that on too many campuses big-time revenue sports are out of control."

Reform was needed, the commission stated, offering its own conservative, yet oddly optimistic, program for universities to follow. One of the eighteen members of this esteemed panel was Donna Shalala, chancellor of the University of Wisconsin. Her own school's athletic department was a stew of red ink and negativity, and this made me even more curious. How would she fix things in her own kitchen?

The reporter in me was fidgeting. A friend of mine from Madison, John Roach, constantly twisted my arm. He said things such as "You wouldn't believe what's going on up here," and "Before you die you have to see Butch's Bologna Bash."

In the end, I agreed. One more book on sport; one more chance for redemption. One more look at people. For in the end, that's what every book is about.

Thirty minutes from my home I would cross the Illinois state line into Wisconsin, and I would know I was a traveler, the adventurer I have always longed to be. There, whizzing past, was Bobby Nelson's Wis-Pride Cheese Store. There was a pumpkin patch, an orchard where you could pick your own apples, a farm where you could saw down your own Christmas tree. There was a porno bookstore, its parking lot full of tractor trailers and motorcycles. There was the Mars Cheese Palace. And there was the Kennel Klub, a roadhouse whose roof was adorned by a huge mouse eating a wedge of cheddar the size of a filing cabinet. I daydreamed. I thought of my days at summer camp in Wisconsin, of chasing turtles on quiet lakes with my buddies in aluminum canoes, the lily pads whispering under the gunnels. I had miles of reverie before and behind me.

It was a fine ride. I enjoyed it all. May you also.

Acknowledgments

OF ALL THE KIND PEOPLE WHO HELPED ME AT THE UNIVERSITY OF WISCONSIN, there were three who rose far above the call of duty. Al Fish and Pat Richter gave me the run of their place and answered every question I threw at them. Rick Aberman was a true friend and guide. I thank them deeply.

I would be remiss also if I didn't give special thanks to another trio who helped me immeasurably on this project. Editor Jeff Neuman talked me through a lot of blind turns and dark tunnels and always made sense. Peter Rudy, a fine writer and wit, collected information that I needed, but didn't know I needed until he got it for me. Young Chad Millman, a basketball player, driver, reporter, sounding board, buddy, and now fellow *Sports Illustrated* employee, did everything necessary, including hanging out with me during one of the best summers of our lives.

1

IT WAS MAY 1986, AND LIFE WAS GOOD AT THE UNIVERSITY OF WISCONSIN. In the preceding months winter had blanketed the fair town of Madison in snow and ice, but the students had weathered the storms in the warm interiors of State Street bars (where it seemed anybody not wearing diapers could belly up for a beer), the ice fishing on the nearby lakes had been better than usual, the traying down Bascom Hill had been delightful, the usual late-night dorm lounge debates over the existence of God and the horrors of imperialist hegemony had raged like nourishing campfires throughout campus, and all the while the promise of a verdant prairie spring had kept the youngsters' spirits up, allowing them to view the cold and snow as just part of the beautiful backdrop on the stage where they frenziedly pursued truth, knowledge, and pedal-to-the-metal fun.

The grownups—the faculty and administrators—were fairly sanguine, too. All of them wanted more money, of course, but most knew deep in their hearts they were blessed to be employed by this great university in a charming city of 180,000. Better to be underpaid in heaven than overpaid in, say, Starkville, Mississippi. Wisconsin is a unique state, and anyone who arrives from another part of the country quickly realizes as much. Grounded in the work ethic of the Eastern Europeans who became dairy farmers in settling the rolling land, Wisconsinites believe in the value of hard labor and serious education. Being a student at the University of Wisconsin is an honor to the state's residents, and working at the university is perceived as a prestigious way to make a living. With a total enrollment of 43,000—30,000 undergraduates and 13,000 grad students—and a flock of highly respected instructors and researchers, the University of Wisconsin at Madison (its full title) is routinely ranked among the top thirty or so universities nationwide with regard to educational value and academic integrity. A 1988 poll conducted by *U.S. News & World Report* that ranked American universities according to their overall academic reputation listed Wisconsin seventeenth in a group that included almost four hundred schools. The *Froke Guide to Colleges 1993* gave UW-Madison its highest academic ranking, making the school just one of eight public universities to receive a five-star rating. Virtually any kind of poll examining the things a university deals in—education, diversity of thought, dollar value, potential of graduates in the workplace and so on—shows UW to be near the head of the class. Not only is Wisconsin the nation's fourth largest institution of higher learning, but its total budget of $1 billion is the largest in the country. *Big* and *good* are words often used to describe the university. In 1986 UW was feeling good about itself in a big way, charging through the materialistic eighties with a contentedness that was soothing to both the school and to Madison residents who had weathered the divisive turbulence of the radical sixties and the uncertainties of the inflationary seventies.

This contentedness carried over to the athletic department; the department virtually embodied good cheer. With a budget of more than $10 million to support twenty-seven male and female sports, the department often came dangerously close to not paying its bills, but somehow by the end of each fiscal year it always managed to balance its budget. Athletic director Elroy "Crazylegs" Hirsch, a former Wisconsin football star and a man who rarely met a beer he didn't like, bubbled with enough enthusiasm to put a happy spin on anything short of pure disaster—and there were no pure disasters at Wisconsin.

Though never a powerhouse like Ohio State or Michigan, the UW football team chugged steadily along under regular-guy head coach Dave McClain, with minor successes and always the promise of better days ahead. McClain's overall record was an unremarkable

46–42–3 in eight seasons, but he had led the team to a peak of sorts in recent years, going 7–5, 7–5, 7–4, 7–4–1 from 1981 to 1984 and garnering appearances in three postseason bowl games. The bowls were obscure ones, to be sure—the Garden State Bowl in 1981 (a 28–21 loss to Tennessee); the Independence Bowl in 1982 (a 14–3 win over Kansas State); the Hall of Fame Bowl in 1984 (a 20–19 loss to Kentucky)—but they were bowls all the same. Before McClain came along, no Wisconsin football team had played in a bowl since 1963.

The football Badgers had faltered somewhat the previous season, 1985, going 5–6 in a rather schizoid campaign that included a 12–7 win over mighty Ohio State and a 14–17 loss to lowly Northwestern. But that was okay; losing a few games, even to lessers, was always okay at Wisconsin, as long as 77,745-seat Camp Randall Stadium, the eleventh largest college-owned stadium in the country, stayed pretty much filled. And as long as the goofy, giddy Badger fans were allowed to drink and party and rock in the stands as if celebrating some bacchanalian festival known only to themselves, the cash would keep flowing into the box office. Average attendance at Badger home games had not dipped below 70,000 for twelve consecutive years, despite the fact UW had winning teams in only half of those seasons. Fans cheered anything good their teams might do, seldom booed the bad, drank themselves silly (at least some did), and then stuck around for the wacky "Fifth Quarter," a cornball postgame ritual of participatory singing, dancing, sentimentality, and profanity led by the UW band and cheerleaders.

Though attendance rose or dipped slightly with the performance of the team, it never fell to precarious levels. A .500 season would mean chaos and bankruptcy at a place like the University of Michigan, but at Wisconsin it just meant it was time for fans to have another beer and start thinking about next season. Football basically paid the way for the other school sports, all of which (except hockey and, in a good year, basketball) lost money on their own, so it was a fortunate thing that UW students and boosters didn't demand perfection of the football squad. There seemed to be an essential empathy with the football team among Wisconsin fans, a decency that probably arose from their having seen the way random, uncontrollable events could bring hard times or prosperity to even the best farmers back in Antigo, Friendship, and Black Earth, that allowed them to tolerate such things as back-to-back 4–7 seasons (1979 and 1980) without protest. If a herd of Holsteins could give less milk due to random electrical surges delivered to their udders by faulty milking machines—as often happened on Wisconsin dairy farms—then a football team could go sour for equally uncontrollable reasons.

As the crowd gathered for the annual spring football game in May 1986, such stoic acceptance was replaced, as always at this time of year, by a sunny optimism. The day itself helped create the feeling; the sun shone down on the students in the stands, many of whom had brought coolers and blankets and Frisbees with them and who quickly turned the stadium into their own beach party. McClain, who was dressed in a bright plaid shirt and a neon-blue blazer, was in good spirits as well. "He looked like he was going to an Easter celebration or getting ready to play golf," recalls George Wilcox, then a sports reporter for the *Daily Cardinal*, the student newspaper. The forty-eighty-year-old McClain's only real problem was determining who would be his quarterback for the fall: red team helmsman Bud Keyes or white team QB Mike Howard. Wilcox interviewed McClain after the game and remembers him as being "upbeat and smiling the whole way."

McClain, whose salary was a mere fifty thousand dollars a year, was one of the lowest-paid coaches in the Big Ten, but he wasn't driven by money. "He was an eternal optimist," says his wife, Judy. "But he knew Wisconsin with its history and nature was never going to be in the top three in the conference. He had drive and he worked hard until game time, then whatever happened, happened. He slept like a log the night after a game. And the night before, too."

He slept well that weekend, and on Monday, as Wilcox's game story was hitting the local distribution points around campus, McClain was back at the stadium, preparing to do his usual vigorous physical workout. He walked past baseball player Scott Cepicky, who was pedaling on a stationary bike near the wrestling room and kidded him about missing the spring game. Cepicky was the team's punter, but McClain had given him permission to play in a baseball game against Illinois on Saturday. "I guess you're a big-time baseball player now," winked the coach. "Too good to punt."

"Hey, you'll just have to pay me more money," Cepicky laughed.

Cepicky, from St. Louis, was close to McClain. "He was my father away from my father," says the young man, now a first baseman in the Chicago White Sox organization. The two talked about everything, including the fact that McClain's family had a history of heart problems, that McClain's mother, father, and brother had all died from heart ailments. That's why McClain stayed in shape, to try to ward off the genetic threat.

"But he never got down," says Cepicky. "He smiled all the time—he loved being around young guys. He used to say, 'I know my days are numbered. When I'm gonna go, I'm gonna go.' But it didn't upset him."

Wearing a rubberized suit, McClain worked out, pedaling furiously on a stationary bike, and then went into the sauna, where he took a seat next to Dr. Stephen Zimmerman, a physician in the university's medical school and a casual friend. The two men talked briefly about the spring game, and McClain commented on how much he had enjoyed taking the senior football players out the night before to a restaurant in New Glarus. Then he wiped sweat from his brow and sighed.

"I feel like I have the flu," he said. "Or maybe it's just a hangover from last night."

The men chuckled. Zimmerman left the sauna briefly to cool down in the shower, and when he returned he noticed that the coach seemed to have nodded off. "He was snoring," recalls Zimmerman. "He'd been talking when I left. He was still sitting up when I came back in."

In moments McClain was making no sound at all. This was more than sleep. The doctor felt his own heart race. He grabbed the coach and laid him down on the floor and threw open the door, screaming for help. He began CPR on McClain, and within minutes paramedics had arrived to take the unconscious man to St. Mary's Hospital. But it was over; Dave McClain was dead of a massive heart attack.

Dr. Zimmerman wrote a letter to Judy McClain later, telling her that in his professional opinion her husband had not suffered at the end. Scott Cepicky rode his motorcycle to the McClain house a couple days later to tell Judy how sorry he was and to apologize for not being able to attend the funeral—he had a damned baseball game he had to play in. Most people in Madison mourned the loss of a good man, not knowing how important that one man had been to the financial health of the athletic department, or how his passing would serve as the dividing line between old and new days, between innocence and cynicism, between good-natured sport and cold-hearted business, between the way the world used to be and the way it is now.

"Nobody had ever mentioned the word *budget* before then," says Wilcox. "When McClain died it was the beginning of the end. That's when everything changed."

2

IT IS MID-DECEMBER 1990, AND SNOW FALLS FROM THE GRAY SKY, DUSTING the streets of Madison in powdery white. Rick Aberman, the psychologist for the University of Wisconsin athletic department, steps out of the Dave McClain Athletic Facility, takes a breath of the chill air, checks his watch, and begins his daily run. Lean as a marathoner, with long curly hair and sharp, youthful features, the thirty-five-year-old Aberman could almost pass for one of the star runners on the Badgers' cross-country team as he trots gingerly over the icy asphalt.

Plumes of vapor jet from his mouth as he turns right out of the parking lot and heads up Monroe Street past the bunkerlike Copper Grid Bar, where half pints of brandy to go are sold only on football Saturdays (all other days you have to drink your brandy in glasses inside), past the legendarily grubby Mickey's Dairy Bar, where a full, nearly palatable breakfast can be had for less than three dollars, and onto the sidewalk that will lead him past shops, cafés, and banks to the thirty-two–acre University Arboretum that nestles up against the south shore of Lake Wingra. Skinny as he is, Aberman thinks nothing of the cold. He is from Minneapolis, and running through all kinds of weather is one of the things that delights him about his solitary sport. A few years ago he ran on a day when the windchill was sixty degrees below zero. That was kind of stupid, he admits, but you gotta do what you gotta do. Run around the indoor track in the Fieldhouse? Never. Talk about boredom. Plus, when he goes for six or seven miles through the streets and countryside, he gets into a zone where he can think.

Aberman's position in the athletic department is an unusual one, perhaps a unique one among all major colleges. He was hired four years ago to help athletes with their mental health. He wasn't there to be a motivator, or to concern himself with an athlete's performance in any way, except as it affected the athlete himself or herself. The young people who came to see him—of their own will; he merely made himself available to them—were his patients, and his responsibility was to them as individuals trying to understand, and cope with, their roles in what was becoming a full-tilt business rather than amateur sport.

Aberman had earned his undergraduate, master's, and doctoral degrees at Wisconsin; he had, he realized, spent more than a third of his life in Madison. He knew that his position within the athletic department was something of an anomaly, one that reflected one of the best features of the state itself, and also some of its inherent contradictions.

Though Wisconsin always ranks high on any national list of "healthy" states—that is, places with low infant mortality, accessible health care, clean air, low violent crime rates, good hospitals, and the like—it also leads the nation in morbid obesity. Almost one-fourth of Wisconsin men and one-third of Wisconsin women are obese, meaning they are 20 percent over their desirable weight. Aberman sees these people everywhere he goes: in their snowmobile suits in the winter, in their deer-hunting camouflage and international-orange outfits in the fall, in their shorts and T-shirts in summer, in their Wisconsin-red pants and Bucky Badger sweatshirts in the spring. There are over a million of them in this state of five million citizens. At five feet eleven inches and 140 pounds, Aberman moves cautiously among these people, looking at times in his wiry mobility like a representative of another species.

And why are so many Wisconsinites plump? Surely, it has to do with the fact that this is the Dairy State, that cheese and cream and butterfat are exalted products here—the lifeblood of the farming industry, unquestioned staples at many a Wisconsin dinner table.

Wisconsin perennially ranks first nationally in its number of milk cows, in milk production, and in butter production. It also is first in the output of American, Muenster, brick, Italian, and blue cheese, and second in Swiss cheese production. And then there are the bratwurst and knackwurst, the beloved repast of Wisconsin's vast German and Eastern European population. And, of course, there is all the drinking; beer in Wisconsin is virtually another form of water. The state's Major League Baseball team is, after all, the Brewers, while its pro football team in Green Bay commemorates the cholesterol-building meatpacking industry. Add in the whiskey and brandy for all those nights spent sitting around the poker table at deer camp or hanging out at a roadhouse in Wautoma or hunkering down at a neighborhood bar in Milwaukee or Appleton or Sheboygan and you have a virtual recipe for bad health. A recent study ranked Wisconsin second in the country in its number of drunken drivers on the state roads. The Budweiser Beer theme song was adopted in 1973 as the UW favored fight song and—with the word *Wis-con-sin* replacing *Bud-weis-er*—played by the school band whenever it performed.

And yet the state was so progressive in so many ways. Its university passed the nation's first hate-speech law, making it illegal to say bad things about one's fellow students. It was home to both the Progressive Party's presidential candidate (and former governor) Robert "Fighting Bob" LaFollete *and* the neo-fascist U.S. Senator and paranoid Commie-baiter Joseph "Tailgunner Joe" McCarthy. The great architect Frank Lloyd Wright was born in Wisconsin. So was filmmaker Orson Welles and artist Georgia O'Keeffe. And so was Liberace. Madison is where the student anti–Vietnam War riots exploded through the streets in the sixties, but it's also the place where the athletic department stages in its Fieldhouse an annual fund-raiser called Butch's Bologna Bash, named for a booster who grinds sausage in his garage and attended by ten thousand fans and many UW athletes, all of whom ingest huge quantities of fatty meat, cheese, and beer while singing "If You Want to Be a Badger" and dancing in the corridors of the creaky old building.

As his feet fall on the muffled turf of the Arboretum, Aberman thinks, as he has before, that maybe it is time for him to get out of town and move on with his life. But maybe not. Things have gotten so screwed up in the athletic department: everybody is feeling the stress of the current situation. The department is $1.95 million in the red, though the deficit is closer to $6 million if you count deferred maintenance projects and needed cash reserves. This is mostly the result of declining football attendance, increasing costs, and bad management. So much of the problem goes back to the day Dave McClain died, and to the way things were done stupidly, naïvely, and backwards from that moment on.

First, McClain's assistant, Jim Hilles, was made interim head football coach for 1986, but was given no power. The department canned him after one 3–9 season, and recruiting was hurt by the lack of stability in the program.

Next, Elroy Hirsch hired North Dakota State football coach Don Morton in November 1986. Morton came from an NCAA Division II program and knew little about the pressures of leading a Division I Big Ten team.

Half a year later, in May 1987, Wisconsin hired a new athletic director, Ade Sponberg, who happened to be Morton's buddy and the former athletic director at North Dakota State. Sponberg had been responsible for overseeing North Dakota State's eighteen Division II sports with an annual budget of $1.6 million. UW had twenty-seven Division I sports and a 1987–88 budget of $10.4 million.

Continuing the backwards hiring procedure, UW named Donna Shalala, the former Hunter College (N.Y.) president, its new chancellor on New Year's Day, 1988. She should have been hired first, so that she could have hired the athletic director, who in turn would have hired the coach. A stunned Shalala was greeted with the news that football revenue for the 1987 season was seven hundred thousand dollars short of budget and that the athletic department's resources were gone.

Football attendance went even farther down the pipe in the next few years, following the downward spiral of Morton's ignoble teams. The Badgers went 3–8, 1–10, and 2–9 from 1987 to 1989; average attendance dropped by almost 10,000 each of those years—from 68,000 in Hilles's only year, 1986, to 59,300 in 1987, to 49,300 in 1988, to 41,700 in 1989. At that rate, the stadium would be a parking lot by 1993.

To start the 1989 season, Wisconsin lost 51–3 to the University of Miami on national television, leading state senator Gary George to call for "drastic action" in the athletic department because of such "humiliating defeats." Morale in the department reached an all-time low.

Most of the athletic department buildings and fields are crumbling or substandard; the Fieldhouse, built in 1930, is without question the most primitive basketball facility in the Big Ten; the men's and women's soccer teams never know from day to day where they will be practicing, due to a lack of available space. The era of computers seems to have skipped the bookkeeping side of the department entirely. And yet everybody was so saddened by McClain's untimely passing that the department quickly went out and built the $9.5 million McClain Athletic Facility, an enclosed eighty-yard football field with elaborate locker, meeting, and coaching rooms, even though only 7 percent of the funds needed to pay for the structure had been raised.

Late in 1989, Shalala fired Sponberg, then "reassigned" Morton to another, undisclosed, "job" within the university, before giving him some cash and booting him out of UW entirely. Then Shalala and the board of regents hired Pat Richter as the new AD; he then hired former Notre Dame assistant Barry Alvarez as the new head football coach—all at substantial pay increases over the salaries of their predecessors. A new accountant named Tami Holmquist came in from the private sector to make sense of the books; a bean counter/head-chopper with the unlikely name of Al Fish was sent in by the state government to see what the hell was going on in this little byzantine enclave; and now nobody in the department knows which side is up.

A report on the athletic department status was recently written by a group called the Long-range Planning Task Force, a committee put together by the university to make recommendations to the athletic department on how to cut out the nonsense. Among the comments: "Planning should have occurred long ago. . . . Football is of primary concern, as it is the major source of funding for our non-income sports programs." And then the kicker: "The past is unacceptable."

But there was also a thought expressed by the committee that showed how the predicament at Wisconsin was part of a problem that extended far beyond the boundaries of this state. Big-time university sports bring entertainment to the masses and money to athletic department coffers, but the product, noted the report, had to be "exciting, entertaining, and competitive" to draw fans and revenue. To make sports programs all those things, athletic departments must throw more and more money at the process itself, to buy a competitive edge. It was a crazy, vicious cycle, with nobody willing to stop it. "What is occurring," the report summed up, "is that the cost of collegiate sports programs, in general, is out of control, and knowledgeable people in the field know it."

Aberman knows he is not a big contributor to the problem; his paltry salary is less than what a first-year mail carrier makes. His task is to deal with the consequences of this system, as it affects the lives of the nine hundred or so young men and women for whom the whole structure supposedly exists.

Aberman jogs out of the fields and trees and back onto the Monroe Street sidewalk, feeling the warmth his body has generated in the cold. As he heads back toward the debt-ridden McClain facility, he thinks fleetingly of his mentor, family therapy pioneer Carl Whitaker, the man who taught Aberman so much when he trained under Whitaker at the university hospital. In his book *From Psyche to System*, Whitaker listed a number of axioms and homilies, sayings to ponder and take strength from, and one often pops into Aberman's mind: "A person, by definition, is one who is alone." This is true. Aberman had always felt somehow outside the mainstream, a loner who liked people but didn't quite share their agendas. His parallax view gave him a perspective that was like that of a man in the cold looking in through a window at a crowded family gathering. It was a gathering he wanted to join—the athletic department—but he wasn't sure how to do so.

One other thing strikes him like a bolt from the blue as he slows to a walk in the parking lot: the athletic department building, the main entrance right there in Camp Randall Stadium itself, looks remarkably like a giant wedge of cheese.

3

Barry Baum walks swiftly toward Vilas Hall, where his creative writing class is meeting. He keeps his head up, looking at the faces of students passing him by, wondering how many of the students know who he is, and how many of them would attack him if they did know. At five feet six-and-a-half inches tall, Baum is shorter than almost every male he passes, but it is the very large students—the athletes—he is most concerned about, the big football players who might want to give him a piece of their minds.

Not that he is overly concerned even about that. A native of Brooklyn, with more than a few mannerisms of the classic city guy from Flatbush Avenue, he has thick skin and a basic cheerfulness that carry him blithely through the world. He is always smiling about something or other, and he knows only one way to go at the small problems of daily existence: with full-tilt, optimistic assertiveness.

He has been a sportswriter and columnist for the UW student newspaper, the *Daily Cardinal*, since 1987, and he prides himself on taking on the tough issues other student reporters—particularly those limp-wristed milquetoasts at the rival, conservative, establishment-tool *Badger-Herald*—won't touch. He has written about the lousy basketball teams at UW; the bad job done by Steve Yoder, head basketball coach, the financial straits of the athletic department; the poor facilities in and around Camp Randall; the losing attitude of the entire campus; on and on. But he never got a rip-roaring, nasty, mean-spirited response from any of his subjects until he took on the new Alvarez-led football program.

It started with a story he wrote on the front page of the *Daily Cardinal* on November 2nd about third-string center Erik Olsen, who had just quit the team. Under the heading UW FOOTBALL PLAYER QUESTIONS DISCIPLINARY ACTION Baum told how Olsen was forced by offensive line coach Bill Callahan to run the stadium stairs for making repeated mistakes in a pass protection drill during a midweek practice. Olsen ran until he vomited, "with his helmet on," Baum noted, and then rejoined practice "without a break." Overall, the story was balanced and fair, reporting mostly facts; Callahan and Alvarez were both quoted, as was starting center Dave Senczyszyn, who said, "I would question making someone run for one mistake, but it wasn't one mistake with Erik Olsen."

Olsen himself was not quoted, having talked to Baum but then requesting that his comments be kept off the record. Baum honored that request. Line coach Callahan showed a degree of cynicism and toughness that Baum duly noted, letting the coach's words speak for themselves:

"A lot of players throw up," Callahan said. "They eat before practice and run around a lot. It's no big deal."

Apparently, Callahan, who acknowledged that different coaches use different techniques to discipline their players, will not change his.

"Is there a limit to the amount of mistakes a player can make? Sure, I made him run some stairs. That's really tough, isn't it?"

So what was the big deal? A player quit, a coach acted tough; it was college football at its usual. The problem centered on Baum's opening sentence, which read, "Reports of possible abuse have surfaced concerning Erik Olsen . . ." and the headline mentioning "disciplinary action," which Baum did not write; it was penned by the *Daily Cardinal* sports editor Mike Bresnehan after Baum filed the story. Small points, perhaps, but not to Alvarez, who was outraged by the story. He had sports information director Steve Malchow inform

Baum at a football press conference that Baum would not be allowed to talk to coaches or players anymore. Shortly thereafter the *Daily Cardinal* received a letter from fifteen offensive linemen ripping Baum and the paper for printing the story.

Entering Vilas Hall, Baum stops to pull the letter from his briefcase and read it again. "You should be ashamed, Mr. Baum," it begins. "You had no right to accuse our coach of abusing his players. . . . We don't deny that coach Callahan has worked us harder than any other coach that we have ever had. But he does this out of love. . . . To write a story like you did shows us just how ignorant a journalist you really are, Mr. Baum. To manipulate people into answering loaded questions like you did only proves one thing—that you, Mr. Baum, need to retake a course in news reporting. If you would have taken a little more time to talk to a few more people, like the whole offensive line, none of this garbage you call a story would have been printed." The tirade was signed, "The 1990 Wisconsin Badgers Defensive Line: Nick Polczinski, David Senczyszyn, Rick Godfrey, John Filiatraut, Ben Hoffman, Jim Basten, David Rapps, Chuck Belin, Brian Patterson, Mark Lynch, Brady Pierce, Jeff Miller, Jeff Rasmussen, Mike Verstegen, Tyler Adam."

Baum puts the letter away and heads up the stairs. Loaded questions? What loaded questions? Coach, do you often run players until they puke? What's loaded about that? It's as basic as you can get. What was he supposed to ask—Excuse me, sir, may I kneel at your feet? He is a trained journalist, after all, not an apologist, not a jelly-spined PR flack! So he had been banned from interviewing anybody on the football staff or team; he couldn't interview certain employees or students at the very institute of higher learning where he paid tuition and worked on the student newspaper, ostensibly to report campus news to his compatriots. He didn't understand it at all. Wasn't there a First Amendment anymore? The adult world mystified Barry Baum.

In truth, if you questioned him closely, Baum might not even be sure what the First Amendment says; he just knew he wanted to be a hard-driving shoot-from-the-hip journalist like his hero, Peter Vecsey, the wise-guy New Yorker who was then writing about the NBA for *USA TODAY*. The *Daily Cardinal* was going to be his launching pad, but how could he soar when he could barely talk to his own football team?

After class, Baum wanders over to Dotty's to order a chicken sandwich and ponder his floundering career as a scribe. Dotty Dumpling's Dowery is a little hamburger joint a block from the stadium on Regent Street. There are strange dolls, antiques, and sports relics stuck to the walls and hanging from the ceiling of the noisy, dilapidated, order-from-the-counter restaurant. "Tough times for newspapers," Baum says. "Even the *Cardinal* is losing money. I get six dollars a story now, and I used to get eight dollars as a freshman. So sometimes I string for the *Dubuque Telegraph-Herald*, if I'm already at a game and they need something. They pay fifteen dollars for a feature and twenty dollars for a game." He shrugs. It's not a big amount, he admits, but a check is a check. It means you're a pro— though sometimes even that is debatable.

Baum licks barbecue sauce off his fingers and says, "It's funny, this business. I covered the Packers-49ers exhibition game here for UPI, who never pay—they still owe me money—and I called Dubuque and asked if they wanted a game story. I mean, I was already at the game, so how much would it cost them? Twenty bucks? They said no, they couldn't pay for it, because it wasn't in the budget. So I wrote it anyway and sent it to them. And they ran it huge in a big box on the front page of sports."

Baum laughs outright at this. Everything he has done has been a struggle: The short Jewish kid who wanted to be a hoops star in the Big Apple (he actually was the starting point guard for his St. Ann's School team in Brooklyn Heights); the New Yorker trying to make it in America's Dairyland; the college student with average grades trying to transfer into the School of Journalism as a sophomore, being accepted on the strength of his good cheer and unbridled chutzpah—he sees the humor in all this. Consider the letter of recommendation written by one of his teachers, broadcast news professor Tom Grimes; Baum took three courses from Grimes, and Grimes wrote, "I can say without reservation that he was the most outstanding journalism student I've had in my nearly ten years of teaching. . . . When Barry applied for admission to the School of Journalism last year, his grade point average was just a little below the minimum average necessary for admission. In 99 percent of the cases, such students are denied admission. Not only was Barry admitted, but the testimonials from faculty to his energy, intelligence, industriousness, and overall high quality as a professional were endless. The department chair had to call order—literally—so we would have a vote to admit and get on to other business.

"What most distinguishes Barry from other students is his re-portorial persistence. The man has no shame! He simply won't back down. I've seen him confront university officials with embarrassing information, which he's dug up, and be berated and otherwise vilified by those officials at press conferences and in print. All other undergraduates I know would have cowered and slunk off. Not Barry.

"As the department chair stated in his recommendation of Barry, Barry will succeed in the profession regardless of his GPA. We could either bow to the inevitable, and allow him in the program, or keep him out and see him succeed anyway."

Tough times, thinks Baum again. Not that he's depressed. It's just that things seemed more clear-cut back when he was younger and really full of spit and vinegar, when he was a ball boy for his beloved New York Knickerbockers from 1984 to 1987, for instance. "I knew no one back then," he says wistfully. "I got the job by pounding the pavement, by writing letters to Mike Saunders, the trainer. I found out he was the guy to know. I called the Knicks constantly, telling them all I wanted was an interview. I was fifteen, and finally I had the job."

He also somehow talked his way into hosting his own cable TV interview show on one of Manhattan Cable's public access channels, calling the program *Courtside with Barry Baum*. "It was channel D, the same one that after midnight had psychics on, crazy people, sex stuff with Robin Byrd, the sex queen," he recalls. "When I was with the Knicks they weren't very good—Bill Cartwright got hurt, Marvin Webster got hurt, Truck Robinson did, Bernard King. I remember a starting lineup of Darrell Walker, Louis Orr, Ron Cavenall, Pat Cummings, and Rory Sparrow. They went 23–59, 24–58, 23–59—very consistent—during my three years. And my show was always touch and go, too. One night Al Lewis, Grandpa Munster on *The Munsters*, called up and said he wanted to talk, but he didn't turn down the sound on his TV and we got too much feedback. Another time Louis Orr showed up twenty-seven minutes late for the show, which was only twenty-eight minutes long. He walked on wearing his hat and coat and the show ended."

Baum relished his nights as ball boy, feeling the energy of the Manhattan crowd at Madison Square Garden washing over him, convincing him that playing sports or talking about sports or, better yet, writing about sports was his destiny.

"My first game as a ball boy was unreal," he says. "Opening night, a sellout with nineteen thousand people, and I sat under the basket with a towel to wipe the floor if somebody fell. Isiah Thomas went down at midcourt and I ran out and started wiping, and he was just lying there forever, so I wiped around him, like he was a body—it was so scary, just an amazing thing with all those people and the noise and the lights. Then early on a net got caught on the rim, and Hubie Brown, the Knicks' coach, is yelling at me, 'Get the fucking net!' Screaming at me. I went out, but what could I do? I was only five-four at the time. Another ball boy jumped up and got the net. Hubie, he used to scream and make everybody so *tense*. The players were so nice, but the coaches . . ."

Baum finishes his sandwich and furrows his brow. His thoughts have returned to Wisconsin, to his unfathomable battle with Alvarez. His mission is so straight ahead—get the news, make some amusing comments about the news, get people to read the news—that he marvels at the complexities surrounding that simple chore. Street-smart and aggressive, Baum is also one of the most naïve people on earth.

"I don't get it," he continues. "Why are coaches like they are? Why do they have this . . . *attitude?*"

Presently, his focus changes and he thinks about what might have been at Wisconsin had a couple of coaching legends made their way to Madison. "Bobby Knight was going to come here, you know," he says. "And Bo Schembechler was coming, too. This was a while ago, but with Schembechler, they put him in a hotel far from campus, didn't tell him what was going on, and he said the hell with this place. Imagine that—Knight and Schembechler! As a writer, I guess, well, it would be fun to go to an NCAA tournament or the Rose Bowl every now and then."

His smile fades, though, as he realizes the predicament such snarling dictators might put him in. "I did talk to one of the writers at the *Indiana Daily Student*, and he told me, of course, that Knight doesn't give interviews to student writers. I asked him why, and he said, 'Because he's Knight.' He only talks to this guy Bob Hammel of the Bloomington paper, a guy who goes everywhere with Knight. What is that? If they didn't allow everybody to come along, I wouldn't go. How does a guy like Hammel know what to write, when you're just like somebody's PR guy?"

Questions, learning experiences, hypocrisy, hidden agendas, power, rules of the game—Barry Baum, student of this thing called the real world, struggles with his lessons, making progress but always being amazed by each new page in the book. He pays his bill and walks past some loud girls dipping french fries into pools of ketchup. He walks across campus to the parking lot where he keeps his maroon 1989 Nissan 240SX, a surprise gift from his father two years ago for doing well in school. He needs to run some errands today and he fires up the car. The Wisconsin license plates read BBFB.

Barry Baum from Brooklyn, of course.

4

THE SNOW IS STILL FALLING SOFTLY AS ATHLETIC DIRECTOR PAT RICHTER, athletic board faculty head and chairman Roger Formisano, and administrative official Al Fish walk into the oak-paneled main hall of the Madison Club, the elegant private eating establishment frequented by the movers and shakers of Madison's business and political world. The lovely, old four-story red-brick building is located only three blocks from the state capitol building and just a half mile from the eastern edge of the UW campus. The building perches like a boathouse high above the shore of Lake Monona, one of the four main lakes that bisect Madison and give the city so much of its seasonal charm. But right now Lake Monona is frozen and desolate as the arctic tundra, and Richter shivers as he looks through the large windows at the back of the Madison Club.

"I wish they'd do something with that," he says, waving at the stark shoreline with a touch of disgust in his voice. "Back in 1954 they were going to build a Frank Lloyd Wright building, a convention center that would go out over the lake. It would have cost four million back then. Now they've resurrected the proposal and it'll cost thirty million."

Fish and Formisano nod. How Madison.

This town, many have noted, often paralyzes itself with fits of self-examination and furious debate over the obvious. While Madison pondered every aspect of a much-needed fairly priced convention center designed by the most famous architect in American history, other towns simply went out and built the damned things (without Wright's touch) as fast as they could, leaving Madison in the dust, convention center–wise. "Madison is a great place to be against something," is how Fish puts it. A tall, cheerful, witty, and sometimes downright silly man, the thirty-nine-year-old Fish had recently read a book called *Madison: A History of the Formative Years* and found in it several passages that delighted him with their accurate depiction of the modern Madison mind, even though the book addressed city history from 1846 to 1920. One paragraph in particular sang to him:

> At the core of the Madison personality was an intense awareness of the city's extraordinary natural beauty and the honor of being *both* the capital of a great commonwealth and the home of its university. Madison leaders were terribly proud of this distinction and sought to redeem the great promise inherent in these rare circumstances. The challenge of fulfilling the exciting potential of these circumstances brought out the dreamer and the doer in an unusually large number of citizens. It lured people away from their pleasures and duties, made them . . . take sides in controversies almost against their will. . . . This is not to say that Madisonians worked to achieve the *same* goals. In fact, the city's heterogeneous, relatively affluent, and well-educated population were notorious for their alacrity to argue about almost anything. The months and often years needed to reach agreement on many issues were almost legendary.

Amen.

"All Frank Lloyd Wright's known around here for," says Formisano with a shrug, "is for moving to Spring Green and being a famous adulterer."

Fish looks out at the snowy landscape and comments on the high school football star from the Deep South who came to Madison recently on a recruiting trip. "The kid wore his coat and gloves even when he was indoors. Never took them off. He just stood there and looked at the snow, like it might come inside."

Shortly the group is joined by head football coach Barry Alvarez, a sturdy, olive-skinned, balding man of forty-two with piercing blue eyes under hooded lids. Dressed in slacks and a bulky wool sweater, Alvarez, who has just finished his first season at Wisconsin with a 1–10 record, has the prematurely weary look of a man who knows conclusively that the world is unfair.

Basketball coach Steve Yoder soon walks in, dusting snow from the shoulders of his overcoat. Short, blond, blue-eyed, with the intensity of a debt-riddled car salesman, Yoder always looks as if disaster lies waiting for him just around the corner; in that regard he resembles Alvarez, and this may be more a function of a "revenue sport" coach's job than of his genetic makeup. Yoder always seems on the verge of being fired for some reason or other; last season his team finished 14–17, this year it is 3–4 and needs to do well to keep the critics down. Finally, hockey coach Jeff Sauer, fresh from leading his team to the 1989–90 national championship, walks in. Sauer is forty-seven, with thinning hair and one permanently bloodshot eye. He needs no one to help him run his incredibly successful hockey program, but he is continually upset with the way the NCAA and its rules committees and the half-witted athletic department constantly try to undermine his juggernaut. Hockey will pay its bills, win games, pack the Dane County Memorial Coliseum with raving beer-chugging fans, and even throw some cash into the school's coffers—if everybody would just keep their mitts off him and his boys.

Richter, a tall, athletically built man who starred for the Badgers as an end on the legendary 1963 Rose Bowl team (legendary because in nearly three decades, UW has not been close to a return to Pasadena) before playing nine years in the NFL and earning his law degree at Wisconsin, is not a demonstrative, banner-waving charismatic leader. The guidance he brings to any group comes from quiet perseverance and hard, reasonable, solid work, not from tub-thumping or point-running. (Hot-flash creativity and ebullience are more Fish's characteristics, and Richter and Fish work well together because of that, the way a skilled straight man and a good comedian mix.) Small talk with the guys, friendly joshing and sports chatter—those are the things that come easiest to Richter, the things he seems to enjoy most.

"You're the only guy I've ever known," says Richter to Formi-sano, "who keeps his ties in the front closet with the overcoats."

Formisano chuckles. "That's because I take my tie off as soon as I walk in the door to my house. I don't leave it on to impress the kids."

All this locker-room sparring ends abruptly when Chancellor Donna Shalala, all four feet eleven and three-quarters of her, walks into the hall in front of the private dining room where the group will eat. She's wearing a white blouse with blue polka dots, a blue skirt, and a cardigan sweater, and her short, dark hair still has a few un-melted snowflake crystals in it, sparkling in the light. Her electric smile flashes from man to man, putting each at ease, but also letting each know by its glimmering radiance who precisely is in charge here. Though a foot and a half shorter than Richter, Shalala seems through sheer physical exuberance to dwarf the man. The others, too.

She is chilled to the bone, she says. "I just walked over from the capitol," she tells the men. Then she shakes her head, still smiling. "Those legislators aren't paid enough. They drive me crazy, they're so dumb."

She means it, too. Shalala always says what's on her mind, no sugar-coating tolerated. "Thirty-five thousand dollars isn't enough for a person in that field. Maybe for four months' work, but not for what they're supposed to do. The best this state was run was when the agricultural interests ran things. A bunch of farmers, young farm-ers, with good ideas."

Shalala, one of the fraternal twin daughters of James and Edna Shalala—a real estate salesman and a physical education teacher/lawyer of Lebanese descent—grew up in an inner-city neighborhood in Cleveland and resembles a farm maid about as much as a dragster resembles a tricycle. But she admires anyone who works hard, knows his job, and pursues excellence. That pursuit is a holy thing to this woman who just a month earlier was called by *Ladies' Home Journal* "arguably the most important woman in academia today." She was hired in January 1988 from Hunter College in New York City, a Division III commuter school, and readily acknowledged there were things she didn't understand about a huge research institution like Wisconsin. "What I understand is excellence," she said when she was hired. Of UW football, she told the *Milwaukee Journal*, "There are farmers in the fields who stop when the game comes on. From one end of this state to the other, there are people who haven't gone to the university, who don't have kids at the university, but who identify with the Badgers. They are taxpayers. They want winning teams, but they want honest teams. It has to get better."

She is here today to meet with her athletic department, to keep the dialogue going about improvements, the deficit, recruits, anything at all, and to keep the wavering department compass aimed precisely at the big *E* in Excellence. She doesn't buy the notion that success in big-time revenue-producing sport is counter to the mission of an academic institution, or that a civilized school such as Wisconsin might not want to get down in the mud with such rough-and-ready football powers as Miami, Auburn, and Texas A&M. To this human dynamo, a workaholic and perfectionist who was so hands-on at Hunter College that she personally tested floor waxes for the school's hallways, striving to be the best does not run counter to anything, except to losing.

This is not a common perception at Wisconsin. When Shalala canned Don Morton, the *Daily Cardinal* skewered her with a cartoon showing her clinging to the mast of the sunken athletic department ship, screaming to an empty ocean, "Take a swim, Don Morton! I can handle this alone! Full speed ahead!" But Shalala is nothing if not a team player, adept at making others catch her enthusiasm and work hard because of it. She was scorched by the nastiness she found when she went to Washington, D.C., to work for the Department of Housing and Urban Development under Jimmy Carter in 1977, and she learned how vulnerable a lone struggler can be. "I got chewed up," she has said of that experience. "I thought of myself as aggressive, but I didn't know what aggressive was. . . . There were times when I thought I wasn't going to survive. I would go home and actually cry myself to sleep, I was so exhausted and depressed."

Now she is the first woman ever to head a Big Ten university and one of only two female presidents in history to preside over a major research university, the other woman being Hanna Holborn Gray at the University of Chicago. Of course, the University of Chicago dropped big-time sports over a half century ago, so Shalala's reign is unique. She wants to get along with her athletic staff while guiding them into the future, not only because she likes camaraderie and excellence, but also because she is a pioneer for her sex in the sports world, and history will note clearly whether she measured up to the tough guys or not. And she hates to lose.

All the men defer to her, though Fish is the least fazed by her status. Fish is the only real political animal in the bunch—other than Shalala herself—a career bureaucrat whose specialty is backroom analyzing, lobbying, and trouble-shooting for state administrations. Before he was appointed to his post overseeing the athletic department, Fish was the head of the Division of Policy and Budget for the State Department of Health and Social Services. Before that he was an adviser to former Wisconsin governor Anthony Earl, a budget analyst in the Department of Administration, and a program evaluator for the Legislative Audit bureau. He knows that when his time is up in whatever job he's in, when his political boss (whoever it might be) loses the election, Fish will hit the road. "That's the business I'm in," he says cheerfully. But he also knows he's so good at what he does that he'll never be unemployed for long. Every owner needs somebody to balance the books and collect the fees; every king needs an assassin.

Fish got his current job supervising the athletic department's reformation after he read the state-mandated audit in February 1989, which described the department as a mess beyond belief. Fish wrote to the chancellor's office outlining how he would solve the athletic department's problems, pointing out four major steps he would take: 1. expand fund-raising; 2. increase ticket sales; 3. increase advertising and promotions; 4. snare more money from students and the state. All were good ideas, but it was Fish's understanding of the psychological maneuverings needed to pull off the plan that was inspired. "This [plan] will . . . signal many interest groups that management is calmly and decisively addressing the financial problem," he wrote. "[T]he organizational structure and staff should be reviewed. This needs to be done carefully to avoid the appearance of looking for scapegoats. . . . This crisis can be an opportunity. The fact that it has been a high-profile story in the media can be used to involve more people and organizations in the solution. The University should not react defensively, but acknowledge the problems and take . . . highly visible actions . . ."

He concluded by stating, "I am very interested in working on this issue. . . . Naturally, I would prefer a permanent position, but I understand the need to act quickly. I am willing to use other means to begin working within a week or two. . . . I would like at least to maintain my current salary of $57,000 per year." Shalala promptly hired him at $67,500 annually. She knew that if he could do just a fraction of the things he said he could, Fish was the bargain of the decade.

The athletic department audit from state auditor Dale Cattanach's office, the report that had prompted Fish to write his letter, had fairly nauseated Shalala in early 1989. The follow-up report she received just two weeks later didn't settle her stomach, either; in that report, dated December 5, 1990, Cattanach said that one year after the original audit the department was still a disaster. "In fact," he wrote, "at the end of fiscal year 1989–90, the cumulative deficit was $1.95 million, which was about $1.2 million more than at the close of fiscal year 1987–88, despite $1.6 million in new revenue provided by the Legislature and the University."

The department was still a sinking ship, even though Fish had hit the students for ten dollars per semester in "segregated fees," which brought the department $760,000 annually, and had nailed the faculty with 50 percent increases in parking fees, bringing in another $480,000. Fish also had refinanced the state bonds covering the McClain facility, reducing annual debt service payments by $360,000. But these moves weren't nearly enough. The football team stunk; attendance was dismal. The athletic department machine, old and overloaded as it was with twenty-seven sports, 165 employees, and 900 student-athletes, seemed resistant to tinkering and tire-kicking. The state auditor had no faith left in the contraption. "(G)iven the Department's past difficulties . . ." wrote Cattanach, "we question the Department's ability to meet its estimated budget for fiscal year 1990–91. . . . The Department continues to encounter serious financial difficulties."

Shalala knew it was cutting time. An athletic department run this poorly could undermine the spirit of the entire university. Donors could hardly be expected to give cash to a black hole of waste and incompetence. The grand plan for campus-wide excellence could be broken on the racks of athletic mediocrity, leaving the little hot-shot from New York who talked big and failed bigger, looking like a fool.

"The truth is, we want a football team as good as the university," said nuclear engineering professor Gerald Kulcinski, head of the ad hoc committee that had recommended to the athletic board that Don Morton be fired. Other UW supporters were even more restless; one state legislator suggested Wisconsin hire former Oklahoma coach Barry Switzer to crank up the football team. Switzer had left Oklahoma after a spate of NCAA violations and player crimes had rocked the Sooners' program. State senator Joseph Andrea of Kenosha told reporters that he couldn't drag himself to a recent Badger game, even though he was a huge football fan. "Why do I want to watch an exercise in futility?" he said.

Shalala glances out the window at the bleak landscape. Some of the season's first ice fishermen have set up on the far side of the lake, looking like microbes in a white laboratory dish. Shalala still has her trademark smile, but she means business. Everybody knows that. She talks to Alvarez about the possibility of having a late-starting football game at Camp Randall Stadium, to bring in more people, fans who would prefer to be entertained at night rather than in the middle of Saturday afternoon. But they agree there could be problems with that. Richter brings up the perennial downside to such experiments: Give fans a whole afternoon to drink, and you can count on a lot more trouble during the game and after it. Shalala nods. She has talked to people at other universities that have tried late games, and they warned her about rowdiness. Shalala is on record as saying that alcohol abuse is the number-one problem on college campuses today.

Shalala laughs, amused with the debate. The whole problem is really such a simple one: Put a good team on the field and people will come, no matter when the game is played. Students come in large numbers, anyway, God bless their souls. But they have no money, and they don't pay the same ticket prices as the public, and they don't make donations to booster clubs, and they don't lighten your burden as you travel around the state trying to drum up financial support for the school from adults who have money.

"You know," says the chancellor, "the trouble with the usual one o'clock games is they're too early for the students. Really. I talked to my niece about it and she said, 'There isn't even time to *eat breakfast* before games.'"

Everybody smiles at this. Here they are, mature, professional adults trying desperately to understand the habits of a group of people with which they have so little in common.

"What a strange breed," says Shalala.

5

PAT RICHTER WALKS THROUGH THE MONROE STREET PARKING LOT, GAZING, AS others have before him, at the stone cheese wedge that is the main entrance to this great university's athletic department. The wedge is actually the east end of Camp Randall Stadium, with most of the offices of the 160 or so employees stuffed like air pockets in the upper recesses of the cheese. The structure supports about a quarter of the rows of stands in the stadium itself, so that the cement rows serve as the roof for the department: one man's ceiling is approximately 19,000 men's floor. When a game is in progress and fans are stamping their feet, the noise and vibration in the offices is terrifying.

There is an industrial-strength metal door that you can use to get into the building, but the principal entrance is a rolling, ten-foot-high garage door a few feet to the right. You can literally drive a truck into the UW athletic department. Once inside the building, often accompanied by gusts of arctic wind and exhaust fumes, one has to walk partway down the cement driveway and then up two flights of gum-stained cement stairs to get to the athletic director's office. There are no elevators in the building. The other coaches' and administrators' offices are up several more flights of stairs and then down hallways so narrow and dark they seem to have been lifted stone by stone from a medieval castle. The walk to Steve Yoder's tiny basketball office on the fourth level, for instance, is so difficult, particularly for older or infirm people, that the parents of some recruits have never made it up there, simply staying by the tacky garage door while their sons were given a sales pitch on high.

Though seemingly lost in ancient times, the Wisconsin athletic program is far from a failure across the board. Many of its nonrevenue sports teams—from men's and women's cross-country to crew to women's soccer to women's volleyball—compete for conference and national titles. Just three weeks ago, the Big Ten champion women's volleyball team blew out perennial threat Illinois in the Fieldhouse in front of a national record crowd of 10,935. Middle-distance runner Suzy Favor was recently awarded the 1990 Jumbo Elliot Award, the Heisman Trophy for women's track and field. Moreover, UW's athletes have led the Big Ten in All-Academic honors for four straight years, with one hundred and one Badger athletes making all-academic squads this year, compared to sixty-nine athletes each for Northwestern and Ohio State, the second-place finishers. The traditionally powerful hockey team has won four national titles in twenty-eight years.

It is four days before Christmas and time for the department's year-end party. Richter pulls his overcoat tight against the icy wind and clutches a Christmas present to his ribs—his sore ribs. Something always hurts him from the old days, back when he played four sports at UW and became the last athlete at the school to earn nine varsity letters, after which he went on to play nine collision-filled years in the NFL. One day he sat in his office and randomly listed the damage he'd been dealt, touching various parts of his body as he spoke: "Left shoulder separation as a freshman in 1959; gash over right eye against the Steelers, 1968, sewed up in the locker room, no anesthetic; two broken noses; chipped teeth; lip ripped away from teeth, thanks to Larry Wilson of the Cardinals; two broken collar bones, 1960 and 1965; cracked ribs; torn kidney in Hall of Fame Game, 1965—doctor said, 'Drink a gallon of water and call me in the morning'; chipped bones in both big toes; broken little finger, left hand, 1969 preseason; broken knuckle on ring finger of right hand, 1962; torn thigh muscle in high school; torn right hamstring with Redskins sometime; dislocated right thumb in baseball; hit in the left ear with a fastball in college, peeled it like a grape; right knee cartilage, training camp, 1971."

The scars and the awards and the history are precisely why Shalala wanted Richter. He was making over $150,000 a year as the vice president in charge of personnel at the Oscar Mayer plant in Madison and took a cut to $139,000 when he signed on with UW. Like several of the others on the reform team, Richter was swayed by the challenge of righting a listing ship and by the Badger blood in his veins, and not a little bit by the chance for some real ego gratification. Where else, after all, but at UW itself could he be constantly praised for something he performed for fun over a quarter of a century before? As Al Fish says, "We kept telling Donna, 'We don't know who we want for athletic director, but we need the perfect AD, somebody like Pat Richter.' His name kept coming up, even though he wasn't a candidate. Finally she said, 'Well, why don't you just get *him*?' I did, but it was like luring a bear out of hibernation."

But the bear is into the act now, and after he walks upstairs and gives his secretary, Sonja Christenson, the present—for which she smiles warmly—Richter straightens his blue blazer and blue tie with the little red Santa Clauses on it and heads back down the stairs to the National W Club room at the far end of the driveway/hallway beneath the stands. He enters the large windowless room with its cheap wood paneling and all-purpose reddish carpet and walks straight into the rollicking athletic department year-end party. These are his people, like it or not. He heads to the bar for a drink.

There he encounters his predecessor, sixty-seven-year-old Elroy "Crazylegs" Hirsch, the athletic director from 1969 to 1987. Hirsch is now a "consultant" for the department, earning almost forty thousand dollars a year for performing vaguely defined duties that could best be described as promoting Badger-awareness through golfing, handshaking, backslapping, joke telling, and partying. Right now these duties also include bartending.

"A little libation?" Hirsch asks with a big, happy-days smile, his trademark silver flattop shining in the overhead light. "How about a brandy old-fashioned? Wisconsin leads the nation in brandy consumption, you know."

Richter settles for a beer. If Richter is somewhat aloof and uptight, Hirsch is his opposite. A former Badger football star himself, ol' Crazylegs is a relic from a kinder, gentler, harder-partying era. Legendary are the tales of Hirsch standing entire barrooms of Wisconsinites to Brandy Manhattans (brandy and vermouth mixed with assorted cherries, olives, onions, or even—God forbid—pickled asparagus stalks); leading everyone in the Bud song; doing one-armed pull-ups; kissing babies; telling tall tales; pounding down the Old Styles and Michs and Millers and Buds and Leinenkugels like a camel guzzling water at an oasis; dancing fevered polkas with charmed ladies; whipping crowds of happy farmers, insurance salesmen, truck drivers, waitresses, professors, lawyers, and housewives into paroxysms of UW feel-good enthusiasm. Often as not, Crazylegs would use the frenzied moments to gently twist a few arms and get folks to ante up some cash for the department. No matter what the football team's final standing might be, if Crazylegs was doing good, the athletic department was doing good.

"Wisconsin was never a great football power," former University of Michigan athletic director Don Canham told the *Chronicle of Higher Education* in a March 1990 article assessing Wisconsin's problems, "but Elroy, by sheer magnetism, brought that whole state together." An article in *Isthmus*, Madison's much-read, ultraliberal, pull-no-punches weekly newspaper, was a little more critical. "The former UW athletic director was a bigger mascot than Bucky during his tenure in the go-go 70's and early-80's, when Camp Randall was always full for football games and money didn't matter. Crazylegs was better than Ronald Reagan at making people feel good, but was equally adept at running up bills his successors must now pay."

The last statement is not completely accurate. Hirsch did not actually pile up debt; he simply helped the department mainline funds from a football team that seldom finished in the top of the Big Ten but always finished in the top fifteen in the nation in attendance. Ol' Legs was like the grasshopper who fiddles away the summer while the ant saves for the snowy day. Elroy didn't borrow food from anyone; he simply left an empty cupboard when he excused himself from the table.

No matter, he is the bartender today, and Richter bows to him by starting his end-of-the-year speech from midway between the bar and Hirsch's red Wisconsin jersey, number 40, framed under glass and hanging on the west wall like a vestment.

"It was just about a year ago that Elroy slipped me into the red jacket," says Richter to the assembled coaches, administrators, and secretaries, many of whom have worried looks on their faces. Fifty-one positions have been changed or done away with in the department in the last year, and who knows who's next. Al Fish alone looks mellow. "It hasn't been easy—we all know that," Richter continues. "We think we have the right programs in place, but they keep trying to hammer us in the press. This city is always like that. That makes it tough for morale, but we're excited about the people who are here to help us face the problems and move into the future successfully. Intercollegiate sport is at a crossroads. Everybody knows that. We have to clean up the show, but survive financially."

When Richter's speech is done, the party surges onward. One of the revelers is recently hired associate athletic director Jim Bakken, a former kicker for UW who went on to play sixteen years for the St. Louis Cardinals and still holds the NFL single-game field goal record with seven. Beyond that, the fifty-year-old Bakken's credentials for his current job, which pays $47,500 annually, are somewhat uncertain. Though he did serve as the athletic director for small St. Louis University for five years, he resigned that post in 1988 and most recently had been working as an account executive for the Smith Barney brokerage firm in Madison. Just prior to that, however, he had been found guilty of failing to pay enough tax on income obtained from a St. Louis investment group and was sentenced to three years' probation and ordered to perform community service as punishment.

But then, his current job itself is a little unclear. Though listed as associate athletic director on the university pay list, Bakken's more precise title, according to Fish, is director of external relations. It is not clear what Bakken should do to fill this role, nor what he does do. He seems to have one of those pork-barrel niches that have always been a part of athletic departments and bureaucracies everywhere, the kind that are so hard to weed out of a system, but which steadily drain funds from the till. No one will openly admit it, but it seems Bakken was hired at least in part for his gridiron glory, and the fact that he was Richter's football roommate during the 1961 season.

"Every year the Packers play an exhibition game here in Camp Randall," Bakken explains to a couple of listeners. "An exhibition is an exhibition. So we need something to stand out. So I'm exploring having a concert in the stadium along with the game. You know, the Beach Boys."

What about a top-forty band or maybe something off the wall, like Metallica or Motley Crue, a listener asks.

"Never heard of them," says Bakken, whose youthful face is framed by white hair that makes it hard to tell if he's old or young. "Somebody asked me a while ago about Fleetwood Mac. Never heard of them, either. I like the Beach Boys."

A listener asks Bakken if this would be a way to get back into the high life, make some dollars for the department, return to the glory days of Wisconsin football history.

"Wisconsin has no football history," states Bakken.

A MONTH LATER THE ETERNAL SNOW COVERS THE ROLLING FIELDS OF CENTRAL Wisconsin like a thin cotton blanket. The sun is bright, but the temperature in Madison is five degrees, and each time the garage door to the athletic department opens, the boiler at Camp Randall cranks up another notch.

Inside the W Club things are also heating up. The athletic board, the eighteen-member committee of faculty and business people that oversees the workings of the athletic department, is meeting to discuss business. Since the University of Wisconsin at Madison is a state school, the management—even of its athletic department— begins with the governor of the state, who is currently Republican Tommy Thompson. Thompson, along with the state legislature, appoints the board of regents, who in turn select the president of the UW "system," the affiliation that controls the thirteen branches of the university statewide in cities such as Whitewater, Eau Claire, Stevens Point, Milwaukee, and, of course, the flagship campus in Madison. The acting system president is Kenneth "Buzz" Shaw, a former UW basketball player. It is the president's role to appoint the chancellor of the Madison campus—currently Shalala. The chancellor then appoints most of the athletic board, which—with the chancellor's guidance—approves the athletic director. The athletic director hires the coaches, who in turn hire their staff (after approval from the AD). The food chain works up from the lowest oarsman on the crew team or scrub catcher on the baseball team back through the athletic director and all the way to the governor, and hence, the people of the state; it goes back down the same way. That, at least, is the theory behind the organization. Sometimes, as one might expect, it seems as if in the athletic department nobody is running anything at all.

The meeting begins with a discussion of security, the result of a disturbance at the recent Wisconsin-Iowa basketball game. A group of demonstrators protesting the declaration of war in the Persian Gulf pounded menacingly on the doors of the Fieldhouse and chanted antiwar slogans while the ESPN-televised game was in progress. Associate athletic director Joel Maturi noted that the rare television exposure no doubt contributed to the incident; some members of the board pressed Maturi to develop a plan to prevent further demonstrations, though Maturi reasonably believes that there is only so much an administration can control. Free speech does still exist on the UW campus.

Next on the agenda is the hiring report. Ten new people have been hired in the last year, notes a board member, but fifty-one have been hired since 1989. The employees who have left, says Fish in an aside, "took early retirement, were redirected, relocated, encouraged to find other employment, given career counseling, if you will." He chuckles to himself. "Many of them are suffering from Al's-Hammer Disease." He thinks of the biggest axing he did, which was also the most unpleasant. "When Don Morton was let go," he says, "I remember cutting the check for three hundred and thirty thousand dollars, giving it to the attorneys, and then going home and getting sick."

Next is a report on Title IX progress at UW—that is, the efforts being made to get the athletic department to have the same representation and funding for women's sports as for men's, as required by the NCAA's federally mandated gender equity rule, commonly referred to by its title number, nine. Currently, the department is far out of whack in both numbers and cash devoted to women's sports. A report from the Equity Committee, one of seemingly hundreds of committees analyzing almost everything the department does, suggests three remarkably obvious solutions to the dilemma: "1) increase the number of sports offered for women; 2) reduce the number of sports offered for men; 3) provide for some combination of both 1) and 2)." Such is the glory of academic research.

The board members themselves are an interesting group, ranging from the truly academic to the business-oriented. Linda Greene has given the report on gender equity; she is a law school professor and a former hurdler on the UW track team. Her low-key presence is balanced by the always questioning Cyrena Pondrum, an English professor whom Fish calls "a major pain in the ass." Other members include Charlie Thomas, a black public school principal in Chicago; Susan Lubar, a sales division manager for the same Smith Barney that once employed Jim Bakken; Jim Hoyt, the dean of the UW journalism school; Gerald Kulcinski, a former UW football player and now a UW nuclear engineering professor ("A big fusion guy," says Fish. "You can't say he's dumb; he *is* a rocket scientist."); and Merritt Norvell, a black IBM executive and former UW football teammate of Richter's. Norvell's interest is clearly focused on football, since one of his sons, Aaron, is a junior linebacker and another son, Jay, is a graduate assistant coach for Barry Alvarez. Such familial interest would seem to cause a problem for a board member who supposedly should make his judgments on ethics and business acumen rather than on emotion, but then Richter himself is not an unbiased helmsman—his son, Barry, is a rising scholarship player on the hockey team.

During a break, Fish joins some of the local sportswriters in the hallway to discuss the real burning issue of the moment: the fate of leading hockey scorer Sean Hill for the upcoming critical game against Minnesota, ranked fifth nationally to UW's eighth. In Wisconsin's last game, a 6–3 loss to hated Denver University, Hill checked a Denver player so viciously that he broke the young man's neck. The check was the kind that occurs several times a game in college hockey, except for the little follow-through elbow flourish that Hill delivered. The injured player will have to wear a metal halo screwed to his skull for months, and it seems certain his hockey career is finished. Still, the Wisconsin backers—including Fish and Richter—think Hill should not be suspended by the league for the blow. No one knows yet what the league commissioner, Otto Breitenbach, a former associate athletic director at Wisconsin, intends to do.

The talk turns to deer hunting, a bane to the woods of Wisconsin and UW football attendance for a couple of weeks each fall, as a half million hunters charge the shrinking forests of the state armed with brandy flasks, orange caps, and enough firepower to hold off most of the militarized nations on earth. Everybody has seen road signs shot to smithereens, read about the cows with COW painted on their sides still shot dead, and heard about the hunters who have blown their own heads off while looking down the barrels of their guns to see why the things wouldn't fire. Rob Schultz of the *Madison Capital-Times* grimaces and tells how he was following a car last deer season, a vehicle with a dead and bloody deer lashed to the roof, when both he and the deer-toter turned off the highway onto a cloverleaf. "During the turn the deer flew off the car and I ran right over it," he says. "It just destroyed the bottom of my car, bones and guts flying everywhere. I honked at the hunters to let them know, but then I figured the hell with them. Jesus, what a mess. I still can't get rid of the smell."

What a place, the writers all agree. What a wonderful, fun-filled place.

6

It's Monday night, and that means it's hockey night at State Street Brats. The bar, owned by senior defenseman Bob Andringa's parents, is the hangout for the team, a no-frills drinking establishment with video games, tables for dining (bratwurst, naturally), overhead TVs, and a stuffed gnu on the wall. Team captain Andringa himself isn't here tonight, though his mother is tending bar and seventeen of his teammates are tossing down pitchers of beer. Word is that Rob is studying for a big midterm tomorrow.

"Don't say he's studying," pleads Sean Hill, laughing and swigging from his plastic cup. "Say he's hung over."

Dennis Snedden, the talented senior left-winger, is the chairman of the Monday Night Club, and he surveys the guys as they talk about hockey, girls, hunting, drinking—the important things. A couple of players work the Super Chexx hockey video game, while others start a game of Thumper, with the loser of each round chugging his beer. Jacques Auger, a French-speaking freshman defenseman from Quebec, enters the bar and is greeted by Snedden and the others. One of Governor Tommy Thompson's daughters is also at the bar; she has been dating Auger, and she lightens the testosterone-laden tone of this meeting, if only a little. Forget the fact that at least half the players here are too young to be legally drinking alcohol; this is Wisconsin, and these are the mighty ice Badgers.

Chris Nelson, a tall, slender, junior defenseman from Los Angeles, comes out of the rest room and Hill calls to him. Nelson is that rarest of people in big-time hockey, a black man. He thrives on his uniqueness, wearing number 8 on his jersey and calling himself "the Eightball." His license plate reads SOUL N ICE.

"We've been trying to get Chris to grow an Afro," says Hill, grinning. "A big one."

"Like Doctor J," says Barry Richter, who then recounts the time his dad took him as a boy to see the Milwaukee Bucks play the Philadelphia 76ers so they could watch the great Julius Erving, and then the marvelous Dr. J didn't set foot on the court. "I don't think I ever got over that," says Richter sadly.

A blond-haired player in a red flannel shirt, sporting a swollen black eye and a cast on his right hand, sits down at the table. He has a very young, almost sweet-looking face, marred by the shiner, but he has a cockiness that seems at odds with his physical presence; he looks to be about five feet eleven inches tall and weigh about 175 pounds. His name is Matt Buss, he's a redshirt sophomore forward from Plover, and he has never played in a varsity game. He is a good student, but not a particularly good hockey player, at least not yet, and his arrogance seems to spring from his fierce desire to be like the stars on the team, to be accepted as one of the gang, a tough guy who's as macho as the sport demands. He wears his cast like a badge of courage, though the injury did not occur on the ice; he broke his hand in a fight four days earlier in a bar.

"It was four on one," he says proudly. "One guy hit me, and I looked over and knocked him out. Then I started hitting another guy, and I just really messed up his face. Then my hand broke, but I kept pounding him." Buss drinks his beer. "Then the cops came. But no charges were filed. I told them I was a hockey player." He smiles. That's all there was to it.

Just as Buss finishes his story, two players start to yell and push each other near the pinball machine. Richter and Hill have moved to the bar, where they are downing "Snakebites," shots of Yukon Jack and sweetened lime juice, which Mrs. Andringa has fixed for them. "Those guys just don't like each other," says Hill matter-of-factly of his arguing teammates. Mrs. Andringa walks around the bar and shouts, "Oh, come on, guys—don't get in a fight!"

The players chill out and immediately the incident is forgotten. The rhythm of the bar is a little like a hockey game itself—violence seems ready to rise from the action at any time and then dissipate just as quickly. A number of girls come in, acquaintances of the hockey players, and it is clear that almost everyone in the bar is either a player or a player's friend. This seems to be by design; the combination of alcohol and hockey aggressiveness would not mix well with a crowd of outsiders.

A young woman offers Hill some candy that is attached like buttons to a paper strip. Hill eats the candy. Then he eats the paper. "Roughage," he says.

At 2 A.M. Dennis Snedden stands up and bellows, "As chairman, I now have to clear this place. Let's go!"

As Duane Derksen, the starting goaltender, rises and puts on his coat, he pauses to look again at the ring on his finger, the ring with the red stone with the W on it surrounded by four zirconiums. It is his national championship ring, and it means a lot to him. Still, there are times when he wonders how much it means to others, those who aren't part of this hockey family. "We're the best team at this school," he says. "But it's still like we're not quite number one."

That position, he says, is held by the cursed football team. Not for what it's done on the field, but for what it might do some day, if Alvarez ever delivers on his promises. It's not fair, Derksen knows, but that's how it is.

THE NIGHT OF THE WISCONSIN-MINNESOTA HOCKEY GAME, RICK ABERMAN eats his pregame meal at Dotty's. Taking orders is Jenny Kruzing, a former UW soccer player now in grad school. Aberman knows her, as he knows many of the athletes currently playing sports at the school. He has counseled several of the current women's soccer team players, just as he has counseled several of this year's men's hockey team members. The athletes' problems are mostly the same as other young people's—drinking and drug problems, love problems, family problems, academic problems, anxiety problems—with the added stress brought on by the hazards of their sports. *Why does the coach treat me like that? What do I do when I'm injured? Why am I afraid to be as good as I can be? Who am I when I'm not an athlete?*

Aberman has his concerns about the athletic department and its financial spasms and the way those churnings can affect the athletes.

He spends a good part of every day simply watching various teams practice and mingling with the players and coaches, to let them know that he is around and is approachable. More often than not, interested athletes will sidle up to him while he prepares to jog or while he's standing rinkside or on the sideline or even riding a stationary bike in Camp Randall or at the fieldhouse known as the Shell, and ask him whether it would be all right if they chatted with Rick a little about a problem that has come up—nothing important, of course, but maybe if he had a minute sometime. . . .

Breaking down the athlete's initial distrust of a stranger, a stranger moreover who will hear the secrets of the person's life, is the hardest part of Aberman's job. That and getting athletes to realize that talking about their problems, pursuing their own psychological health, is not a sign of weakness, not the behavior of sissies and losers. The best way Aberman knows to ease the path to his door for athletes is simply to let them see him hanging around and appearing nonthreatening. As a result, he probably spends more time watching college sports than any other adult not in a position of authority.

He spends a fair portion of his time watching the hockey team and chatting with coach Jeff Sauer to see if any skaters have problems that he can help resolve. Hockey is a violent sport, and at UW it is a crowd-pleasing event that routinely packs the Coliseum to capacity with nearly nine thousand screaming fans. UW has led the nation in college hockey attendance for an astonishing twenty-one straight years, setting an NCAA single-season record—one that may never be broken—in the 1981–82 season, when, in twenty-eight home dates, the hockey Badgers drew nearly a quarter million paying fans.

The UW skaters themselves are historically a rowdy lot, and sometimes Aberman feels that the attention they get only exacerbates certain juvenile behavior patterns they have already developed. Madison police know the hockey team well, as do the owners of most State Street bars.

Aberman attended the recent board meeting, and he knows how badly the team, Richter, and coach Sauer want bad boy Sean Hill to play tonight. Unfortunately, the commissioner of the Western Collegiate Hockey Association, the league to which the Badgers belong, has suspended Hill for at least one game.

Hockey is not generally a revenue-producing sport at the collegiate level, but it certainly makes money for Wisconsin, because the team is able to pack the large, modern arena which the school rents from the county government, and because that arena sells beer. Fans come to watch the Badgers win, but they stick around because the beer flows so freely in the "beer garden" in the foyer; home games seem more like a party than an athletic contest. Some ticket holders never make it past the kegs to their seats, spending entire evenings without so much as a glimpse of the ice, reveling instead in the time-honored Wisconsin tradition of "pounding down a few." It is a rare luxury for a college to be able to serve beer and profit from it at one of its teams' home games; NCAA rules prohibit the sale of alcohol at sports events on college campuses. UW avoids that restriction by using a nonuniversity facility located off-campus for its hockey games.

Adding to the athletic department's financial concerns is the NCAA's recent reform-minded ruling that will cut hockey games from thirty-four a season to thirty-two. The move will cost UW approximately one hundred thousand dollars in revenue. "Why don't they just leave us alone?" Sauer had moaned of the NCAA and all the other meddlers who just want to mess up a program he had perfectly under his control.

The frustration must have filtered swiftly onto the rink, where every rush to the net by a Minnesota puck handler nearly starts a fight with one or more surly Wisconsin players. Barry Alvarez and his wife, Cindy, sit behind the south goal, along with unpaid assistant coach Jay Norvell and four football recruits. Three of the recruits are black, and one is from Florida, and none of them are familiar with this strange sport wherein speeding, helmeted players with big sticks try to knock each other through the Plexiglas walls. A fight breaks out on the ice directly in front of the recruits, and the young men stare with wide eyes.

Alvarez watches them, wondering if this is such a good recruiting ploy. A few days earlier he had brought in a "burner" from Mississippi, and the kid had stayed on campus two full days because of a big snow that delayed airline flights. The recruit's sponsors and varsity team members had taken the high schooler "traying"—sledding on school cafeteria trays—and the kid had dug it, had thought the whole winter experience was as cool as could be.

"He committed to us three different times," says Alvarez, who can only hope that all the players who have said they will come to Wisconsin will still sign binding letters of intent twelve days from now, on February 6th, the official day of reckoning. "He was coming here, no question. Then the last time he committed, he said Jackie Sherrill was working him and now it's touch and go."

Sherrill is the legendary coach who resigned from Texas A&M a couple of years ago under a cloud of NCAA charges which brought the school's football program a two-year probation. Sherrill left with nearly three quarters of a million dollars in Aggie buyout money, lay low for a time, and then last year accepted an offer to be the head football coach/messiah at hardscrabble Mississippi State. Alvarez knows the recruiting game. The recruit runs a 4.3 forty. Jackie Sherrill will find out if the boy likes grits or greens. He'll find out where his daddy hunts. He'll work the kid the way a master baker works dough. Sherrill is the man who, just to psych his boys before a skirmish with the University of Texas Longhorns, brought a bull onto the Mississippi State practice field and castrated it. Alvarez's eyes say what his heart knows: He'll never see the burner here again. (Sure enough, the kid signs with Mississippi State within the week.)

So. Alvarez turns back to the hockey game, which UW is losing, 2–1, and finds his new recruits. Another fight erupts directly in front of them, and the youngsters seem to enjoy it. Al Fish is sitting nearby with his four-year-old daughter, Molly. Neither of them seems distressed by the violence, either. Brawling is such a part of Wisconsin's hockey tradition that most fans would probably be greatly disturbed if it ever were eliminated.

Shalala and Richter are also at the game. The chancellor seems to relish contests of any form, rooting and cheering her Badgers on. Richter is grumpy over Hill's suspension, making all kinds of excuses for the savage blow that nearly paralyzed a young man. "The thing that bothers me," he says angrily, "is that a check like that will happen five or ten times in any game. And what about the liability here? The Denver kid had a congenital neck problem and I heard he maybe isn't completely okay. Does this mean anything legally? It shouldn't. I mean, my son is on the team, and I don't want unnecessary rough things, but . . ."

The rough things keep on coming, though, as the fourth fight of the game breaks out early in the third period and the band begins to chant, "Asshole! Asshole!" Play stops as a brawl explodes in the stands near the Minnesota bench. One of the Minnesota players,

Sean Fabian, brandishes his stick and climbs partly over the Plexiglas barrier in an attempt to get at a heckler before his teammates pull him back. The entire arena rocks with the "Asshole!" chant as police wade into the melee. Fifteen minutes go by as the cops try to restore order, the players on the ice shuffling back and forth while looking up into the stands in amazement.

When play is finally allowed to resume, Minnesota scores quickly to put the game out of reach, 5–2. The match degenerates into a parade of macho posturing at this point, with near-fight following near-fight.

In the locker room after the game, Aberman chats with some of the Wisconsin players. Aberman is not upset by the fights—a native Minnesotan, he understands and accepts the code of hockey—but he wonders if the players are mature enough to know that fighting can often get in the way of production; that winning, not intimidation, is the ultimate goal. Sometimes Aberman wonders about the maturity of all the kids on this party-hearty campus. One of the athletic board members, Jim Hoyt, the dean of the school of journalism, shared that same concern recently. Hoyt also attended the game tonight, and as he watched one of the hockey fights wax and wane, he commented on his separate role as chairman of Shalala's recently formed committee on fraternity and sorority issues.

"Two years ago we had huge racial problems on campus," he said, "with the precipitating event being a fraternity's mock-slave auction in which members dressed in blackface. That spearheaded reform in which, among other things, we forced fraternities to hire resident advisers and have regular series of educational programs at their houses on such things as date rape, alcohol abuse, and racial sensitivity." Part of the problem in the racial area, Hoyt knows, is that many Wisconsin students have had practically no contact with black people until they get to UW. It's not that the kids from Hayward and Wild Rose are racists, it's just that some of them are out of touch, victims of their own environmental deprivation. After all, the state's populace is 92 percent white and only 5 percent black (the other 3 percent are Native American, Eskimo, Aleut, Asian or Pacific Islanders, or Hispanic). Moreover, the state's largest city, Milwaukee, has more residents of a single ethnic heritage—48 percent are of German descent—than any other metropolitan area in the country.

Aberman, who is Jewish, generally shrugs off the insensitive comments he hears. If the whole state is a trifle immature, he often thinks, then it is also rather naïve. He smiles almost warmly, recalling the time associate AD Joel Maturi, a devout Catholic, had spoken to him in anguish over the failing morale in the athletic department and what could be done to improve it.

"Why can't we just be more Christian?" Maturi asked plaintively. Perhaps realizing the indelicacy of his words, Maturi quickly explained, "I don't mean anything religious by it, Rick. I just think people could say hello to people more often. You know, be more *Christian*."

Maybe that would do it, Aberman thinks. Maybe old Joel's got the answer.

7

THE SNOW BLOWS SILENTLY PAST THE WINDOWS OF AL FISH'S CORNER OFFICE, continuing the endless-winter motif that drives seemingly sane Wisconsin human beings to such acts as snowmobile riding, ice golfing, and of course ice fishing. Fish himself prefers to play basketball in late January, indoors, although occasionally he'll break down and go cross-country skiing with his wife at night along the edge of frozen Lake Mendota, partly for exercise and partly to look in the windows of the fancy homes along the shore. "They all have their blinds up, because to them the lake is their backyard," Fish explains. "It's not like window-peeping or anything."

Behind him on the wall, above the volcano-red carpet and cheap, 1950s-style paneling, is a poster that shows Bucky Badger at the wheel of a red Corvette. DRIVE THE BADGER SPIRIT, says the sign, WITH UW PERSONALIZED LICENSE PLATES. APPLICATIONS AVAILABLE AT YOUR LOCAL MOTOR VEHICLE OFFICE.

Wisconsin residents can now buy a vanity plate with the university seal on it for forty-five dollars, twenty of which goes to the athletic department. This was Fish's idea, and he smiles every time he sees a car tooling down the road with one of the plates on its rear bumper. He knows a fundamental axiom that, remarkably, still eludes many in positions similar to his: Selling things—license plates, shirts, key chains, bibs, caps, underwear, wall space, goodwill, teams—is how you make money. Al Fish will put anything up for a bid, and if the bid is good enough—and the moral damage isn't too great, and no laws are broken in the transaction—he'll sell it.

Fish spends every day facing one essential problem: How is he going to cut the budgets of most of the sports teams and still keep the coaches happy—and do that while increasing the football budget and basically giving football emperor Alvarez everything he wants? He shrugs. He'll just do it. Roll up the sleeves and put on the velvet glove, because it must be done.

He looks at the other poster on his wall, the one that shows a fierce Badger football player under the message WE'RE GIVING MIAMI EVERYTHING WE'VE GOT. INCLUDING 290 POUNDS OF BRADY PIERCE. Pierce, one must assume, is the player displayed. Fish shrugs, then chuckles. That promotion kind of got away from us, his look says; it made that opening 51–3 loss all the more humiliating. Well, not "us" exactly; Fish hadn't officially arrived on campus yet when the poster was created. But that was the loss that led to the legislative call for "drastic action."

"In the last couple of years we've made fundamental change in the entire university," says Fish. "If we don't get adequate money to hold to a certain level of quality, then we'll offer less, but keep the quality. With students, we'll just cut enrollment. With sports, we'll have to do something, too. It's simply taking responsibility for your own quality rather than blaming others. Over at the capitol they're looking at a projected deficit for the whole state of eight hundred million dollars in about two and a half years. With a total state budget of twelve billion, that's not terrible, but the budget is always supposed to be balanced. It's in the constitution. So there are some hard choices to be made, for everybody."

Shalala's hell-for-leather pursuit of excellence has made the university's educational mission more elitist than populist. The chancellor wants things to be the best they can be, and if that means fewer people will be involved in the good things, so be it. Let the common folk go to other schools in the state—that's why the other campuses exist; Madison will be like Florence and Rome and Athens all rolled into one. Fish supports that vision, athletically speaking.

"Do you do a few sports well or do you just limp along?" he asks, noting that UW has more varsity sports—twenty-seven: men's and women's teams in basketball, indoor track, outdoor track, cross-country, crew, swimming, tennis, gymnastics, fencing, golf, and soccer, as well as men's football, hockey, wrestling and baseball, and women's volleyball—than any Big Ten school except Ohio State, which has thirty-one. "This is a philosophical question. And my answer is there are hundreds of universities and colleges around the country that do things at a lower level. I played on the Luther College, Iowa, golf team as a student, that's how good I was. Division III. One year we went to the Division III nationals in Seguin, Texas, where we got creamed. I drove my '66 Malibu down there and we stayed in dorms for four dollars a night and brought our own towels. Luther's contribution was to give us golf balls, and hey, that was fine.

"But this is different here. There is an element of elitism at work in our plan. As you move up the ladder there are fewer and fewer people of top caliber, and to attract them—those elite athletes—you need good facilities and the best coaches. Which costs money. Money is what it comes down to. The more you spend, the higher your team rankings." Fish looks at his blackboard, where he has scribbled some figures and made some crude charts, adding up certain costs and income. Millions of dollars dot the board like wallpaper designs. Arrows point this way and that. The word *football* is prominent. So basically he's talking about the relief that would come from filling the football stadium again. Is that all there is to it?

"Yes, yes," he responds. "Yes it is. Every ten thousand extra people per game per season brings you six hundred thousand dollars. Net." He shrugs at the simplicity of the equation. "Net. So you can see that when we went from averaging over seventy thousand people a game to thirty-nine thousand [the turnstile count], it was like driving off a cliff.

"I see hundreds of athletes coming through Wisconsin leaving with more than they had—time management skills, discipline, teamwork—things they got from playing sports at the highest level. I have no empirical data to prove that they got these things from sports, but I think that it's true. And it's good. At the same time, I don't think these are benefits that others can't have by being in the marching band or being involved in other intensely felt things. It's just that if we're going to do these things, any of them, let's do them well."

If there was one notable off-field thing that wasn't done well in the old days, it was the bookkeeping for the department. Nobody worried too much about the cash that rolled through Camp Randall as donors gave, tickets were sold, and checks were written. As long as everything worked out at the end of each fiscal year, everybody had a good time and no employees went to prison what problem could there be? So many elements of the athletic department budget and accounting system were arbitrary, convoluted, nonsensical, or virtually untraceable anyway, that the whole process of making order of what came in and what went out was largely ignored. The machine always managed to keep lurching along, no matter how screwed up finances were. Moreover, there was no new, organized computer program that the head accountant could have slipped into his laptop to straighten everything out, because there was no computer. Virtually everything former business manager Dick Schrock did was done on paper. Vast ledgers and books with his handwritten numbers and adding-machine tallies loomed everywhere around Schrock, like the trappings from a Dickensian scrivener's office. If the UW athletic department had existed in any century after the invention of numerals, paper, ink quills, and candle power, its accounting procedure would have been not too different from what it was in the 1980s.

By the time Fish came in, the tabulating had gotten completely out of hand. One day he tried to make some sense of some numbers and simply couldn't. Money was missing. There was no way to deny it. "It was about eighteen hundred dollars," says Fish. "There were three IOUs in three different cash boxes." Stunned, Fish called Schrock in and asked him what was going on. *IOUs? in a multi-million-dollar business?* Was Schrock stark raving mad?

"I said, 'Where is this money?'" Fish recalls. "And Schrock says, 'Well, I had to pay some bills fast.'"

Fish almost fainted. "What? We have means for doing that!" He ordered Schrock to show documentation for each IOU by the end of the day or there would be hell to pay, if not legal consequences.

"Schrock did the budget at his kitchen table," says Fish. "Not even with a computer, just on an adding machine. He came in that day with little handwritten receipts explaining where the money had gone. I mean, it was nuts. He had his hands on the money in the department, to pay for travel, sweatshirts, purchasing of equipment, Bucky Badger stuff, and things like that, and he could get his hands on the ticket money in the safe downstairs."

Fish promptly gave Schrock his walking papers and began a

search for a new accountant. Fish laughs now at the way the book-work used to be done, though he didn't find it amusing at the time. It's possible, he comments, that charges could have been brought against Schrock, though there wouldn't have been much point to it. The bungling no doubt was done without malicious intent; it was, well, just *that*—bungling. You don't whip a dog for not knowing its circus tricks; you get a new dog for the act. And where is Mr. Schrock now? Fish shrugs.

"It's like Argentina. He is off the face of the earth. Disappeared."

IT'S MID-AFTERNOON, AND FISH NEEDS TO TAKE A WALK, ONE OF HIS SLAPHAPPY strolls through the entrails of the athletic department, into the maze of hallways and rooms and storage areas and cul-de-sacs that make up this primitive structure.

"I'm fried," says Fish, heading out of his office. "I like to take a couple hours every week just to walk around and see what's going on, anyway."

His first stop is in front of a door midway along a forbidding-looking hallway that could have served nicely as a set in *The Fall of the House of Usher*. Fish pulls out a ring of keys, fumbles for a while, then unlocks the door and flips on a light. "Look at this," he exclaims happily, pointing at the dusty trophies, boxes, and paraphernalia stacked to the ceiling in haphazard mounds. There is part of an old Bucky costume. A team badminton plaque. Old cheerleader uniforms. Fish rummages through a box and pulls out a T-shirt celebrating the CRAZYLEGS RUN 1987. On the front is a cartoon of Elroy Hirsch, smiling widely, his legs twisted crazily around each other; on the back is a map of the state with the Heileman's Old Style beer logo inside it and the words WISCONSIN DOES IT WITH STYLE. Nobody knows this stuff is still here. Nobody cares.

Fish laughs with genuine glee at the absurdity of this collected junk. "I owe my position to the disaster I inherited," he says, relock-ing the door and moving on, "so I can't complain."

He continues past the small offices that are dark and silent and then reaches a door at the north end of the building. Opening it, he is issued into a well-lit, carpeted, drywalled, and tastefully decorated office area that houses only the football program and, on a lower level, the men's hockey office. The contrast to the dungeonlike facilities for the other twenty-five teams is so abrupt and complete that one has the feeling of having left a prison galley for the opulence of the captain's stateroom. The feeling is both accurate and intended.

"You just leaped seventy years," says Fish.

Football at a Division I university has nothing whatsoever in common with a sport such as, say, indoor track. All the pressure is on the football team, and all the glory goes to it as well. The attitude of superiority oozes from the players and coaches and the staff that caters to them and it rains down on all the other athletes: We are the warriors; we take the risks; we are above you. Barry Alvarez sometimes literally seems to strut through the athletic complex, his minions following like the entourage that follows a machine politician or a heavyweight boxing champ. No other UW coach could even imagine receiving the desperate exaltation Alvarez received from boosters, sponsors, and UW fans—before he had coached a single game on campus. That fervor was captured on a billboard that loomed over the beltway south of town: it showed Alvarez with his arms raised to the heavens, signaling either a touchdown or a miracle, or both, next to the words HAIL BARRY!

Fish stops in front of framed photos of Wisconsin's sixteen football Academic All-Americas. One of them is Don Davey, the graduating senior defensive tackle who has just been honored as the first four-time Academic All-America in NCAA history. Another photo is of Pat Richter, 1962, in a narrow tie, button-down shirt, and houndstooth jacket. Fish looks at the plaque of the man who is now his boss, at least on paper, and tilts his own head back and forth. "I don't know," he says quizzically. "A dork or a nerd?"

He moves on through the football complex, coming to a large room that hums with the sound of many video machines and computers editing tapes and printouts for the players and staff. "This is all lease-to-buy over five years," says Fish of the equipment. "Costs a little over a hundred grand per year. It's incredible. You want to know what Iowa does on third and ten, it'll search it all out for you and put it together." Whether UW wants the high-tech video stuff or not, it pretty much has to have it, Fish adds. "The Big Ten made a rule in 1990 that everything must be on video." For all sports? He smiles, shaking his head. "For football."

Fish leaves the main office area and cuts over to the McClain facility, using the enclosed, carpeted, and heated catwalk that rises above the street and attaches to the complex like a bridge to a shopping mall. He looks through the large glass wall on the second floor down at the spectacular expanse of indoor green—eighty full yards of football field—and nods. The air-conditioned turf-covered room is for the exclusive use of the football team on those days when the coach decides it's too cold, wet, hot, sunny, snowy, windy, humid, dark, or buggy to practice outdoors. Other sports teams may use the facility for running and the like, but never, never when the football team has designs on the place. How, one can't help wondering, did Badger teams manage to play football for, oh, the past hundred years or so without the benefit of such a lovely structure?

"McClain wanted it," says Fish, gesturing at the building. "When he died, that was what put it over. It cost nine and a half million dollars. They raised five million dollars and financed the rest with the state." Riding an emotional wave of sorrow and do-gooderism, the athletic department built the structure without bothering to collect the funds to pay for it. A good man had died; here was his pyramid. Nobody seemed to mind that when the go-ahead was given to begin construction, the athletic department had raised just 7 percent of the needed cash; it was still the go-go eighties and debt was just another tool in the tool belt. Trouble was, nobody at UW had any money to make the loan payments, either.

Fish recently refinanced the debt through state bonds and now has the department making payments of about $450,000 annually until the year 2009. The department would still be in the black if the McClain facility had not been built, but it just wouldn't be . . . big-time. "This is kind of the rock of our sports program," says Fish, proudly.

He turns and walks over to the 130-seat auditorium—football use only—that features theater-style chairs, blackboards, a large film screen, and inspirational words painted on the walls. TRUST . . . COMMITMENT . . . LOVE . . . BELIEF.

"That comes from Barry," says Fish.

He walks down the stairs to the football team's magnificent locker room and weight room and then once more into the old part of the building, to the fourth floor, where the basketball coaches have their cell-like chambers. Fish unlocks the door to basketball assistant Ray McCallum's office and stares at the old and ugly furnishings. "They, too, have carpet problems," he says, looking at the ratty fabric covering the floor.

Fish walks across the main drive to the Shell, the fieldhouse that provides courts and weights and a track for intramural sports as well as for some of the non-revenue varsity sports. Fish observes the student basketball games in progress and the joggers making their rounds, and he declares, "*This* is *access*. For the masses. Not for the elite."

He stops at the nearby ticket office and is pleased to see a sign on the door reading, HOCKEY—NO TICKETS AVAILABLE. BOTH NIGHTS. He stops in front of a worker at the counter. "Hi, Ruth," he says. "Any other sellouts?"

"Not right now," says the woman.

"How about basketball, can we average over ten thousand?"

"Yeah," she says. "I think we can do that."

Fish smiles. He likes to hear that. A mediocre team in a dreadful facility, but the program will do better than break even. Another step toward black ink.

He next walks up to the women's athletic offices—also in the old part of the stadium—and finds administrative program manager Laurie Irwin standing by the receptionist's desk.

"How do you think people would feel if we got rid of the pompon girls?" Fish asks her.

Irwin works with the cheerleaders, pompon girls, and Bucky Badger entertainers. She has gray hair and a no-nonsense demeanor.

"Not good," she replies.

"Hey, just floating trial balloons," says Fish, raising his hands.

Next Fish goes back down to the hockey office, which, like the football offices, are nicely appointed and reflect the sport's status as a moneymaker. Coach Jeff Sauer is engrossed in recruiting minutiae, and Fish stops only long enough to say hi to secretary Nancy Olson, who sits in front of a sign that warns I SUFFER FROM PMS—PUTTING UP WITH MEN'S SHIT.

"Hi," says Olson. "Whatcha doing?"

"Firing people with new chairs," says Fish, noting that the woman is perched on a chair that is newer than anything outside this wing of the department. Olson laughs. Hockey is a very small but efficient golden goose, laying itsy-bitsy golden eggs. Only a fool would tamper with it.

If anything or anybody should be on guard in this department, it's the low-profile sports and their coaches who bring nothing but bills to the table. No fan interest, no great booster support, no recognition, no big deal. Fish wonders if any of the people under him have realized that the easiest way to cut expenses would be to take the axe to entire sports and chop them off like dead branches. Has anybody been reading between the lines? Do these happy, trusting souls understand that no job is sacred—not when there's a budget to balance and excellence to pursue?

He roams back up the stairs, then stops just for fun in the hockey locker room. He looks at the equipment—the tools of ignorance, as the gear is sometimes called. He's tired, wiped out from all the work he's been doing to fulfill his promise to the state auditor and the chancellor. But troubleshooting is his milieu, his chosen field, and he can't let it get him down. He picks up a sweat-soaked goalie's mitt and looks at it thoughtfully.

"Ever smell a hockey glove?" he asks cheerily, extending the thing.

The stench is ungodly.

8

DONNA SHALALA, THE HUMAN THOUSAND-WATT LIGHT BULB, CLIMBS INTO HER automobile and explains the circumstances behind her ascent to the post as the highest-profile woman leader in American education. "Of course, Hunter had a woman president before me," she says, pulling out of the driveway of the UW chancellor's house—her house now—a stately three-story structure with a basketball hoop by the garage. "Plus, the school had been a women's college until 1964. And then, it all happened so *fast*. I wasn't looking for that job. And I wasn't looking for this job."

She pauses for a moment, aware of the innocence of character such blind good luck seems to suggest. She's not an innocent, not by any means. Her nickname, the one she earned during her stint as assistant secretary of HUD, was "Boom-Boom." It came from her gung ho, roll-up-the-sleeves, twin-cannon approach to solving whatever problems might lie in her path. Shalala often seems naïve, guileless, and so full of boundless energy that she could be mistaken for an eager rube who just fell off the hay truck in the middle of the big city. But rubes are not called Boom-Boom. And Shalala has always known what she was doing—maybe not exactly where she was going or by what path, but at least where she would end up. And that, of course, was the realm of power.

She grew up in Cleveland, a fine student and a feisty athlete who excelled in softball and tennis and seemed unaware that the world might place obstacles in her path to success. Even as a child she had a confidence that propelled her to simply go out and take charge of things. Her mother, Edna Shalala, a physical education teacher, attorney, and fine tennis player in her own right, tells of the time a tornado bore down dangerously close to the family home. Edna assisted Donna's twin sister, Diane, into the house, but could not find nine-year-old Donna anywhere. "I became quite alarmed," Edna later told a reporter. "I didn't know where she was. Finally, one of the neighbors told me, 'She's directing traffic up at the corner.'"

"How long am I going to stay here?" says Donna Shalala now, responding to an observation that she seems like a frog leaping toward bigger and bigger lily pads—Peace Corps volunteer in the early sixties; Guggenheim Fellowship scholar; earner of a doctoral degree in social sciences from Syracuse University in 1968; teacher at City University in New York, Yale Law School, and Columbia University Teachers College; director of the Municipal Assistance Corporation of New York City, an agency established to restore that city to fiscal stability in the early seventies; HUD official in the late seventies; Hunter College president from 1979 to 1987; and now big boss at the fourth-largest university in the country. "Well, I like this job," she states. "I have no plans to go anywhere."

She drives carefully down the icy road that leads toward campus. The tip of the Capitol building rises like a thimble above the brick-and-stone buildings that house her teachers, coaches, students, and administrators—her charges. "What's above this?" she asks. "I don't want to be president. What else would I do?" She thinks for a moment. "Maybe run a foundation or a corporation. But this is quite a job in itself."

She pulls into a parking place near the small restaurant where she often eats dinner. She steps onto the sidewalk without glancing at the bumper sticker on her trunk, the sign that has an *I*, a heart, a drawing of Bucker Badger's head, and a football on it: I Love U.W. Football. Though she is a member of the Knight Foundation's Commission on Intercollegiate Athletics—the august group of university presidents brought together to study college sport and make blueprints for its reform—Shalala is an unabashed booster for her own teams' successes afield. Excellence is what she wants—more W's than *L*'s. When people warn of the corruption that invariably undermines sports programs that are eager to climb the ladder, Shalala says simply that it won't happen at Wisconsin. "I think we can do it right," she proclaims.

She prides herself on being as involved with the football team as she is with the English department. She has personally helped recruit a number of star gridiron prospects, shaking their hands, asking about their high school teams, even going to the airport to greet the boys as they step off the planes. Of course, Shalala is so gung ho about her UW students generally that she has greeted many nonathletes at the airport as well, going so far as to carry their luggage and give them personal tours of their new dormitories. But football is different. That's where people see whether you're tough or not, whether your state is as nasty as mine, whether, in a sense, your being four-eleven and three-quarters and a woman means you can't fight. If she could be a standout second baseman for the West Boulevard Annie Oakleys the year they won the Cleveland city girls' softball championship under the coaching of George Steinbrenner (then a college student), Shalala figures, then her football players can be good students and athletic stars at the same time. What's so tricky about it? She will just infuse everyone with her enthusiasm, and the grades, wins, and prestige will fall into line.

While waiting for their house to be built in Madison, Barry Alvarez and his wife lived for a few months on the second floor of Shalala's own home, creating for Shalala one of her favorite stories about the closeness she feels toward her standing army, the football team, and its general. Alvarez often ran into other Division I coaches who complained that they had very little contact with their respective presidents or chancellors. "Hell," Alvarez would counter with a smile, "I'm *living* with mine." Shalala always laughs when she tells the story, because it shows that she is tough and hungry and in on all the boys' jokes that don't normally circulate in refined ladies' company. One of the first things Shalala said to Alvarez when he arrived on campus was, "I hate to lose." He smiled right back at her and said, "Me too." That is another story she loves to tell.

Of course, what Shalala is best at is getting good people to serve under her and then, as she says, "letting them run their own show." Since she is always pumped up and inquisitive, Shalala often finds candidates for her employ in places where other administrators would never look. Such was the case when she appointed Roger Formisano to the athletic board. She just happened to be sitting next to him on an airplane, got into a conversation with him about risk management, his teaching field, discovered he was a UW professor, and enjoyed what he had to say about a number of subjects. "I liked the way his mind worked," says Shalala. "And I liked that he liked kids." So she appointed him to the board. Simple.

"When I first got to Madison," she continues, "I was given a list of the usual cast of characters, people who had been waiting years to get on the athletic board. But I asked my staff to pull the list of faculty members who had season tickets to football, basketball, and hockey games. On that list were distinguished professors, many of whom would never have had their names considered for board positions. What bothered me was that everyone had told me that board members were either hostile toward athletics or were the other extreme, absolute jocks who couldn't have an independent view. So I found a first-rate economist like Bobbie Wolf, who went to games not just because of her husband but because she loved games, and appointed her. Then I appointed Linda Greene, a member of the law faculty, because I remembered when I recruited her to teach in our law school that she was a world-class middle-distance runner. Then I got the name Emily Comstock from someone just in conversation, and when I asked a staffer to get her résumé, I found out that not only does she hold an important position in the education department here, but that she was once a women's basketball coach at Michigan Tech. And nobody knew that. So I appointed her."

Shalala's ecumenical approach has given the board a diverse point of view, but the problems confronting members are the same as the ones confronting athletic boards everywhere: How do you win games, maintain academic integrity, and balance the budget at the same time? For Shalala, the dilemma is worth attacking with vigor, for she has never questioned the moral and educational value of big-time sport.

"I was very competitive in athletics," she says. "Cheerfully competitive. My house was full of trophies. I was the Cleveland tennis champion from age ten to thirteen, and a lot of my competitiveness came from my mother, who was a nationally ranked tennis player in the thirties. She's eighty-one now and still plays and wins in senior tournaments. I really think that my concentration and discipline comes from my training in sports. Tennis taught me how to focus and get rid of distractions. People ask me what I think about on the tennis court and I say, 'Nothing.' Nothing. When you're totally concentrating, you're not concerned about anything else except what you're doing."

Despite her focus, résumé, intellect, and energy, Shalala was still a long shot to take over at Wisconsin, because she had no experience managing a large athletic department. "The glass ceiling for women getting control at large, academically prestigious universities has always been athletics," she says. "There is no woman in a comparable position to me. Hanna Gray runs the University of Chicago, but that's not Division I. My friend Margaret Ross Barnett just took over at the University of Houston, but academically that school is not particularly prestigious. We rank number one in the nation among public universities as a research school. We have the largest budget of any university in the nation, a billion dollars. Wisconsin is big-time in everything."

It is, and Shalala got her job because she was perceived as being big-time herself, despite her inexperience with corporate-sized football staffs and NCAA Final Four television revenue-sharing. But then, the athletic department's woes were mostly financial, and who better to handle them than someone who used to give lectures on how a city of ten million could avoid fiscal collapse? Still, she was not prepared for the athletic department chaos which unfolded, as she likes to put it, "in front of my eyes."

She grimaces as she recalls reading in the papers about the decline in football revenue for the school, something she had not been warned about. "I said to our athletic director, Ade Sponberg, 'What are we doing without this income?' And he said, 'There's no problem.' So I said, 'Maybe you'd better bring the budget in so I can look at it.' "

Sponberg brought it in, and the chancellor looked at it and almost gagged. "I discovered the whole mess myself," she says. "Ade assembled all these people around the room, and they didn't know what their budget numbers were. One of my fields of expertise is municipal finance; I actually *know* about budgets. I teach things like state budgeting and the like, and here were all these people who had a deficit building up that was unbelievable and nobody—not the Athletic Board, not the athletic director, not the deputy athletic director—nobody knew what the real numbers were or where everything was headed.

"You know what it reminded me of? The New York financial crisis, the one I worked on in 1975. I called my friends back in New York and said, 'I can't believe it, I'm going through it again!' I knew the culture of public bankruptcy, of dealing with people who didn't know the numbers, how to pin it all down, basically nice people of goodwill who just couldn't lay out any kind of strategy.

"The people here were unwilling to face reality. They didn't know how to think about it. And if we didn't change things fast, we would have gone straight down the tubes. We wouldn't have had money to start the sports the next year. We couldn't have paid for the scholarships. I literally mean we were bankrupt. Chapter Eleven. We would have had to pay the athletic deficit out of the university's instructional budget, and that would have affected the educational programs of the school. There was no official declaration of insolvency, because it was just like the New York City situation in that there were funds—in this case, ticket money—coming in every year. But we caught it just before it got completely out of hand. We changed the management of the company, we stretched out the debt, and we got a strategic plan. Just like you do with a bankruptcy."

One of the first things Shalala did when she sensed the depth of the athletic department sinkhole was to contact an expert and ask for advice. The person she called was the legendary Don Canham, the former University of Michigan athletic director and the acknowledged father of collegiate sports marketing and salesmanship. Canham, a former NCAA high jump champion while a student at Michigan in the early 1940s, came back to his alma mater in 1968, saw the primitive way Wolverine sports were being promoted, and promptly went about whipping up so much business for the University of Michigan athletic department that by 1991 the department had a budget of $30 million. Back when Al Fish was still a pimply high school kid, Canham was acting on the axiom that people will buy almost anything related to big-time college sport, as long as you sell it to them with fervor. Canham's marketplace was as vast as his imagination. He used direct mail and high-concept advertising campaigns to sell everything from Michigan football tickets to maize-and-blue golf umbrellas. In his first year he saw that the famed Michigan-Ohio State football game was not going to be a sellout in

Ann Arbor, so he did something unheard of—he took the ten thousand remaining tickets down to Columbus, Ohio, and sold them there. *To Buckeye fans.* Since then, Michigan has played over one hundred consecutive home games in front of crowds in excess of a hundred thousand, and has led the nation in home football attendance for nineteen straight years.

Canham came to Madison as a favor to Shalala, refusing any kind of stipend, and sifted through the rubble of the UW department. Shalala had lunch with him, "very publicly," as she puts it, so people would know the serious stuff had begun. Canham declared that it indeed was a mess and that Shalala should kick the department into the twentieth century by getting competent people in place and doing all the modern things that Shalala intuitively felt should be done. Folks in Madison sensed that if nothing else, the new chancellor was smart enough to know who had done things right in similar situations. "Bringing Canham in gave me instant credibility with the sports press," she states.

She was aware, however, that all things are not equal in education or sport. "Sure, the playing field isn't level," she says of the different academic standards that exist at different universities. "That's why we're trying to get reform into sport, change minimum academic standards and rate of progress towards a degree and all sorts of things like that. Everything the Knight Commission does to raise academic standards will help Wisconsin—what we're trying to do is organize the country so everybody does the same thing at the same time. It's not easy to put education and sport together, but the choice here at Wisconsin is either to put the two together or get out of the business."

Shalala's goal is to make the University of Wisconsin a multicultural democracy, reflecting her belief that in a perfect world nobody cheats, lies, abuses others, cares about race, color, gender, or hairstyle or does anything less than give 100 percent in the lab and on the football field. While she favored the concept of a hate-speech code when the issue came up on campus, she ended up opposing the actual rule that was drafted, because she insisted it should not restrict anything said in the classroom or during an artistic performance. Valhalla must not have speech police marching through its domain.

Nor did Shalala take kindly to football coach Don Morton's

demeaning statements about the role of sport at an academic institution. "He described the athletic department as the toy department of the university," she says. "And from the moment I met him, I resented the description. It's too serious a business for that. People sitting in a stadium at a sports event becomes a bonding experience. It gives everybody a sense of community, of belonging to the institution. It's like other big communal ceremonies, like commencements, wars, religious events, Thanksgivings, family gatherings. But there are very few things that are shared by seventy thousand people."

One thing that stunned the chancellor when she came to Madison was the attention the local media gave to UW sports—a quirk of journalism brought about because Madison was big enough to consider itself a big city but far too small to have the buffering scale of a place like, say, New York, or even Milwaukee. People wanted the sports gossip, she was told, and by God, the media was going to give it to them. Even if it was just college stuff.

"When we had a press conference on [the firing of Don] Morton," she recalls, "there were more TV cameras there than there are TVs in the state. When my friends in New York ask me, 'How important is college athletics?' I tell them, 'When I fired the football coach, they interrupted the soap operas to show it. The *soap operas*.' I'll never forget that.

"One woman I know, who's married to a sports nut, told me she never read the sports pages until all this started here. 'Now I'm addicted,' she said, 'I was fascinated by the Morton-Sponberg thing, and now I read the sports pages every day. It's like a soap opera.'" Shalala had laughed then, and shaken her head. "It still amazes me," she says now.

Later that evening, at a party at Shalala's house for the National Indoor Women's Tennis Tournament that is being held at the new and modern Nielsen Tennis Building—named for its prime donor, Art Nielsen, a UW grad and founder of the famed TV ratings company—Nielsen himself is talking to a group of people, dredging up athletic stories that show how much, and at times how little, college sport has changed in the second half of the twentieth century. "In 1941 I qualified for the nationals in tennis," says Nielsen, eyes twinkling in his craggy face. "I went to Harry Stuhldreyer, one of Notre Dame's legendary Four Horsemen and then the athletic director here, and I asked him what the plans were for me regarding the nationals. He said, 'There aren't any.' I said, 'But I've worked so hard,' and he said, 'You know, tennis isn't a major sport.'

"Then he looked at me, opened up a desk drawer, opened a cash box, and started peeling out tens. When he got to one hundred dollars, he said, 'Is that enough?' I looked down and then I said, 'You know I've got a partner.' He counted out another hundred dollars and closed the box."

End of story. Everybody smiles. The good old days.

9

BARRY ALVAREZ TAPS HIS FINGERS ON HIS WOODEN DESK TOP AND LOOKS AT HIS
trusty recruiting coordinator, Rob Ianello, who stands beside him
like an aide de camp at the general's elbow. Today is the official
NCAA signing day for this year's crop of football recruits. Ianello,
dark-haired, in his late twenties, with a touch of Southern drawl in
his voice from his days as an assistant at the University of Alabama,
has worked hard to upgrade the quality of player who will wear the
Badgers' red and white in future years. This year's batch of athletes
seems better than anything Don Morton brought in during his tenure, but then, with kids you never know. You don't even know for
sure that the ones who swore on their family Bibles they'd attend
UW will really come across and sign on the dotted line once D-day
arrives. And it has arrived.

"Palermo can't take off," says Alvarez with nervous distraction.
He looks past Ianello and out the window at the fog that shrouds the
campus. He is speaking of assistant coach John Palermo, who is stuck
at the Madison airport when he should be flying to Minnesota to sign
stud fullback/linebacker Matt Nyquist to a letter of intent. "It's five
and a half hours by car to where the kid lives, the other side of
Minneapolis," says Alvarez firmly. "He'll drive if he has to. I guarantee you that."

A couple of players signed at the most recent UW home basketball game, but the others will have to be hunted down in their hometowns and watched while they sign up: put the pen in their hands, give them the big smile and the reassuring joke or two, wink at Mom and Dad or whoever is legally in charge, pet the dog, ignore the crying babies and ringing phones, and then when the athletes have scrawled their names on the letter of intent, put the document in the briefcase like a fragile artifact and head out to find the next fickle teenager/assassin before he defects to some heathen place such as Ann Arbor.

"Jaeyson Wilson, from Tampa," says Ianello with a slight nod of his head, like a man recalling a dream. "He committed to us on Sunday morning. Wide receiver. Damn good. Then Kentucky got to him. On Monday. We went to see him on Tuesday, but that was it." The kid was long gone.

Alvarez thinks of Derrick Taite, the flash from Moss Point, Mississippi, the youngster who loved UW to the max before he was gobbled up by the Jackie Sherrill all-Dixie show. "He was here and we had sixteen inches of snow," says the coach, gazing again into the fog. "Went traying by the observatory. Loved the snow. Never seen it before . . ."

Alvarez goes silent for a while. Suffering seeps from the lines in his forehead. Then, abruptly, his face lights up, he smiles broadly and says one word: "Maniecki!" He is thinking of Jason Maniecki, a monster lineman from the Wisconsin Dells. "This is a big kid," grins the coach. "Parents from Warsaw. Moved to this country at age ten. Family runs a couple motels up in the Dells. The Shamrock is one of them, I think."

Alvarez looks down at a list of players' names on a pad of paper and crosses Maniecki's name off. Praise the Lord, the young man has signed and is safely in the fold. "At a banquet he told me he was going to sign," says Alvarez. "And then I looked out at the crowd and his parents weren't looking at me, and I thought, 'Oh, God, no! No!' And I was in a panic, but then his dad comes up and says of some other recruiter, 'They brainwash him! They brainwash him!' "

Relief flooded back into Alvarez's soul at that moment; he was on the side of the angels once again, the Manieckis' savior, their ally against the ruthless horde that would sell Jason a bill of goods, lure him to a campus where no one would care about him as a student-athlete, where he would be just a piece of meat and not a unique University of Wisconsin *human being*.

"This is a man," says Alvarez dreamily. "Big, thick neck. Two hundred seventy pounds and cut. He just won his second state heavyweight wrestling title. His opponents run from him."

The reverie leads Alvarez to think about the talent that escapes yearly from Wisconsin to other Big Ten schools and universities nationwide, simply because UW has such a poor reputation in football and because previous coaches tolerated the brawn drain as part of their fate. "The first thing we gotta do," says the coach, "is build a wall around this state. We can't let our best players get away. Every year there are seven to fifteen Division I players we better keep.

"This kid, Jamie Mignon, the All-America linebacker from Appleton, we thought we could get him. But he went to a damn Michigan camp as a sophomore. These football camps are just recruiting camps—sure, they all are. We had six hundred kids at our own camp last summer, with a number of prospects. We just have to promote it more."

Ianello leaves to work in his own office as Alvarez pulls out a UW football camp brochure and glances through it. Disguised as a folder containing explanatory information about a low-key, mid-June football camp for average sports-minded kids, the high-gloss, full-color, five-page brochure is actually a recruiting tool to lure future studs to the Madison campus before they've developed all-star reputations or allegiances to other schools. The brochures are basically unregulated by the NCAA, and they are, as Alvarez notes, a critical weapon in the battle for the hearts and minds of future stadium-filling ballplayers.

"Recruiting is finished today, but tomorrow we got five coaches going in-state and four going to Chicago to drop off camp brochures at schools and leave questionnaires for kids," he says. "We'll call every high school in this state before May." Alvarez thinks for a moment and then yells loudly, "Boomer! Boomer!"

A short, plump, smiling middle-aged man limps into the room.

"Boomer," says Alvarez, "how many high schools in this state?"

"Four hundred fifty," says the man. "Playing football, public and private." He looks around, sees nothing more is needed from him, and leaves. His real name is Pat O'Connor, but everybody calls him Boomer. Alvarez doesn't know why.

"He was here when we came here," explains Alvarez with a

shrug. "I thought, who the hell is this? We were trying to clean up the image of the place and didn't want guys like him walking around, looking like that, in sloppy clothes. But we were trying to figure out what was going on with recruiting, because none of us had any idea, and in a couple of weeks we found out he's like a computer, he knows everything about recruiting—guys' size, weight, who's committed where. He gets faxes daily from scouting people, he's just a recruiting nut. So we get him to wear a tie and clean up his act, and now we list him as Volunteer Recruiting Secretary. He's a funny little guy, lives with his mother. Never been paid."

Alvarez starts to say more but is interrupted by a yelp from Ianello, who is standing in the doorway.

"Cory Raymer, line one!"

Alvarez picks up his phone and says with a big, relaxed laugh, "High-sticking anyone? Great to have you aboard!"

Raymer, Ianello explains, is a hockey player as well as a football standout. "He kills people," whispers Ianello, as Alvarez chatters away. This kid is in the bag. He's sitting at home with UW assistant Paul Jett, signed, sealed, and waiting to be delivered.

"Is your dad there?" asks the coach. "Let me talk to him, okay?"

Alvarez covers the phone and looks pleadingly at Ianello.

"Mark!" Ianello whispers.

"Mark," says Alvarez. "Thrilled to have your son! We promise to take care of him."

Alvarez hangs up and sits back, waiting for the next call to come through. He is buoyed by the recent conversation and feeling better about his chances of success at this school. "We're starting to get players comparable to those on the teams we're playing," he says. "They weren't before."

He straightens his tie and removes his glasses and places them on his desk. "The butt-kissing is over," he says in a new, firmer tone. "That kid, Jaeyson Wilson, he'll have to be de-recruited down there at Kentucky. He thinks he's the program. I told him we'll win whether he comes here to Wisconsin or not." The coach realizes this sounds a little heady. "Of course," he adds, "that was after I was pretty sure we'd lost him."

IN THE SMALL ACCOUNTING OFFICE ACROSS THE HALL FROM PAT RICHTER'S office, Tami Holmquist hunkers over pages of budget requests from the various sports teams. Holmquist is a certified public accountant who joined the athletic department last fall as its official business manager to replace Dick Schrock and attempt to bring some order to the bookkeeping methods used by the department. She is young, energetic, and already somewhat overwhelmed by the inertia of this bureaucratic monster that just keeps gobbling up money.

She smiles without humor, her freckled cheeks rounding into circles, as she surveys the numbers. "Most of the budgets are in, but not all," she says. "Most seem to be running about twenty percent over last year. Some are more." She shakes her head. "Football wants all charter planes for away games. None of those games are more than five hours away by bus, most are less, and I could save twenty-five thousand dollars per trip if the team went by bus. Football is seventy-four percent over last year on its travel budget."

Holmquist seems truly dazed by what she is dealing with. She thinks back to her acceptance letter, the one she wrote to Pat Richter last August: "Let me reiterate how pleased I am at getting this position. I was hoping I would, as I feel it is the perfect job for me and I know that I will fit into your organization well." But there was never any budget looniness like this back at her old accounting firm of Suby, Von Haden & Associates. Is she fitting into this organization well? she asks herself. No, she is not. She has already had a run-in with football strength coach Scott Raridon, in which he insulted her for questioning his equipment purchases, and she has felt the scorn of Alvarez simply for suggesting that the football team, like every other team, must live within its means.

"When I first got here there was a large order for pants, shorts, windbreakers, and parkas for the football coaches," she says. "I called in Scott Raridon to ask him about it and he said, 'Who the hell do you think you are to question me?' I just said, 'It's my job,' but I gave them the money eventually. I had just paid a bill for football coaches' clothing for twelve thousand dollars, and I just wondered, *why am I spending more*? But I gave them . . ." She leans over, opens a drawer, and flips through a file. "About two thousand dollars extra."

After that she had a discussion with Fish about Raridon, asking, "Who is this guy? Is there something I should know?" Fish responded by saying there had been some troubles with Raridon in other matters. "Want me to yell at him?" he asked.

"No," she replied, not wanting to appear to be a whiner. "I can handle this myself."

But could she? The whole mathematical nightmare of the department's finances as well as these strange, aggressive men acting as though they must be served by underlings—it was overwhelming to her.

"You know, if you apply an overhead to all three revenue sports, each one turns out in reality to be a loser. The only real plus was men's basketball, and that was only from the CBS-TV contract. It's crazy. The sports have never been done that way; people only look at the directs, not the other things. With football there are no charges for cleanup, maintenance, or security at the stadium, the offices, the McClain facility. And the administration up here is not written as an expense, but they take a lot of our time, budget, and support areas." Holmquist looks out in the hallway. "Steve!" she yells.

Steve Malchow, the sports information director, who came with Alvarez from the University of Iowa two years before, pops in. He is a tiny, bespectacled young man, who also at times has been stunned by the athletic department's primitive workings. Holmquist asks him how much time he and his assistants spend on each sport.

"I would say at least half our time on football," he says. "Twenty percent on basketball, twenty percent on hockey, and ten percent on all the rest." He smiles zanily. "Hey, it's like when I was at Iowa—fill the stadium, and all your problems disappear!"

Malchow leaves and Holmquist looks back at her numbers and files. She takes a deep breath and shrugs. Maybe it's too soon to make any judgments about the program or the people in it; after all, she's been here only five months.

"I should have all the budgets by the end of the week," she says. "Maybe it'll make sense then."

10

AL FISH STUDIES THE YOUNG MAN SITTING IN FRONT OF HIM. FISH WEARS HIS most kindly, reasonable, empathetic expression, the one that says, "You know me—I'm just a regular guy trying to do what's right."

The young man's name is Chris Tipton; he is a senior from Rockford, Illinois, majoring in advertising and political science. He is a student government leader, an elected member of the Segregated University Fees Allocation Committee (SUFAC), the group that has an interest in anything the university brass does that might involve siphoning money from the general student body. This is the second year that all UW students are being forced to pay a ten-dollar-per-semester fee that goes straight to the athletic department to help it pay its debts, and Tipton wants to know why. While the fee doesn't sound like much—just the cost of a few pitchers of beer at the Kollege Klub or Jingles or half the price of an economics textbook, it nevertheless means a free and clear $750,000 for the athletic department. And many students don't like the idea of giving up anything—even ten bucks a term—to a branch of the university they see as having so little to do with its academic mission.

Fish looks sweetly at Tipton and says, "I want to give you an overview of this whole mess."

The clean-shaven, short-haired student is neatly appointed in pressed jeans, a starched yellow shirt with a polo pony on the breast, horn-rimmed glasses, and Top-Siders. He seems eager to hear the important man's tale.

Fish explains to him that the department is $1.95 million in debt and that about $4 million worth of deferred maintenance costs also lurk on the horizon. "However," says Fish, as if from one friend to another, "the state picks up eighty percent of the cost of maintenance. What happens is, we build the facilities, like Camp Randall, then we deed them over to the state after we've paid for them, and then we can do a million dollars' worth of maintaining them for just two hundred thousand dollars." Of course, Fish fails to mention that Camp Randall Stadium itself was built seventy-four years ago on land that once housed a Union military training center during the Civil War, with a starting grant of fifteen thousand dollars—a very large sum in those days—from the state legislature, but that's not relevant just now. He's selling Tipton on the efficiency and frugality of the department.

He explains that people in this state want champions in the field, and the athletic department must winnow, repair, and upgrade to provide what the citizens demand. It is a simple, patriotic mandate. "Nothing was done on computers here, it was all done on typewriters," Fish says. "I mean, it was *scary*. So we're investing in computers and systems we never had before. One of the biggest things we're developing is a fully automated box office. Right now tickets are an incredible headache, but with the new system, we'll probably save fifty to seventy thousand dollars just on the printing."

Tipton nods with understanding. He knows about selling and persuading and dealing; that's what he's majoring in. Spending money saves money in the long run.

"All of these things are going to cost money, of course," continues Fish. "But our theme is that everything we spend should buy permanent improvement. People have suggested we have a telethon, a Save Bucky campaign, something like that, to bail us out. But that's short-term thinking. What do you do next year? So we won't be conducting any charity drives. We'll be doing it ourselves."

Good old roll-up-the-sleeves effort is the closing pitch today: Not only is the department frugal and proud, but it is also as tough as a Wisconsin trapper. Tipton nods again, though he knows (at least subconsciously) that his basic question has not been answered, only tap-danced upon.

"We want to keep the student fee until we get our debt reduced," Fish says the way one pal might tell another about the teensy-tiny dent he put in the borrowed lawn mower. "That's our proposal."

Tipton squints and looks at the floor. "My personal feelings aside," Tipton says, looking up, "I don't know if SUFAC will go along with that. Some people on the committee, quite frankly, are political activists who have no interest in athletics. Only two or three out of the eleven go to games, like myself."

Fish nods. He understands. He brings up other matters of interest to Tipton—the "Bleacher Creatures" student section at Camp Randall, the use of student passes for entrance to games ("Last year a lot of students threw their passes over the bleachers for others to use," warns Tipton), improvements to the Fieldhouse. "I sat way up there for the Michigan game," says Tipton, thinking about the rickety old building. "Behind one of those 'minor obstructions.'"

Fish smiles and says, "Our ticket man calls those 'leaners.'"

Fish continues explaining the other methods the department will be using to raise funds, so that Tipton will know the students are not being fleeced, noting that ethical considerations always come first in these fiscal matters. There was, for instance, the recent ill-fated athletic department fund-raising operation put on by a Madison car dealership that had to be quashed before it turned sordid and possibly criminal. "Kaiser Ford had this campaign where they basically said, 'Test drive a car and ride with a cheerleader,'" says Fish, frowning with indignation. "It was on the radio for about three hours, until I called up and reamed them out. It had sexual overtones. I mean, *think* of who might come in for a ride. The cheerleaders cancelled."

After a suitable pause to show his disgust, Fish continues, looking at Tipton with sincerity. "But there are many inoffensive ways to market things—license plates, phones, credit cards, on and on. So we don't have to ask you for more. And one other thing. We're not in the business of access here, we're in the business of making quality. We will be cutting sports."

This dollop of inside information gets Tipton's attention, as well it should. There has been a buzz throughout the department and parts of campus that sports will be axed to trim fat, but no one on Richter's staff has made any official announcement to that effect. "What about women's volleyball?" Tipton asks. He is a women's volleyball fan.

"It's safe," says Fish. "And the sports that remain, their budgets will go up."

"Well, this is encouraging," says the student. He strokes his chin, thinks. "Again, I just want to prepare you for the reception you're likely to get when you try to extend the fee. There will be a lot of cynicism because of what has happened here in the past."

Fish nods with understanding. "We're dealing with a lot of people who don't believe athletics are important or should be part of the academic process," he says. "I'm not worried about that. In many ways, I was the same as a student." Again, the bonding thing—Fish and Tipton are brethren, on the same page.

"The chancellor envisions this to be a permanent thing," says Tipton. "She seems consumed with instilling in the students that this is a permanent fee." He looks warmly at Fish. "You seem honest," he says.

Tipton then asks about having concerts at Camp Randall to raise money. "In May of '88 we had Pink Floyd and it was successful," he says. "I attended and had a good time. But we haven't had any more concerts. Why?"

"We tried with Springsteen, McCartney, and the Grateful Dead," replies Fish, "but they all go to Alpine Valley for guaranteed multinight deals for a million dollars. But we are shooting for somebody for next summer and spring."

"Who?" asks Tipton, perking up.

"If I tell you, you can't tell. Can't get rumors started."

Tipton shakes his head. "No, I won't tell."

"The Beach Boys in August," says Fish conspiratorially. This gets no response. "And in the spring, Genesis and Phil Collins."

"Oh, wow!" Tipton looks delighted. Then his smile fades. "Phil Collins—aren't you shooting too high?"

"We need the revenue," says Fish with a shrug. "I can't spend months on a project if all we'll make is ten thousand dollars."

The student ponders this. A capitalist himself, Tipton works part-time for the Wisconsin State Lottery, helping the state shake cash from its citizens so it can then provide services for the people that they could have paid for themselves had they not spent so much on lottery tickets.

"Where were you before you came here?" he asks Fish.

"Health and Social Services. The state. What are your plans?"

"I interviewed for a sales position with Oscar Mayer, and it went real well," says Tipton brightly. "I wish Pat Richter had been here today, so I could talk to him about it." Richter is off with the hockey team in North Dakota just now.

"Chris, you wouldn't want to be in a marketing job here, would you?" asks Fish.

"Here?"

Fish nods.

"What kind of pay?"

"Mid-twenties."

"Not bad. That's not bad."

The meeting ends with both men agreeing they'll stay in touch and with Tipton stating he'll think hard about the job possibility. They shake hands and Tipton leaves. Fish sits back comfortably. That went well, he is thinking. Will Tipton be able to swing the SUFAC members to the side of the department?

"He's a conservative, hard-core Republican," says Fish. "Some of those kids are antiwar radicals. They'll never vote for this. But it doesn't matter. Donna will override it."

It's such a sham, anyway; you just let the kids think they run the university, then when it comes down to closing time, the real political animals rise and do whatever is necessary. Shalala, like Fish, is nobody's fool; she may be a champion for the downtrodden in society, but she knows how to get what she needs, too. Just now Fish is more concerned with the young man he has just dealt with than he is with lining up straw votes for the student fee. A perplexed look crosses his face.

"If he's good, I'd hire him," Fish says. "But it worries me when a kid is twenty-one and that right, that conservative. He works for the state lottery? At that age I was a nihilist with long hair, rebelling against society, you name it. Jeez, he doesn't have property taxes or anything! He wanted advice? Advice? I couldn't give him advice. I was too busy manipulating him."

Does that sound too cynical? Sorry. There is something a little larger than simple sports funding going on here, than squeezing a few bucks from post-adolescents. "Look," says Fish. "We carry the identity of the state with us. We *are* the state. Our sports are nationally known—for people who used to live in this state, who maybe live in Arizona now and still love Wisconsin—I mean, that's *us*. The

Badgers. We've had ten Nobel Prize winners here, but who can name one? People can name Barry Alvarez, though. That's reality. People in this state talk about beating Ohio State and Purdue, not about science grants. That's reality."

THERE IS NO SIGN ON RICK ABERMAN'S DOOR SAYING SHRINK OR PSYCHOLOGIST or THE DOCTOR IS IN. His office next to the football locker room at the McClain facility is not advertised in any way. "I don't want a sign," says Aberman, relaxing at his desk between seeing athletes. "I don't want a sign that says 'IF YOU'RE CRAZY, WALK IN THIS DOOR.' I work hard at making this an okay place to be, against that old school of thought that says if you need help, you're weak."

Aberman knows that athletes have psychological problems, the same as everybody else. And he also knows that dealing with those problems sometimes can be the hardest thing an athlete does, and the most beneficial for his or her career. "If you just identify the problem, get help, deal with it rationally, you can become a much better athlete," he says. "Take eating disorders. For years people denied them entirely: 'Not on our team!' But eating disorders are a big part of sport—for gymnastics, wrestling, cross-country, track, basketball, volleyball, swimming, and other teams, especially for women. Being anorexic or bulimic doesn't help you. Just recently I was seeing five women athletes, all on laxatives, binging and purging. You do that, you lose fluids, electrolytes, your body finally breaks down, and it's just very dangerous. And it will threaten your career."

On the coffee table by his couch is a pamphlet entitled "The Road to Disordered Eating: How Do I Turn Around?" Inside there is a chart of a road leading from "Normal Eating" to "Anorexia Nervosa." Aberman has gently offered the pamphlet to many female athletes.

"One sport that bothers me just by its very nature is women's gymnastics," he continues. "It creates problems, because the athletes don't want to look like women, they want to look like little kids. They don't say, 'This is college, we're women now, we shouldn't get graded down because of it.' But it's like cross-country, they don't want big boobs or hips because they get in their way. It puts the athletes in a dilemma; becoming a woman is like a career-ending injury. Some of them train continually, not because they want to, but because they're afraid of what they'll become if they don't—women.

"A couple of years ago female gymnasts who came to practice just a pound overweight were punished and could not practice. Their coach, Terry Bryson, put them in a room, closed the door, and told them to think about it. Well, I finally went to Paula Bonner, the women's AD, and she talked to Terry, and the three of us met and worked out a weight policy. I didn't want to be in a disciplinary role, because that's not my job. But I was forced into it by the lack of action by anybody else."

On the wall of his office is a poster of Albert Einstein with words stating GREAT SPIRITS HAVE ALWAYS ENCOUNTERED VIOLENT OPPOSITION FROM MEDIOCRE MINDS.

Aberman doesn't feel that he is blessed with an Einsteinian mind, but he does sometimes feel that his rational approach to addressing the problems of UW athletes—who are, after all, just college students—is not what the athletic department really wants from him. It's much easier for coaches to understand the function of the sports trainer, a person who fixes ankles and knees and shoulders, things you can see, than it is for them to figure out a guy who helps players deal with overbearing parents or depression. Aberman works on heads, and that's troublesome. He was hired, of course, to do just that, to help athletes with their head problems. His very hiring was a tribute to the essential decency of the state and the university itself; only a liberal, nurturing school would care enough about its athletes' mental health to put a man such as Aberman on its athletic department staff. Aberman is unaware of another administrator like him at any other Division I school. Oh, there are sports shrinks at some schools, but they are in place to help athletes reduce stress, focus energies, "image," meditate, and basically kick butt afield. Aberman is at UW to help athletes become healthier people, period. Hired under another regime, he often wonders whether Richter or Fish would have brought him aboard if the choice were theirs. After all, what's his contribution to the bottom line? Not much.

It's late now, and Aberman closes up shop and heads over to the old weight room in Camp Randall to see his buddy, assistant strength coach Steve Myrland. There are only a handful of athletes pumping iron in the room—women mostly—and Myrland, a sturdy but not musclebound man with a wry grin, is telling them to stretch. "Be sure and hang," he says, pointing to a iron chin-up bar overhead. The women flex their broad backs, walk to the bar, and take turns hanging limply from the bar.

Aberman and Myrland chat casually. They are both outsiders: Aberman the iconoclastic headshrinker, Myrland, the strength coach, who emphasizes limberness and wants to write novels. Myrland's small, old-fashioned weight room itself puts him out of the mainstream; this room is for members of the "minor" sports—God forbid a rower or runner or female volleyballer go into the gleaming, high-tech vastness that is the football weight room in the McClain facility, run by Scott Raridon. That palace is only for revenue producers. Myrland detests Raridon, not only for his supercilious attitude toward non-gridders, but also because he thinks Raridon is untrustworthy, a petty man who loves acting as emperor. Though hockey players bring in money—to the tune of about fifty thousand dollars per home game—and could lift in the McClain gym or anywhere else they wanted, most of them work out in "Steve's" gym rather than the football gym because of their respect for Myrland. The strength coach talks squarely to them, and they appreciate that.

As Aberman and Myrland prepare to go to tonight's game at the Coliseum, they discuss the quirks of the hockey players on the UW team. The most unusual player is Sean Hill, the bad-boy defenseman who will be making his home-ice return tonight after his suspension following the Denver game.

"He's tough and durable and he doesn't whine," says Myrland. "But he's not really coachable. He gets in shape his own way—I can't do anything with him. He's a loose cannon, which is part of his genius."

The two men climb into Aberman's half-frozen car, shivering as the heater blasts out icy air. "Ever hear the expression 'All the tools, no tool box'?" says Myrland. "That's Sean."

In the game against the University of Alaska-Fairbanks, Hill quickly scores a goal and UW takes a 2–0 lead. Hill then seems to drift off into a zone of complacency, skating casually as though enjoying a glide along Lake Mendota. "He's a good kid," coach Jeff Sauer said before the game. "But you never know what planet he's on."

The Badgers have to scramble to escape with a 5–4 victory. In the locker room afterward Sauer watches as his players undress and head off to the shower. The warriors who look so intimidating in their skates, helmets, and pads, reveal themselves to be basically normal-sized young men with innocent faces. Still, this is the proving ground for many players who will go on to lucrative careers in the National Hockey League. Standout junior goaltender Duane Derksen two years ago was playing behind Badger goalie Curtis Joseph: Joseph now has a million-dollar contract with the St. Louis Blues. Twenty-four former Badger skaters are currently playing in the NHL, and a number of them have made the NHL All-Star team. If the money is right, there are several current Badgers, Derksen and Hill prime among them, who might desert immediately for the pro league.

"We have all kinds of kids coming through here," says Sauer, "all with different goals. Some won't be here long. Some just want to play college hockey. Sean Hill." Sauer shakes his head, smiling weakly. "Old Sean." It appears he has more to say, but he just smiles and walks over to talk to Aberman.

Outside the locker room door, Pat Richter and his wife, Renee, wait with other parents for their sons to emerge. Renee is cheerleader-cute, with braces on her upper teeth, and while she waits she thinks about all the time she has put into promoting and assisting her son's hockey career. Aberman had said earlier how amazing hockey families are, unlike any other families of young sports stars. "Some of those families," he said, "are incredibly dependent on the performance of the son for their self-esteem. They live for the hockey player. They travel with the kid's team from the time he starts in midget league. It's a whole different dynamic for me to deal with those families."

But Renee Richter thinks mostly of the not-always-pleasant hours she spent lugging her son and his pals to distant places so they could play, and she could watch. "You should drive back from Green Bay sometime with six hockey players in a station wagon in the dead of winter, when it's so cold everything is frozen solid, except the equipment," she says. "Odor? It's an experience."

Finally Barry Richter saunters out, glasses on, hair wet, a wild-patterned red tie hanging around his neck.

"Where did you get that?" says his dad, the AD, in awe.

The son groans, shrugs. He's bored. He's got things to do. His parents follow him as he heads for the exit.

AL FISH HAS GONE TO PURDUE UNIVERSITY IN WEST LAFAYETTE, INDIANA, TO look at the new scoreboard the fellow Big Ten school has erected in its arena. A similar scoreboard for UW—one with the space around the stats-keeping lightbulbs rented or leased to various advertisers—could mean more money for the Badgers' sports kitty.

In his athletic department office Pat Richter says, "I think Al just wanted to get out of town." But he's joking. A high-tech scoreboard with advertising on it is something that could bring great pleasure to Fish, the way a new train set brings joy to a child. There is a growing concern, however, that revenue from such advertising might come under scrutiny from the Internal Revenue Service. The IRS has been looking closely at all university athletic department moneymaking schemes, seeing some of them as business ventures subject to taxation rather than as not-for-profit fund-raising. Ohio State was recently nailed by the IRS for not paying taxes on scoreboard advertising, for instance. "I think we're exempt from that," says Richter. "The money we would make from something like this is plowed back into the university. It's called—what?—'unrelated business income,' I think."

At this moment, though, Richter's mind is not focused on the money-making schemes of his sidekick Fish, but rather on the recent disturbance which occurred in the women's basketball program.

Just two days ago, starting junior point guard Amy Bauer quit the team, citing "personal reasons" for leaving. Her quitting came just one day after women's basketball assistant coach Mike Peckham was suspended by Richter for, as Richter stated in a letter to Peckham, "alleged violation of item number 5 in your contract." That item deals with compliance with the various rules and policies of the University of Wisconsin, the Big Ten conference, and the NCAA. Though nothing more was publicly stated by the athletic department about the reasons for Peckham's suspension, rumors flying all over campus suggest it had something to do with sexual hijinks—specifically that Peckham and Bauer, the all-time assist leader for the team, have been having an affair. Bauer's quitting immediately after Peckham's suspension only added fuel to the rumor fire.

Word was already leaking from players and others close to the team that in a tense team meeting on February 20, head coach Mary Murphy berated Bauer and demanded that she apologize to her teammates for her relationship with Peckham. A married man with two small children, the thirty-two-year-old Peckham was hired by Murphy when she became head coach in 1986; he worked primarily as the head recruiter and academic coordinator for the team. A handsome man with thick brown hair and an easy smile, Peckham has remained silent about the disciplinary action, adding to the mystery. Word was that team members had seen the player and the coach kissing, somebody else had supposedly seen them in a hot tub together on a road trip. The stories were titillating and were spurred on by the fact that Bauer, a willowy, five-foot-ten-inch blue-eyed blonde, was unquestionably the prettiest woman on the team.

Barry Baum was on the story fast. His front-page article in the *Daily Cardinal* featured a picture of Bauer on the left and Peckham on the right under the heading WOMEN'S BASKETBALL PLAYER BOLTS FROM TEAM. In the story Baum mostly catalogued all the people who refused to talk to him about the event: Richter "replied, 'I can't comment on that.'. . . Murphy also declined to comment . . . Bauer refused to comment Tuesday night . . . Three other team members would not speak . . . Peckham would not disclose why he was suspended. . . . Peckham would neither confirm nor deny . . .''

It was a masterpiece of non-information gathering, with each question that went unanswered leading the reader farther down the road of implied disclosure. It followed in the great journalistic tradition of telling one's story while seeming to know nothing, of asking your subject, "Could you please answer yes or no to the question Have you stopped beating your wife?" Basically, the reader saw a smiling Amy Bauer on one side of the *Daily Cardinal* and a smiling Mike Peckham on the other, read that they both were gone, and if you couldn't put that together and formulate some sort of sexual conspiracy theory, you were one dimwitted human indeed.

Pat Richter leans forward in his desk chair, holding a document in his hands entitled "University Wisconsin-Madison Statement on Consensual Relationships." He starts to read the four-page brief, stopping when he comes to parts that seem pertinent to the questions he has in mind. "CONSENSUAL RELATIONSHIPS that are of concern to the UW-Madison are those amorous, romantic or sexual relationships in which both parties appear to have consented, but where there is a definite power differential between the two parties," it states. Richter nods his head and moves on. "Consenting romantic and sexual relationships between *instructor . . . and student . . .* have the potential for extremely serious consequences and ought to be avoided." Several paragraphs later comes the statement, "It is the instructor, supervisor, or other employee who, by virtue of his or her special power and responsibility, will bear a special burden of accountability." In this case, if this case is what it seems to be, that "special burden" is Peckham's load to carry.

"I mean, this just comes down to common sense," says Richter finally. "I'm meeting with Peckham tomorrow morning, and the young man probably just wants to get it off his chest. He says he doesn't want to make waves. Okay, I have to ask him point-blank, the rumor that's going around is . . . she's pregnant."

Talking about this stuff clearly makes Richter uneasy. These were not the kinds of problems he dealt with back in the personnel office at Oscar Mayer. But where there are humans with sex drives thrown in with other humans with sex drives, there will always be problems. That is, if this is even about sex. It could be all about power, subservience, misunderstanding.

"This is different from a corporate problem," Richter says. "Did she receive an advantage out of this? I don't know. I don't think she wants to come back and play next year, though. And I think Peckham is going to leave for his home in North Carolina right after our meeting." He sets his jaw with determination. "It's just common sense, isn't it? What is that saying—'Don't crap in the barn,' or 'don't crap where you work,' or whatever, you know what I mean. It happened, it's weird, but I guess it's not surprising. A lot of our women's coaches are male, and the opportunity exists for things to occur."

He thinks for a moment. "You know, you look at the women's track team—this is just completely hypothetical now—they work very closely with one male coach, Peter Tegen. The possibility is just there."

It's there, too, for members of the same sex to get together in breach of university rules, Richter knows. And there are some UW female coaches who are unmarried and seem to have little romantic interest in males—not that they have interest in the female members of their own teams, but the possibility, as Richter has mentioned, does exist. Mary Murphy herself is unmarried and lived for a time with a female UW administrator, a situation that Peckham has said caused problems for the athletic department.

Fun times, thinks Richter, dropping the pages on his desk. University life. The report he has just scanned was, as it states, developed by the Sexual Harassment Policy Committee in consultation with the Academic Staff Committee and the University Committee, before being "endorsed and issued by the Acting Chancellor." It reeks of political correctness and bureaucratic meddling. How much easier it was for Richter when all he had to do was get on a football field, line up, and kick somebody's butt. All this, and the women's basketball team is a disappointing 11–13 without its playmaking point guard who was averaging 12.4 points and 5.6 assists per game, and sinking fast.

As sleet pours down on a Saturday afternoon in early March, Pat Richter, Renee Richter, and Governor Tommy Thompson, who once was the college roommate of Pat Richter's cousin, sit in the rocking old stands of the Fieldhouse, watching the UW men's basketball team fight to a 26–23 halftime lead over the nationally ranked University of Indiana Hoosiers. The Badgers are ranked nowhere, of course, but they are battlers behind the rugged black senior stars of the team, 6'5", 250-pound forward Patrick Tompkins and 6'6", 195-pound forward Willie Simms.

UW's basketball history is just as wretched as its football history, perhaps even worse, since it should not be as difficult for a school to put together a respectable five-man team every now and then as it is to assemble a top-notch twenty-two man football squad. But after winning the basketball national championship in 1941 and finishing first in the Big Ten in 1947, the Badgers have not come close to winning anything since. They played in their first postseason tournament in over forty years after the 1988–89 season, going 1–1 in the lowly National Invitational Tournament. Though their record that year was just 18–12 overall (8–10, tied for fourth place, in the Big Ten), the school media guide now refers to that campaign as "the historic 1988–89 season."

History is cheap at UW, which is why it would be a nice little footnote today if the Badgers could hang on and beat the hated Hoosiers. In nine seasons, coach Steve Yoder has never beaten a Bobby Knight–led team, but there is always hope in Madison. As a symbol of such optimism, the members of the 1941 national championship team are brought onto the court at halftime to receive commemorative awards on this, the fiftieth anniversary of their wondrous deed.

"Look at that," marvels Thompson as twelve players, all in their late sixties or early seventies, stroll onto the hardwood. "Basketball must be good for you." He sees the last man line up and then notes something else. "Not a minority on the team."

This fact shows as clearly as anything how much elite college basketball has changed in the last half century. Certainly, one major reason UW has fallen behind other schools in basketball is its inability to attract and sign transcendent black athletes.

When the game starts again Renee Richter screeches for the Badgers to hustle. She looks at Knight fuming on the sideline, his ample belly poking out from beneath his red sweater. "He's not a real good role model," she says as Knight shoves one of his players, Pat Graham. "As a human being, I wouldn't let him do that to *me*." She probably wouldn't, either. She is a pistol. She met Richter while both were students at UW, and the sports hero was immediately smitten by the attractive blonde who took no guff from anyone. "All of my cousins went to St. Olaf College in Minnesota to be good Lutherans," she says during a timeout. "But my brother and I went to Wisconsin to become Communists. That's what my dad says."

The scoreboard over center court has just one prominent ad on it, sponsored by the Dairy Farmers of Wisconsin, and it states: MILK —IT DOES A BODY GOOD! The ad is more comforting than the score, which slowly begins to turn in Indiana's favor. UW is just not a very good or very well-coached team. "Come on!" yells the governor to Renee, when she goes quiet for a few moments. "Cheer! We want to party tonight."

But the damage has been done. Wisconsin loses in a near-rout, 74–61, and as the stands empty, the Fieldhouse looks like the old and rickety and uninspiring structure it is. Beer leaks out of the upper deck and drips on Renee's shoulder. At least it looks like beer; there are no rest rooms in the Fieldhouse except on the ground floor, so you can't be certain. When will the school build a new gymnasium? "As soon as he gives us the money," says Renee, pointing at the governor, who is working his way down the narrow aisle.

"We have to be careful about that," says Pat somberly. "A lot of legislators would rather give us the money than put it toward education. We'll probably do something with private funds five or six years down the road." He tells Renee that he and Shalala have even discussed the possibility of renovating this old dump, but that basically there isn't enough room inside these walls to do anything more.

"Maybe Donna will bring back some big money from her travels to the Far East," says Pat wistfully. The chancellor is on a swing through the Pacific Rim area hustling funds for the school. Who cares about Bucky Badger in Hong Kong? "You'd be surprised," Shalala said before she left. Richter smiles. "She's amazing," he says. "If she had her way, she'd level this and level the stadium and build a dome. Don't underestimate her. We'd call it the Donna-Dome."

In the postgame interview room, Tim Locum, UW's skinny 6'4" senior guard and the team's leading three-point shooter, stands disconsolately answering questions about the Badgers' failure to hold on to their halftime lead. Locum is from the small southern Illinois town of Flora, where he was a first-team Class A all-state player who averaged twenty-seven points a game as a high school senior. He has had a good time during his four years in Madison, learning a great deal and making a lot of friends, but he has suffered with the Badgers on the hardwood. "It's the story of my career," he says of the game. "The story of the coach's career. Close, but never quite close enough."

Locum has a wispy goatee, which he rubs as he looks around the room. He spots Barry Baum, who is interviewing another player, and then looks away. Locum is majoring in communication arts and wants to pursue a career in broadcasting journalism when he graduates, but he hopes he doesn't run into many journalists such as Baum in his chosen field. Like a lot of football and basketball players, Locum feels Baum is too opinionated and negative in his reporting.

Ahndi Fridell, the student sports information assistant for Steve Malchow, also looks at Baum with contempt. "He's not very popular around here," says Fridell.

One of Baum's recent columns in the *Daily Cardinal* was entitled "Why Are the Wolverines So Good?"—meaning, also, why are the Badgers so bad. Another, about the end of the Badgers' 1–10 football season, was entitled "Misery Over!" and questioned the progress being made by Alvarez's team.

Baum takes his quotes and leaves the room and retires to the press row midway up the deserted stands to write his game story for the student paper. Janitors and student volunteers sweep the gym, and at three-thirty the UW women's basketball team comes out for a practice. Coach Mary Murphy looks cheerful enough, though the Amy Bauer dilemma lingers on. Baum looks up from his typing and watches the coach. His reportorial instincts kick into gear. Should I talk to her or not? he says aloud—And if I do, what do I ask her? Do I ask her what I know, or do I just keep it easy?

He stares for a while longer, then turns back to his keyboard. First things first. He's got a deadline to meet.

THE FOLLOWING DAY, PEOPLE ONCE AGAIN BEGIN TO FILE INTO THE FIELDHOUSE stands to watch a basketball game, this time to see the UW women's team take on the Lady Hoosiers.

The crowd is different, with many of the early arrivals being young girls and teenaged females with impossibly ratted and curled and moussed hair worn, one must suppose, in the style of rural female jocks. The girls' bangs are teased up like frozen fire hydrant explosions and their ponytails are held back with elastic ribbons. Many of the girls are clearly basketball players themselves, with their sisters and friends and maybe a parent or two in tow. Some of the girls wear their high school letter jackets with the varsity letter in front, often with assorted sports medals hanging like jewelry from the M's and R's and S's. There are other women here, too, older ones with shorter hairstyles and more masculine comportment. Some of them, no doubt, are high school coaches and former jocks themselves. They, like the young girls, are cranked up to see live Big Ten women's basketball.

Coach Mary Murphy paces the sideline, looking intense and driven, even as her team runs its layup drills. Murphy herself came from a tough Chicago Irish family of eight boys and one girl, and she learned to play basketball with the all-out aggressiveness generally associated with the male street game. She was a star guard at Northwestern before getting into coaching, and though she is only thirty-three years old, she seldom plays hoops anymore. "I hardly ever play the game," she said the other day after practice. "I'm too competitive. There's too big a difference between what I want to do and physically what I can. It's too upsetting."

There are perhaps twenty-five hundred fans waiting anxiously for the tip-off, and some of them let out cries of recognition as Chancellor Shalala walks in wearing a Badger-red sweater and skirt. Shalala takes a seat in the stands and confidently answers a reporter's questions regarding the Bauer-Peckham scandal. "We had a tenured professor we got to resign last year over sexual harassment charges," she says. "Pat knows how to handle this sort of thing. The coach had a one-year contract—we can fire him for any reason. The girl will be back next year."

That issue resolved, Shalala watches as Indiana player Kris Mc-Grade chases a loose ball, flies over a row of folding chairs, and very nearly crashes into a metal garbage can. "I like that," the chancellor says. "It means she's intense."

At halftime Shalala goes down to the court to watch as a representative of the Wisconsin Beef Council presents a fifteen-hundred-dollar check, written out on a large cardboard cow, to associate athletic director Cheryl Marra to be used for funding the women's basketball program. Next, a shooting contest begins, with Shalala, who is celebrating her fiftieth birthday, joining in. She misses from ten feet and from fifteen feet, but on her three-point shot, the money shot, she surveys the basket, grasps the ball two-handed between her legs, and lofts an old Rick Barry–style free throw high into the air. The ball descends straight through the iron ring, nothing but twine. The crowd goes wild. Shalala has just won $104 from radio station 104-FM, and she promptly donates it to the women's team.

The crowd sings a spirited round of "Happy Birthday," for which she waves in appreciation. The good feelings flying about are almost enough to obscure the fact that the Lady Badgers sorely miss their dynamic point guard, a five-point win today notwithstanding.

PAT RICHTER HAS BEGUN TALKING FAIRLY OPENLY, AT LEAST WITHIN THE ATHletic department hallways, of the possibility of cutting sports soon to stop the financial hemorrhaging. "On the bubble," he says, "are baseball, men's and women's gymnastics, and men's and women's fencing. Men's and women's crew may have to be capped at a set budget."

The shocking part of the proposal would be pulling the plug on baseball. Richter himself played baseball at UW. But gender equity plays a major role here: Baseball has a quarter-million-dollar budget supporting approximately forty-five men; cut those males and the gender balance tips a little more evenly toward the female side.

Richter is not thrilled about suggesting the cuts. "Elroy tried to see about cutting baseball and gymnastics back in 1972, and the place went crazy. That's why I want to make sure people agree on this. I'm not going into that budget meeting at the end of March and getting blasted out."

Richter—the even-keeled guy—gets a little flustered all of a sudden. "It all comes down to one thing," he says sternly. "Football. If they'd gotten the right man after McClain, I wouldn't be here now!"

The wrong man most assuredly was Don Morton, who followed interim coach Jim Hilles. And, ironically, hiring Morton was one of the final gestures of good old former AD Elroy Hirsch himself.

People who know of Hirsch's football exploits and legendary status as a Badger supreme still often ask what exactly it is that Elroy does these days for the athletic department. In truth, not many folks know that Crazylegs was not even quite as dynamic a football player as his nickname implies. "One of the greatest trivia questions around here is 'How many touchdowns did Elroy Hirsch score in his Wisconsin career?'" says former UW sports information director and walking stat sheet, Jim Mott. "The answer is 'None.'"

Crazylegs's current responsibilities seem largely to revolve around eating, backslapping, and swinging a nine iron. Here is what his office calendar shows his duties to be for the next five months:

March 2	Crew Banquet
4	Don Davey Banquet, Holiday Inn
8–12	Arizona Golf
14	Rounders' Golf
17–19	Naples, Fla.
April 27	Spring Game, Butch's Bologna Bash
28–30	Las Vegas
May 1–4	Turnberry Isle, Fla. Golf
8	Fiesta Bowl, Phoenix
13	Badger Cookout, Milwaukee Zoo
20	Badger Golf, Cherokee
21	Mendota Golf, Madison
June 3	Fond du Lac Golf
6	Janesville Golf
10	Stoughton Golf
11	Oshkosh Golf
17	Monroe Golf
20	Fort Atkinson Golf
21	Glidden Golf
24–30	Blue Line Golf, Blackhawk
26–30	Bozeman, Montana
July 1	UW Baseball Golf, Oregon
5–7	Card Show
10	Prairie du Sac Golf
22	Minocqua Golf
29	Mendota U.W. Golf

And it's still very early in the season.

12

STEVE MALCHOW SITS WITH HIS HEAD IN HIS HANDS, SAPPED BY THE REQUESTS that have crossed his desk.

The most recent one came from state senator Marlon Schneider's office and seemed slightly insane to Malchow. "It all started from when I talked with Barry Alvarez last August and he said he wanted to close the locker room at certain times," says the beleaguered SID. "I agreed, because especially on the road the lockers are too small, and you avoid the problem of women writers and nudity, whatever, if you close the room to the press and everyone else. So now I get a call from some senator's page saying they want to make closing the locker rooms a state law. I said, 'We already close them.' And he said, 'Well, that's why we want to make it a law.' I hung up thinking, Iowa City wasn't like this." (Recently, hockey coach Jeff Sauer was forced to testify at the capitol about the problems of women reporters in the locker room, even though there are practically no female hockey reporters in college sport. Sauer was furious: "I told them I can handle my locker room without a law.")

And then Malchow got a call from the chancellor's office. "They got upset when the war protesters beat on the Fieldhouse doors during that basketball game, which the protesters did because they were on national TV. So one of the chancellor's underlings called and said, 'We'd like you to draw up a list of the remaining games in the order of their likelihood of being protested and send it to us.' I couldn't believe it. *That's* how I'm going to spend my time? I called my dad and told him this was a different place. I had no idea what I was getting into."

AT THE ICE RINK IN THE SHELL, JEFF SAUER WATCHES AS HIS SKATERS RANdomly file onto the oval to practice for the NCAA hockey tournament. Sauer is mad about all the constraints that NCAA reform efforts are putting on his program. "The crap they're pulling on us," he snorts. "Dick Schultz saying, 'Let's play for trophies, not money. Cut back practice time.' You know, Suzy Favor can run on a track, and a basketball player can shoot around, but what can we do? We're just bastards in the wind."

Sean Hill walks across the rubber mats on his skates, ready to join his teammates. He only made second-team all-conference defenseman in the recent voting by coaches and writers, and he ponders this. "It's because I missed eight games," he says. "And because of the thing."

The thing, of course, is the neck-breaking hit he put on the Denver player. Hill finished the regular season with the most points (51) and penalties (122 minutes) on the UW team. "A pretty rare combination, eh?" he laughs. He missed six games with a knee injury and one game because of the suspension; if he had played in every game, he would have had a good chance to break the UW all-time penalty record of 135 minutes set by Dave Maley in 1985–86.

Wisconsin State Journal hockey writer Andy Baggot watches as Hill skates onto the ice. "He actually was on pace for a hundred and seventy penalty minutes, which would have obliterated the league record of a hundred and forty," notes Baggot. Hill is a kind of throwback, Baggot feels. He watched Hill put a nasty check on a North Dakota player recently, knocking him flat. "As the player started to get up, Sean skated over like he was going to help him," says Baggot. "Then he kicked the kid's stick out of his hand." Well, sportsmanship won't get you into the big leagues. Hill's tactics are better appreciated by his peers than by his overseers; in a vote of Western College Hockey Association *players*, Hill was named to the first-team all-conference squad.

Watching along with Baggot in the empty bleachers is Matt Buss, the redshirt kid with the broken hand. He doesn't look happy. School has been going well for him—an aerospace engineering major, Buss is taking such courses as physics, dynamics, and linear algebra, and is holding on to a 3.2 grade point average. But book smarts don't count for much out on the ice, and that's the one place he wants to be.

PAT RICHTER STRETCHES GINGERLY, RUBBING THE RIBS HE INJURED PLAYING IN a faculty basketball game the other day. "Think I broke something," he mumbles to himself. Then he responds to a question about women's assistant basketball coach, Mike Peckham, who has been suspended now for two weeks.

"After reviewing everything, I've recommended to him that he resign," says Richter. "He denied most of the charges, but there was enough corroboration from people—Mary Murphy and others—that I feel this is what must be done. Does he have an attorney? He talked about it. I guess it could get messy."

Richter heads off to the McClain facility to work out, sore ribs or not. "It's one thing to say you're going to get an attorney," he adds in leaving. "Another to do it."

MICHAEL FOX OF FOX AND FOX LEGAL OFFICES, 44 EAST MIFFLIN STREET IN Madison, walks past a coffee table in his waiting room. On the table is a copy of a *Capital Times* article from three weeks ago, with the headline: MAN GETS $1.1 MILLION IN AGE-BIAS SUIT. The plaintiff, one Bobby G. Price, was successfully represented in his suit against his former employer, a large local construction firm, by none other than Michael Fox, with assistance from another Fox and Fox associate. According to the paper, the judgment "is believed to be among the largest ever awarded in a discrimination case in Wisconsin."

Michael Fox, a trim middle-aged man wearing a white shirt and suspenders, has the look of a successful prosecuting attorney. His sharp blue eyes are not the eyes of a man who suffers fools or weak defenses gladly. It is a sign of her business acumen and good fortune, then, that Amy Bauer has asked Fox to represent her in bringing suit against the University of Wisconsin for defamation of character and invasion of her right to privacy.

Like any good lawyer, Fox gets his juices going with the prospect of a new, righteous case. "Richter says some people saw Bauer and Peckham close together in a car," he says. "And some parent called in and said they thought they saw them in a whirlpool, or something crazy." Fox sniffs. "Richter's a nice guy, but I mean . . . People *think* they saw them hugging? Richter's standards are going to kill him. I mean, this is my stock in trade."

Fox takes a wicked delight in going after the big targets and bringing them to the ground—particularly that huge target over on Bascom Hill. "I've sued the university successfully, oh, half a dozen to a dozen times," Fox says. "Everything from academic misconduct to sexual discrimination. One suit was brought against the department of Poultry Sciences. They had this group with the men and women called the 'Yellow Dogs' and the 'Pink Kittens.' The men would bark and pull each others' shirts out with their mouths, and the 'Kittens' would lap milk from a plate. Jesus. Settled for a hundred and eighty thousand dollars."

Fox's focus returns to Amy Bauer. "She's from a family of seven kids—five boys and two girls, and she's the youngest—from a town called Durand." Fox himself is from a family of seven kids, Catholic like Bauer, but those links don't seem too important just now. "What I have to remember," he says, "is that this is a twenty-one-year-old kid who has to live with this whole thing for a long, long time."

Two days later there is a headline in the sports section of the *Capital Times* stating BAUER: MURPHY HUMILIATED ME. Under it is a story quoting Bauer as saying, "I didn't do anything wrong," and that Mike Peckham "always acted appropriately as both recruiter and coach." And there is a summation of a press release from Bauer's attorney, Michael Fox; among other things, the release says that Mary Murphy "allowed false rumors to flourish concerning Bauer's relationship with" Peckham, and that Murphy subjected Bauer "to ridicule and humiliation and destroyed her relationship with teammates."

In the *Wisconsin State Journal* there is a similar article, though in this one Murphy responds by saying that she might consider allowing Bauer to rejoin the team next season, but that Bauer "hasn't indicated she wants to meet with me, and I wouldn't say there is an open door in the statement she released."

The sound one has heard is that of two gauntlets dropping to the floor.

13

THE SPORTS CUTS ARE COMING.

The word has drifted out of the athletic department that Richter and Fish are going to ask the athletic board to approve their proposal to help fix the budget deficit: drop baseball, men's and women's gymnastics, men's and women's fencing, and cap the budgets of men's and women's crew at their current levels. The plan is supposed to save $3.3 million over the next four years and will ultimately cut some seventy to eighty athletes from the scholarship roster. It will also help the department get closer to gender equity in the remaining sports and, above all, will send a message that fiddling-around time is over. The new regime was told to do a job, and by God it's doing it. This budget will be balanced. Let the bodies fall where they may.

None of the threatened sports produces any revenue; none ever has any spectators except mom and dad, a few friends of the athletes, and hard-core aficionados of amateur batting, tumbling, parrying, and rowing. Still, the sports are precisely the ones that universities like to champion as embodiments of the amateur ideal—strenuous physical disciplines that are happily performed by well-rounded young student-athletes for the betterment of body, mind, and spirit. If the great liberal University of Wisconsin doesn't believe in the amateur ideal, what does it believe in? Well, a balanced ledger, for starters.

So baseball is on the bubble, for money and gender reasons. And gymnastics, too, because it is a sport best performed by younger athletes (particularly the women), and because its practice requires too much space and equipment maintenance. And crew is capped because crew members are sturdy and self-reliant and will go out and raise their own funds if they have to. But what's fencing got to do with anything? The entire annual budget for the sport is just $57,000. Practice takes place on the top floor of an old campus building in a room that could hardly be used for anything else. Fencing makes no ripples on campus, but it's never bothered anyone, either.

"You know why you cut fencing?" Al Fish responds straight-faced. "Because how can you cut baseball and gymnastics and *not* cut fencing?"

A MAN STAGGERS OUT OF THE ECHO BAR AT THE CORNER OF BEDFORD AND Main Streets as senior Jim Frueh walks down the sidewalk. Frueh (pronounced *Free*) glances inside, past the closing door with the red W on its front. There are three people at the bar, each motionless, lost in alcohol dreams, quiet jukebox music floating over their heads. The staggering man heads into the night.

"That's where alcoholics go," says Frueh, nodding at the Echo, turning into the alley behind the bar to the entrance to his apartment complex. He climbs to his door on the second floor, enters, and says hello to his girlfriend, Betsy Farr, who is studying in a rocking chair by the window. Frueh is a fencer, one of the two best on the UW team. He is a senior from Oshkosh, majoring in mechanical engineering. He is an intense, serious young man, with horn-rimmed glasses, a narrow face, and a sharp nose. He sometimes appears to be smiling as he talks, but he is not; he is grimacing. He wears jeans, running shoes, and a red Vassar T-shirt that seems a little large for his angular six-foot-two-inch frame. The reason it seems too large is because it is: Frueh normally weighs 185 pounds, but right now he weighs just 175. He recently lost ten pounds in a hospital in South Bend, Indiana, where he nearly died for his sport.

Frueh's expertise is with the épée, one of the three weapons used in team fencing, the others being the foil and sabre. The épée has a three-sided blade, and the target area on an opponent includes the entire body; the other two weapons have much smaller target areas. As the rule book states, with the épée, "whoever hits first, wherever, scores." Frueh has always liked fighting with the épée more than the other two instruments, because épée fighting is a wilder, more daring, nastier form of the sport, and Frueh often feels wild and angry and nasty when he takes the mat. He won the Big Ten title in épée as a junior, after just two years of practice, and sometimes he fought in a fury that made opponents glad that they were covered in protective clothing, gloves, and masks.

"Épée is an old, old dueling sword," says Frueh, sitting on the pea-green couch across from Betsy. "In competitive sport it's not a martial art at all. It's like . . . racquetball." Then he snorts, sardonically. "Fencing. If you're a fencer, people always think you're rich or a fag."

Frueh got into fencing because as a child he was handicapped with severe asthma and never went out for team sports. "I like the *you* against *me*," he says. "Not my team against your team." On his right wrist he has an ugly scar from where he broke his arm in four places after falling off a motorcycle at age sixteen. Part of the reason he began fencing at UW was to help him improve mobility in the wrist. The sport came easily to him, mainly because of his intensity and natural athletic ability. He is a good wrestler and water-skier and is blessed with an uncanny sense of balance. He is also very good at darts. And there is the arrogance, which even he does not fully understand. "When I won the Big Ten, I knew my opponent was going to flèche—that's a running attack—and I pointed my épée directly at his mask, so all he could see was the tip. It was perfect, no depth, just a speck. And then he lunged, and it hit him in the face. And I laughed." In practices Frueh has occasionally become so enraged that he has gotten into nasty fights with his own teammates; once he struck a fellow Badger so hard with his épée that he nearly knocked him unconscious. But even in a frenzy Frueh is aware of the difference between his sport and the actual use of untipped swords in malice. "The épée blade has three sides so the wound will not close," he says. "Nobody who knows anything about the épée would really want to duel anybody."

But at the University of Notre Dame two weeks ago at the Midwest Regional qualifying meet for the NCAA Championships, Frueh crossed the gap between sport and combat. In a ferocious battle against Notre Dame's Greg Wozniak, Frueh lunged at his opponent and struck Wozniak's hand full-force at precisely the same instant Wozniak's épée struck Frueh's bellgard, the metal shield protecting the hand. As the two athletes flew together, Wozniak's épée bent and snapped, the protective tip flew off, and the remaining blade slammed into Fruch's right arm. Fruch felt as though he had been slugged by a heavyweight boxer. He backed up and tried to regain his breath. Seconds went by as he returned to the *en garde* position, studied his foe, and marveled at the fatigue washing over him. Then he felt the blood trickling down his arm, saw the crimson slowly spreading on the sleeve of his white suit, and he knew he was hurt. Someone called an ambulance. The UW volunteer assistant coach, Tony Gillem, a former Badger head fencing coach who was now retired, accompanied Frueh to the emergency room at St. Joseph's Medical Center in South Bend. Frueh was having trouble breathing and his ribs hurt, but the doctors put two stitches in the puncture wound on his arm and assured him that he was repaired. But Frueh didn't feel repaired.

"I was really scared," he says. "I was by myself now, and I started coughing really hard. They hadn't given me a chest X-ray, and the coach had left. I could hear air escaping from my lungs, hear it in my ears, in my neck. I started to lose peripheral vision. I'm an asthmatic, remember, so I knew I was going to pass out. I knew I was really messed up. They told me later I turned pretty blue. But thank God a doctor named Francis Dwan came back, because he thought something was wrong, and he gave me mouth-to-mouth resuscitation. My old coach had left—idiot that he is—I mean, would you leave a friend, anybody, injured in a strange place?"

Frueh grimaces, focusing on something only he can see. He recalls starting to drift while unconscious, not down a tunnel toward light, but toward something. Images ran before his eyes, and he knew he was dying. "I thought about other things, personal things," he says. "It was just . . . personal."

The doctors had not calculated the forces or angles involved in fencing. Yes, Frueh had a puncture wound on his bicep, but his arm had not been at his side at the moment of impact; it had been extended, and the puncture was just the beginning of the damage. Frueh pulls off his T-shirt, rubs the small, healing scar on his arm, and then holds his arm out as though attacking an opponent. Wozniak's blade went through Frueh's polyester double-layered jacket, the plastron shield underneath, his T-shirt, and then, like a needle piercing an apple, into his bicep. But because his arm was held horizontally in front of him, the blade slipped up his arm, under his deltoid, through his ribs and into his right lung, puncturing it the way a nail punctures a tire. In dueling days it would have been a mortal wound. It very nearly was in modern times.

Frueh was placed on a ventilator and spent the next four days in the hospital, the first two days in the intensive care unit. He points to a small red wound on his chest. "That's where they put a tube in to drain off air," he says. He puts his shirt back on, but his anger builds as he thinks of his injury, his school, and the fact that he almost died for a sport that won't exist on campus in a few days. "They told the team co-captain, Tom Miller, to kind of keep it quiet," Frueh snaps. "They didn't even tell the papers, not even the campus papers, you know, that somebody was stabbed. Didn't tell my professors. They might wonder why I'm not in class, don't you think?"

Frueh's story did not appear in any of the Madison papers until four days after the incident, and by that time word was out that fencing was a doomed sport. The insult added to the injury, turning Frueh's sizzling competitiveness in on itself, churning his stomach. What an irony. Even with his injury-caused forfeit, Frueh finished fourth in épée in the regionals, thus becoming Wisconsin's only qualifier for the NCAA Championships. Of course, the tourney starts in two days, and Frueh still can't take a deep breath without coughing.

"To be honest, I'm sick of fencing," he says. "I'm fried. You make sacrifices for this sport, you know. They say make it a club sport. But without a coach, it's a waste of time—you just continue your mistakes. It's not like we get a fucking penny for anything! This is a sport for athletes, not the spectators. I mean, what is college athletics? Fencing's been a varsity sport here for about one hundred years, and the people in it—the students in baseball and gymnastics and crew, too—they're people who actually *attend* college. Football and basketball, those aren't students. Isn't that funny?"

He's not laughing. It's after midnight, and he walks into the hallway outside his apartment door and assumes his competitive pose. He stalks an imaginary foe, right arm shooting forward, left arm held in a graceful curl above his head, jabbing, jabbing, parrying, thrusting, moving down and back on the faded carpet. "The details, the complexities . . ." he says quietly. He lunges and strikes a door with a bang. He retreats. "There are guys who can lunge, who can leap six feet—Michael Jordans of the sport."

His eyes are narrow and cruel. He bounds back and forth, beginning to breathe hard. "I was lucky my opponent was a good fencer," he says. "That he had his . . . épée on my right arm . . . and shoulder . . . where it should be. A bad fencer . . . might have had it . . . in the middle." He strikes his invisible foe again and again.

"The blade could have gone through . . . my neck . . ." Jab. Lunge. "Or my heart."

MICHAEL FOX AND AMY BAUER WALK FROM THE FOX AND FOX LAW OFFICES to the Blue Marlin restaurant on the corner of Pinckney and Hamilton Streets. They get a table for dinner, and Bauer, who is wearing jeans, a white shirt, and a black embroidered vest and white moccasins, places her UW letter jacket with the big white W with two bars across it on the back of her chair. Bauer is attractive in a fit, all-American way: her blond hair hangs below her shoulders, her skin is flawless, and her teeth are pearly white. But she does not smile, there is only bitterness in her voice as she tells her story one more time.

"It started with the two coaches and (women's associate athletic director) Cheryl Marra telling me there was a problem with Coach Peckham, that he'd been suspended because of inappropriate behavior with a player, and that the player was *me*. I denied everything. People may have seen Coach Peckham and I talking, but there was nothing going on. Mary said that everybody, players, parents, had been wondering about us and that players had been going to Pat Richter to talk about whatever was happening. And then I met with Pat, and he seemed uninformed, but nice.

"The coaches said there would be a meeting that night, and they asked me if I wanted to come. I said no, and they said that was good, because the team members would feel free to talk about me. They could talk about Coach Peckham and get their feelings out. Then I would come for practice. I came to the gym and talked to Cheryl in the Reinke Room, and I told her Coach Peckham was a close friend and I needed someone to talk to—my life hasn't been too peachy— and I sought *him* out. My freshman year, my eight-year-old niece had cancer. She was my parents' first grandchild, and I was very close to her; she was like a little sister to me. She lived in Rock Falls, just fifteen minutes from us. You know, I love little children—I'm majoring in education so I can be an elementary school teacher.

"Coach Peckham gave me support. He had a sister who had gotten cancer, and he just helped me out. And my niece recovered, even though she had only a five percent chance of survival. So I feel very sorry for Coach Peckham—he lives and dies for basketball—and I feel like I went to him for help and he got in trouble for it. After this happened, his wife has had me come out and stay at the house. I've baby-sat for them."

The meal comes and Bauer picks at her food. On the court she is graceful and tough and blessed with a sense of when and how things are going to happen. Here, she has no such sense.

"They say he overstepped his boundaries," she continues. "But what are your boundaries? Coaches *want* you to come to them with personal problems."

She takes a small bite of food. "I always felt very uncomfortable talking to Mary," she says, looking down. "I only spoke twice to her in high school. Coach Peckham recruited me. She was a point guard herself; I don't know, maybe that's some of it." Bauer claims she had questions about Murphy's sexual preference. "The team would talk about it. But as long as a person doesn't do anything to me, it doesn't bother me—that's their preference. In a way, though, it bothered me, I guess. It kept me from talking to her. She never gave us her phone number or address. She was like, on a plane, if you lost your luggage and had to write down your address, she was always the last to sign."

This is all personal stuff, though, not court evidence—and Fox knows it. Circumstantial elements. Opinions. Tangential information. Not to the point. Still, Amy Bauer is the one damaged by recent proceedings, and how can she ever prove something didn't happen, if, in truth, it didn't?

"Why did you quit?" asks Fox. "Why not go to the press?"

Bauer looks up quizzically. "Because I was shocked. Nothing like this had ever happened to me."

She goes on to explain again the meeting with the team that Murphy had organized and which Bauer walked in on, how everyone expected her to apologize for something she says she hadn't done, how Murphy encouraged the players to vent their anger at Bauer in the meeting, how Murphy tried to demean her. "She said, 'We have the right to ask Amy anything we want, because it's affecting all of us; it's an adult problem that affects the university.' She was very angry. She said, 'Amy Bauer, you are welcome to come to Purdue for the next game, welcome to start. But you will play by *my* rules, you will not question me. You better change your attitude.' And then she left.

"We never had practice. I sat there. And then I got up and never came back. I couldn't play for her." Again she pauses.

"I had such a great career going," she says. "You know what the rumor is? The rumor is I was pregnant and already had the abortion. I try to be tough, but I cry."

Fox asks her what it is exactly that can make things right for her again.

She looks for a moment as though the tears are coming. She says, "I want my reputation back."

As THE ASSOCIATE ATHLETIC DIRECTOR IN CHARGE OF WOMEN'S SPORTS AT A major university, Cheryl Marra is a rare bird. Not because she is a woman—no, there are many woman associate ADs around the country, most handling the female side of the athletic department. Marra is unusual because she is married, has children, and is clearly heterosexual.

Formerly the women's track and soccer coach and associate athletic director at Dennison University in Grantham, Ohio, Marra, thirty-five, joined the UW staff less than a year ago. She is a lighthearted and friendly administrator, and for the most part she is not faced with the serious dilemmas in women's sports that occur on the men's side—at least not the financial problems inherent to football and men's basketball. Nobody expects the women's side of the athletic department to cause any major ruckuses or scandals, and anything to do with sexuality or the sexual preferences of female athletes, coaches, and administrators is a loaded and generally undiscussed area.

"Nobody wants to talk about lesbianism," says Marra, sitting at her desk on the third floor of Camp Randall. "But you can't hide these things." Behind her a photo of her three small children beams down on her like a diploma of certification.

"You just try to keep all these things professional, but it can be a problem. Parents of recruits want to know the sexual preference of the coaches and the team, generally. And that's in a lot more sports than just basketball." Marra knows there are some lesbian coaches at UW, but that is not a problem, she says, unless it hurts recruiting or a coach becomes involved with a player or acts unprofessionally at any time. But it can be equally dangerous to have a male coach become involved with a female athlete, as allegedly has occurred with Mike Peckham and Amy Bauer.

"A lot of athletic directors won't look at a woman coach if her sexual orientation might become a problem. But it's not always easier hiring a male rather than a gay woman. So what they really look for are married females. And a candidate with children, why, you're golden." Marra laughs. "In all honesty, that's why I am where I am. I'm safe."

She didn't set out on that course with her job future in mind. She got married to her college sweetheart right after school, started coaching, and then the babies just came along. "Believe me," she says, "I didn't do this for career enhancement."

Still, her married life makes her unique among her peer group. "The thing is, coaching is extremely time-consuming. And since women don't have wives at home, taking care of the house and the kids and all the domestic things, being a woman coach is really hard. At Dennison I used the students for baby-sitters, paid them twenty-five dollars a day, and dangled the biggest lure of all to get them: They could do their laundry at my house.

"Still, in my old conference I was the only married woman athletic director. And in the Big Ten I'm still the only one. All the nine others are unmarried. Ten now, since Penn State came aboard."

None of these domestic issues would really matter any more than other personal preferences or habits matter, were it not for the Peckham-Bauer situation and the critical role played by Mary Murphy in its resolution. "What this really gets down to," says Marra, "is a power index—who has power over whom. It gets really difficult. With Amy, her problem is with the head coach, more than anything.

Amy is the one who has chosen not to play. You know, the players had gone to her during the season to talk about what she was doing. Finally they went to an assistant and said the relationship between Bauer and Peckham was getting out of control, it was affecting them a lot, and the assistant told Mary. And she came to me.

"The line you tread in all this is not real clear. At Dennison I had two women coaching men's sports, and here we have three males— Peter Tegen in track, Greg Ryan in soccer, and Steve Lowe in volleyball—coaching women's sports. What it gets down to is, any coach in any sport has to act professionally."

Marra looks at the photo of her kids. The youngsters smile protectively down at their mom.

THREE DAYS LATER RICK ABERMAN RECEIVES A MEMORANDUM FROM RICHTER'S office, a letter sent to all coaches and high-ranking officials in the athletic department. It reads:

> As you know, Women's Basketball Assistant Coach, Mike Peckham, has resigned. Along with this action, it was agreed by both sides that there should be no comments made concerning the situation which might affect Mike's reputation and career. This is considered to be a confidential personal matter, and hearsay would be very dangerous and damaging to Mike and the Athletic Department. Any breach of this commitment could result in disciplinary action.

> In other words, you, too, could walk the plank.
> The big hush is on.

14

PAUL SOGLIN HAS ALWAYS BEEN A MAN DIVIDED, TORN BETWEEN HIS TWO passions—saving the world and playing baseball. The forty-five-year-old mayor of Madison is currently campaigning for his fifth term, but he is not concerned about the reelection task just now. After all, none of his four opponents has ever held public office; one is a gas station attendant, one is a long-haired, bearded street vendor, and one is an unemployed homeless man scheduled to go on trial for allegedly attempting to entice a fourteen-year-old girl into his car last December. The fourth is a twenty-eight-year-old legislative aide to state representative Robert Crowles and looks young enough to be running for student council president.

No, what burns Soglin right now is the state of affairs over at the University of Wisconsin athletic department. "They're thinking about cutting the baseball team!" he says as he takes a seat at the bar of the Golden Dragon Restaurant on Mifflin Street, a block away from the Capitol building. It's noon and Soglin is here to eat and talk about the ponies with his horserace-betting pal and bartender, Suey Wong. "It's a fucking Communist plot! Think of it—a major American university without baseball!"

Soglin can't believe it. He hands two *Racing Forms* over the bar to Wong and then continues his diatribe.

"Really, it's un-American. College baseball doesn't draw crowds. But that's not the point. The point is, *every school should have a baseball team*. I love baseball. I know that if I hadn't wasted my youth being involved in political activities, I could have been a great shortstop. I had a great arm, until I threw it out . . ." He takes a drink from his water glass and seems to grow pensive. Wong wanders up. Soglin orders lunch.

"Threw it out screwing around," he says after a time. "Throwing a large rubber ball at a kid in high school, trying to splatter his nose right into his cranium." Ah well, life must move on. But that does not excuse the apparent boneheadedness being perpetrated over at Camp Randall. "If the purpose of college sport is to make money and entertain, well, okay, then let's close down everything but football, basketball, and hockey! If you start out with the premise that college sports are supposed to be self-sufficient, then any athletic department in the last twenty years that didn't hire an MBA to run the show was remiss in its duties. An AD has always been an old coach that people liked to have hanging around, a guy like Elroy. But he shouldn't have been. He should have been a guy wiring the stadium for TV and learning what *uplink* means. Why did CNN beat everybody in the Persian Gulf War? If an AD can't answer that, he better get out."

Soglin begins to eat his chicken and fried rice. A short, bespectacled man with a bushy mustache, he was elected mayor of Madison when he was just twenty-eight and barely a year out of law school. He has a weary yet bemused look to him, one that no doubt springs from the ironic fact that, after a decade in office, he is now perceived as an establishment politician by some of the left-wing and liberal progressives who supported him as the young "Red Mayor of Madtown."

Soglin keeps his hand in athletics—baseball, that is—by working with his three young daughters on their hardball skills and by devoting himself to his rotisserie-league team—his fantasy squad of major leaguers that competes against other fantasy teams fielded by fellow owners. "I didn't care about the sex of my children at all," Soglin says. "As long as they could throw. The oldest one can snap it at the wrist. They all will *throw* the ball." And the fantasy league, well, sometimes it's harder than anything in politics, Soglin admits. For instance, right now a diner/constituent walks up to Soglin, says hello, and drops the sports section of today's paper on the table.

"It's official," the man says, pointing to the column that proclaims baseball player Bo Jackson is done forever due to his worsening hip injury.

Soglin scans the article, his jaw dropping. "I don't believe it," he whispers. "My only power hitter."

He leaves the Golden Dragon in a gray depression. But the beauty of the spring day and the town he rules soon buoys him. "Back in the seventies, whenever the mayors from around the country would meet here for the annual mayors' convention, I'd make sure to have football coach John Jardine meet with them," he says. "To promote the city, the school. It can't hurt, and I'm hoping to do it with Alvarez at the upcoming conventions."

"It *would* mean a lot to have football back. There are estimates that because UW football is so bad it's costing the city millions of dollars each home-game weekend. Think about it—somebody comes in, you have a minimum of three meals, you have retail sales, clothing, books, souvenirs, hotel rooms, jewelry, gas. And you know what? I'd like to see the Badgers win, just so I can deal with my brother. He's a Michigan grad who lives in San Francisco. Need I say any more?"

He walks to his office, the one with the sign HIZZONER-DA-MARE affixed to its door, and sits at his desk. He spins and looks out his window. On the wall beside him are photos of Soglin with Jimmy Carter, with Fidel Castro in Havana, with a racehorse, with Bob Feller. Beside that last picture is a framed certificate that reads "This certifies that Paul R. Soglin, Date: August 4, 1982, batted against Bob Feller at Warner Park and grounded out to second base."

There is also a terrifying photo, grainy and poorly focused, showing eight cowering young people standing in a hallway, looking straight ahead as though peering into the jaws of hell. This was taken at the Madison Conrad Hilton Hotel on October 17, 1967, during a student demonstration against the Dow Chemical Corporation's involvement in arms production for the Vietnam War. Behind the camera, unseen police in riot gear are marching up the hallway, swinging their batons and clearing a path through the protestors, and what the camera sees is what the police see.

One of the people about to be beaten is a clean-shaven young man, Paul Soglin, and his face alone is unmarked by panic. Indeed, he looks almost lost in reverie as he stares into the lens, gripping the sides of his jacket, lifting it. The mayor looks back from the window now, and glances at the old photo. "I was raising my coat," he says, "so I wouldn't get beaten on my head and neck."

He did get clubbed up high, however, and in the legs as well. He rolls up his left pant leg and shows the scars on his shin. "The skin will split when hit with a billy club," he says, then shrugs. "It's not much."

All that stuff was important, he implies, but it was so long ago, so unnecessary, so unfortunate, so . . . something. The radical anti-war movement died a few years after that—in Madison, anyway—from the kind of grievous miscalculation that often dooms protest movements. Karlton Armstrong, an acquaintance of Soglin's, and Leo Burt, a student, bombed the University of Wisconsin's physics lab in Sterling Hall, killing a man, and that was it. Soglin became an attorney and got into politics, to do good. But often he would stop and think about the beauty and purity of a game such as baseball. It's possible, he still thinks, that baseball has done more good for people in this country than all the elected officials have, than all the do-gooders who would make everything fair and equitable have.

He opens his desk drawer and pulls out a box of Topps baseball cards and slowly examines the contents. On his desk by his phone are several small baseball figurines in various action poses. There are memos on his desk, notes to call this or that important person to haggle over something or other, to make this or that deal, but he ignores them. Instead he looks again at the roster of his fantasy league team, which lies atop his fifteen-page printout listing the strengths and weaknesses of every player in the major leagues. He ignores the grim reality of Bo Jackson's fate and studies instead the pitchers on his club.

"Look at this staff!" he says joyously. "Look at them."

He absorbs the numbers, analyzes them. "I may bring Assen-macher up," he says to himself.

SIX YOUNG MEN WALK THROUGH THE CLOUDLESS 72-DEGREE AFTERNOON TO Camp Randall Stadium, where they climb the athletic department stairs and enter Al Fish's office for a powwow with Fish and Pat Richter. The young men are senators from the Wisconsin Student Association, the undergraduate government council, and their names are Mike Verveer, Jon Van Horn, Jam Sardara, Joel Zwiefelhoffer, Rick Schneider, and Pat Kain. They are not happy about the sports cuts that are going to be voted on by the athletic board tomorrow, and they want the athletic department rulers to know it.

"What's up, guys?" says Fish cheerily.

The young men take seats around the table in the corner of the room and start right in.

"Why are you trying to reduce the debt in four years rather than seven, if it means we could keep the sports?" asks Verveer, who has been elected WSA president.

"We're still blamed for the debt on McClain," answers Richter. "We're under extreme pressure from the legislature. Nobody has said, 'Go slow.' All anybody talks about is the debt."

"The students in those five sports are being robbed of their athletic opportunities," says Zwiefelhoffer, a kid who could pass for a high school freshman. "That's hard."

"I don't disagree," says Richter. "I was called a 'butcher' last night. I don't like that. If there was some other magic out there—"

Fish interrupts. "What can we do to *not* cut sports?" he says. "We've looked at all kinds of budgets. But until we cancel the debt, it's the only agenda."

"But why didn't you consult us?" asks Kain, whose hair falls over his right eye in a modified Prince Valiant do.

"We didn't consult you because we assumed you wouldn't want to pay more," answers Fish. "And even with your student fees we still have to cut sports. Without them, we'd have to cut even more."

Kain doesn't like this answer. "But as a matter of good policy and even law, you should consult students about anything this major," he says.

"Except for getting your nose out of joint," replies Fish tartly, "students *have* been consulted. You have student reps at the board meetings. And besides, we can't go around saying we're going to cut gymnastics three months before we know we're going to do it, because if we don't cut it, it will kill the program for at least two or three years, because every other school will use that as a recruiting tool against us."

Somehow the senators seem to be losing their way. These adults have all the answers; attacking them is like punching an inner tube— the angry stuff just bounces back at the students.

Sardara, an intense, dark-haired junior of Iranian descent, tries another tack. "If we continue the fee, can you guarantee no more sports will be cut? Can you promise?"

"I sure as hell don't want to go through this again in my lifetime," says Richter, sensing compromise.

Fish glows with empathy. "That, in my opinion, is an excellent bargaining chip when the fee comes up again," he says to the students. It's hard to imagine an executive or politico who wouldn't want an Al Fish on his staff, clearing the brush, working the levers, softening the blows, getting things done.

"It's a bitch," says Richter morosely, looking from face to face. "You think I like this legacy? I've got a son who plays here, who's got a lot of baseball friends."

The senators ponder this.

"What about deadweight in the athletic department?" asks Verveer.

"I'll answer that," says Fish. "I've been here two years and seventeen people have sat right where you are and been fired." He neglects to tell them that more than that number have been hired.

"Promises about sports and fees were made to us, not by you two, but Ade Sponberg," says Kain.

Fish smiles. "He probably made promises to Don Morton, too."

The meeting breaks up, and the senators leave feeling somehow less certain about this battle they're waging, about themselves, about life.

"Morton ran a clean program, graduated players, but he gets fired," says Sardara as the six young men walk through campus toward Memorial Union, where the WSA has a fifth-floor office. "That tells you where priorities lie."

The others nod. Around them are the sights of a university stretching, of young people coming out of hibernation on this glorious spring day. But the senators stay focused.

"They're disregarding us, and just about everybody else," says Kain.

"We really don't have a say," adds Sardara glumly. "It's a sham."

In the WSA office some of the senators feel a little better about their roles and about the roles Fish and Richter must play, too. "I respect them both," says Van Horn. "They're both very professional. Hiring Al Fish was one of the best things the department could have done."

"But I'm just not sure they're being paid to do what's best for the whole university," counters Kain. "I'm not that gullible."

All of the senators nod their agreement. They're back in their lair, and their own small world, at least, makes more sense now.

Verveer chuckles. "Donna Shalala wants to go to the Rose Bowl," he says, out of the blue.

Van Horn picks up the thread. "My dad was a professor at Milton College, where all sports were non-revenue," he says. "Here it's so . . . out of line. Expenses just keep spiraling upward. Where does it end?"

"Nobody wants to be the first one to flinch," says Verveer. Nobody disagrees.

AT 8 P.M. PAT RICHTER BEGINS SPEAKING TO A GROUP OF FIFTY PEOPLE IN THE football auditorium of the McClain facility. Assembled randomly throughout the room are most of UW's coaches, as well as a number of baseball players, gymnasts, crew members, and fencers. This was a hastily called meeting, one put together to help Richter explain to those on the bubble just why they are, in fact, on the bubble. The group is sullen. Even the coaches whose sports are not threatened look worried. Who says this is the only swing of the hatchet?

"I can't escape it," Richter says. "If it's not you, it's somebody else. The football team didn't come through, and then there was this little seven-hundred-thousand-dollar surprise—money that just wasn't there. How do you explain that to the average guy? Huh? They say, 'I balance my checkbook, why can't you?'"

Richter sighs. "I haven't been sleeping much. It's unfortunate that because of a lack of bodies in the football stadium, good people have to be hurt. But damnit! We have to do something. I got a call—from a farmer near Columbus—and he said, 'You don't know me, but if you want it, I'll give the department a hundred dollars. I don't have much, but you can have that.' From day one when we made these cut proposals public, that's the only person to ever come forward with an offer like that."

Richter scans the group, looking for sympathetic faces. There aren't many. "Anything I say now is not going to help. I know that. But tomorrow in front of the board I will still be recommending the deep cuts. There just aren't any options."

"How can you say there aren't other choices?" shouts an athlete.

A slender woman stands and says, "You say athletes are limping along. If you asked them, maybe they wouldn't agree."

Richter shakes his head. "We'll come to this point again, no matter what we do."

A baseball player waves his hand in disgust and says, "If the university ever comes to me for a donation, I'll make sure it goes to economics and not the athletic department! I'm from in-state, and I can tell you you're gonna lose a lot of money from Oconomowoc."

This gets Richter a little hot under the collar. "Well, I just got a call from Oconomowoc," he fires back. "And the person said I'm doing the right thing."

"Can't we give the sports a chance to improve?" asks another female athlete.

Al Fish suddenly responds from the sixth row of the audience. "We have to have a permanent solution," he says, showing Richter that he has at least one ally tonight.

People begin to suggest ways the department can make money so as to forestall the cuts—rallies, fund-raising drives, solicitations. How about renting out the McClain football field to conventions or soccer teams or softball leagues?

"The Chicago Bears were here to work out in the postseason," shrugs Richter. "We made a little off them. Not much, a hundred dollars an hour." Obviously, to make a dent in the deficit the Bears would have to conduct twenty-four-hour-a-day workouts at the center from now till Christmas.

Joel Maturi, the associate athletic director who knows about technicalities such as renting out the McClain facility, rises up and sheepishly explains that, all told, the school made about three thousand dollars last year on such ventures. There are building and health code violations inherent in the structure anytime you get more than a hundred or so people inside, he explains. Plus you'd have to cover the turf to have a convention. And you'd need more lights. And electricity. And heating. And air-conditioning. And all sorts of things. "And there aren't enough toilets or exits in the building, so we're not allowed to have too many people in there," he adds.

Why were so few toilets and exits put in a building that cost a fortune to construct? someone asks. Didn't anybody ever think that there might be a lot of people in the building at one time?

Shrugs all around. Nobody knows.

Still, with less than twelve hours until the board meeting begins, the cuts are not official. As this meeting breaks up, groups of athletes and coaches stand in the aisles feverishly discussing ways the cuts can be avoided.

Fish watches the discussions from a distance, noticing men's gymnastics coach Mark Pflughoeft as the coach gestures passionately to a couple of listeners. Fish shakes his head. Poor man. Pflughoeft, forty, has been the men's coach for thirteen years, but in Fish's opinion he's a perfect example of the old-guard athletic department employee who doesn't get it. Pflughoeft himself earns thirty-three thousand dollars a year guiding a team that is proficient but, in modern financial times, irrelevant. "Mark says he has a drawer full of checks from people to help fund gymnastics," says Fish with a snort. "He won't give them to me. I'll bet there isn't two thousand dollars there."

People disperse and Pflughoeft walks out of McClain, crosses the driveway, and goes alone to his tiny office high up in the Camp Randall rampart. The building is dark and still. Pflughoeft leans back in his chair and muses; he has a gut feeling that gymnastics will not be discarded tomorrow, because at a combined budget of two hundred fifty thousand dollars for both men's and women's teams and with so many good students involved—gymnastics athletes have always had among the highest grade point averages in the department—the athletic board really shouldn't see fit to dump them.

He finds himself smiling over his prospects. "I feel pretty good we'll make it," he says. "We're ranked ninth in the nation right now. Plus, I got wind of this whole thing two months ago, so I went out and made some plans, talked to people." He looks almost conspiratorial, like the squirrel who hoarded acorns. "I've got letters of support for me, and I've got checks."

He opens his desk drawer and pulls out four personal checks. He holds them up proudly. They total less than a thousand dollars. "I'll send them back on Monday, if we get cut," he states. "But I don't think I'll have to."

AT 7:30 A.M. ON THIS MARCH MORNING, PAT RICHTER, AL FISH, AND ROGER Formisano meet in Richter's office. The athletic board meeting is just minutes away. Fish looks at his compatriots. "Remember *The Hustler?*" he says. "Jackie Gleason is Minnesota Fats, Paul Newman is Eddie Felson, they've been playing all night, Paul Newman's been drinking and everybody's exhausted. Fats takes off his coat, washes his face, straightens his tie, puts on his coat, and in the greatest line in movie history says, 'Fast Eddie, let's play pool.' "

The three men stand up, walk to the W Club room, take their places at the U-shaped table with the athletic board members, and soon the balls are racked and the game is on. The room is filled with spectators, many of them athletes standing grimly in their letter jackets, their backs against the wall. A number of baseball players in warm-up jackets and caps stand directly behind Richter, Fish, and Formisano, watching the administrators' every move. When baseball coach Steve Land speaks, the room falls silent.

"Look at those plaques," Land says, his voice shaking. He points to the far wall. "Pat Richter is on the left, and Harvey Kuenn [the former UW star and American League batting champ] on the right. Isn't that ironic? We have one Division I baseball team in this state, and we're going to throw it out! One hundred sixteen years!"

He looks at the board members. "Talk about facilities? We got horseshit facilities! But talk about alumni value—tell me what's better than baseball." Land gestures out at the crowd.

"I want the players to come up here." They do, rustling past chairs, assembling in a row in front of the board, looking like pups about to be drowned. "If you can look these men in the eye and say, 'Cut baseball,' " Land states, waving his hand at the athletes, "then do it." He turns from the microphones and leaves the room.

Next, Mark Pflughoeft comes forward to speak. It seems the reality of the situation has finally settled upon him; his sport is truly on the block—grade points, support letters, personal checks be damned. It appears at first that he is going to hyperventilate; then his voice cracks; then he begins to cry. His words are impassioned gibberish.

"We're *not* selfish," he proclaims through his tears. "There is simplicity, there *is* clarity. If we all take a deep breath, we can let these issues go and find simplicity and clarity to do the right thing." He says a bit more, then walks away, to vigorous applause, though the clapping is clearly for his dramatic performance and suffering rather than his insight.

None of the rhetoric matters. Fish and Richter were not stupid enough to have come to this meeting without having the necessary votes in pocket beforehand. Of the eleven board members, eight vote to cut the five sports and cap men's and women's crew at last year's budgets of $180,000 and $150,000, respectively. Even student/athlete representative Elaine Demetroulis, the star tennis player, the Big Ten singles champ and team captain, votes to cut the five sports, an astonishing coup for the athletic department. Her compatriot, men's tennis captain Jack Waite, votes against the resolution; because each student vote counts only as a half-vote, the final tally is 8½ to 3½ in favor of the execution. There will be protest and threats of lawsuits and much saber-rattling by the offended parties in the weeks to come, but basically it's all over. The UW sports ship floats a little higher, if less cheerily, in the water.

In just a few hours spring break will begin for the winter-crazed students at UW. By tomorrow, despair over sports cuts—for those who even give a damn—will be superseded by visions of sand, surf, and cold brews. Daytona Beach, make way for the Badgers!

Fish and Richter couldn't have planned things better if they'd tried.

15

IT IS APRIL AND THE FICKLE SPRING WEATHER LEADS THE STUDENT POPULACE through mood swings as varied as the clouds in the sky. The athletes can now take their workouts outdoors, and when it's warm and bright, they flock the playing fields of campus like field mice. Rick Aberman still spends the better part of his days in the basement of the McClain facility, where the weather never changes and, because of a faulty mechanism or odd power surges, his clock never keeps correct time. It is 2 P.M. now, but his clock, which cannot be adjusted because it is bolted to the wall, reads 6:23.

Aberman looks at the letter he has written to trainer Denny Helwig regarding star distance runner Jenny Kraeger, who Aberman fears is showing signs of anorexia nervosa or some other undetected eating disorder. Kraeger, a senior from Palatine, Illinois, was a walk-on soccer player who showed more proficiency at endurance running and training than she did at soccer, preferring to run for miles rather than endlessly kick a ball. As a junior she was spotted by women's track coach Peter Tegen, who encouraged her to join his team. This was a blessing of sorts for soccer coach Greg Ryan, who according to Aberman had become increasingly concerned about Kraeger's weight loss and fanatical approach to training. Tegen, a dynamic little German expatriate who earned his undergraduate degree from the University of Köln and his graduate degree in English and physical education from the University of Freiburg, is a Svengali-like coach. His female athletes are often overwhelmed by his intensity and charisma, finding in him a father figure and gurulike leader who can push them to successes they didn't know they could achieve.

Kraeger was such a natural at distance running that she finished fourth in the Big Ten Indoor Championships in the 5,000 meters and fifth in the 3,000 meters just two weeks after joining Tegen's track team. During the outdoor season she won the Big Ten 5,000 meters and the 10,000 meters and earned All-America honors by finishing seventh in the 10,000 meters at the NCAA Outdoor Championship, with a personal best time of 33:26. Still, her rail-thin appearance has worried both Aberman and the athletic department physician, Greg Landry. At 5'6" and less than 100 pounds (she admits to 98 pounds, but no one knows her true weight) Kraeger looks like a starvation victim as she moves along the track, her T-shirt flapping loosely against her skeletal arms.

"I'm worried about the possibility of a heart attack," Aberman says of Kraeger. "Your electrolytes can get very screwed up when you don't eat. I've seen anorexics who have begun to metabolize their heart muscles." Female athletes with eating disorders, Aberman knows, are very difficult to deal with. They often deny there is a problem and are highly motivated and diligent in their training. Their weight loss can for a time make them more efficient at their sport, particularly distance running, where every ounce is a burden to be transported for miles. Still, Aberman wonders, where is the coach in all this? Kraeger isn't the only track team member who appears underweight. Junior Heather Rawling, winner of the cross-country run at the 1991 Midwest Collegiate Championship, is so terrifyingly thin that she could double as a model for a World War II concentration camp survivor. Something, Aberman feels, should be done. But what? Tegen, the mentor, has not complained to him. And his teams continue to win: In eighteen years at UW, Tegen has given the school two cross-country national championships and thirty Big Ten championships in indoor and outdoor track and cross-country. He, too, feels the pressure to win in this new, money-first, bottom-line atmosphere.

Aberman walks over to Al Fish's office to discuss another matter, the bad vibes spread by head strength coach Scott Raridon. A tall, fleshy man with blond hair and a furtive look, Raridon has alienated many athletes with his surly demeanor and king-of-the-roost attitude. Why wasn't Steve Myrland promoted to head strength coach when the new football regime came in? Aberman wonders.

Because Raridon was who Alvarez wanted, says Fish—even though Raridon had unspecified difficulties in previous jobs at Nebraska and Notre Dame, including allegations that he had on occasion encouraged football players to use illegal anabolic steroids for muscle gain. The problem—if, indeed, there is one, says Fish—has occurred because Richter had to offer certain things, such as putting Raridon in complete control of the weight program, as part of "the Alvarez package, what we have to do to win." Also, Raridon had to have a good deal of control to justify his salary, which was demanded by Alvarez.

"It's high," says Fish.

"Forty-seven thousand dollars," says Aberman.

Fish looks away. Raridon is not just well paid; he is the highest-paid strength coach in the Big Ten. All those football players—Michigan, Ohio State, Penn State—and he's number one.

Aberman asks about two threatened suits that might be brought against the department by the baseball team.

"They don't have a leg to stand on," snorts Fish. "And some of these coaches are acting as though they can save their sports with big contributions, but where is it? A farmer from Oconomowoc?"

The two discuss other things, and Fish becomes reflective. "You know what surprised me most about all this, Rick?" he says. "Just one thing. How out of context sports are in our society. With all our problems with health care, crime, the elderly, AIDS, drugs, poverty—that really took me. I was so depressed last week. What am I doing in a job where people think this way? I understand it, my head does, but the contrast between this, where you make cuts and eliminate twenty kids who get to keep their full rides, and my last job where if you make cuts you might put a thousand disabled kids out of rehab programs, where people run patients on ventilators up to the front of the Capitol to get money to save lives . . . it's not in the same world. And yet I've been getting anonymous phone calls at home over this. Threatening phone calls."

*   *   *

THE FOOTBALL TEAM IS BEGINNING ITS FOURTH DAY OF SPRING PRACTICE, running through a full-contact goal-line scrimmage in the McClain facility. It has always seemed bizarre to outsiders and even to other athletes that football has essentially two seasons in which players can be injured seriously. But then football is, always has been, different.

A number of hockey players, including Barry Richter, Duane Derksen, Chris Nelson, and Doug McDonald, have come up from their workouts in the weight room to watch the scrimmage from the sideline. Between plays Derksen mentions the big change in the hockey team: Sean Hill left yesterday for the Montreal Canadiens. Word has it Hill signed a multiyear deal and will help the Canadiens, quite possibly, in their imminent Stanley Cup run.

"Nine hundred thousand dollars for three years," says Derksen with a nod. Derksen always got a kick out of the flaky defenseman. There was that time last year when Coach Sauer had the team working a drill in which they rushed the goaltender one at a time, trying to score. "Be creative," Sauer pleaded. Hill dropped his pants to his knees before he skated toward the crease.

"And it's a one-way," adds Derksen, meaning the money will be there even if Hill is sent to the minors for seasoning. "Of course, that's in Canadian dollars, so subtract about twenty percent. But still it's what—$720,000? I think the numbers were $170,000, $210,000, $270,000, and a $250,000 signing bonus. I mean, Canadian, Chinese, who cares—all of a sudden he's got a lot of money." Amazing, really; one day the kid is goofing off in State Street Brats, the next day he's a near-millionaire in the NHL. What a game, hockey.

RICK ABERMAN HAS A CLIENT. HIS NAME IS NICK POLCZINSKI; HE'S A GRADU-ating senior football player, an offensive lineman who stands 6'4" and weighs 320 pounds. He is from Oconto Falls, about twenty miles north of Green Bay, and he wants to play pro ball for a while before using his agriculture economics degree to help him become a stock-broker. As big as he is, Nick is not an overwhelmingly skilled football player; he probably will not be drafted by the NFL, but he's heard that "Denver, Green Bay, and Seattle are high on me." Polczinski is so massive that the first thing an observer thinks is *steroids*. But Polczinski has never flunked a drug test or been accused of drug-taking by anyone in the UW athletic department.

Polczinski's problem has been with Scott Raridon, who has

treated him coldly since Polczinski has insisted on doing his own weight workouts, often in Myrland's weight room. Raridon is such a jerk, Polczinski says. "He tells me, 'If you don't work out in here, I can't tell the pro scouts you've been working out.' I said, 'That's the goddamned stupidest thing I've ever heard. You know how hard I work.' He said, 'Well, I can't lie. I don't see you.' "

Polczinski shakes his head. "That's like saying to the Pope, 'Did you pray today? I didn't see you.' "

But the larger issue for the player has been the general trauma of being a big, visible man playing in a chaotic, unsuccessful, and embarrassing program. Recruited by Dave McClain, Polczinski has played for head coaches Hilles, Morton, and Alvarez, enjoying Alvarez the most, but finding the losing hard to tolerate under all of the men. "Losing is so stressful," he tells Aberman. "I don't like being laughed at. You put in all those hours, but you can never relax. I have a problem with nerves. I throw up before every game, even before big practices."

During Christmas break Polczinski's frustration seemed to bubble over. While working as a bouncer at a local bar, he was arrested for getting into a fight with a patron. The charges were eventually dismissed. "It was all bullshit," he says now. "They accused me of holding a man down while the manager beat him. I told the policeman, 'If I want to beat somebody up, I think I can do it myself.' " But Polczinski had seen Aberman before because of stress, a burden that he struggles to carry.

"You know how hard it is for me to get clothes?" he says. "J. C. Penney has a good big and tall man's catalog, but half the time you order something and it's wrong, doesn't fit. It's hard to be anonymous. I try to be cordial to people, but it just wears you down. I can't go out to a bar and just sneak a beer. Everybody stares." He sighs. "I wish I was five-ten, one-eighty."

"Big people aren't supposed to be sensitive?" asks Aberman.

"Right. I only went out twice after games this year. Two other games I just bawled my eyes out. The Michigan game. But the Temple game was the one that really upset me. I was just physically drained. It came down to the wire, we should have won, but we lost, 24–18. I felt like putting my fist through a wall. I was afraid if I went to a bar I would maim someone. During the season I'd go out running at midnight to calm down. It's not fair to lose that much." He looks down at his enormous thighs, thighs that are never comfortable in street clothes. Even his football pants were too tight; they caused his leg hairs to become ingrown and infected last season. "It just isn't right."

Aberman lets him remain silent for a while, waits for him to continue his monologue, prepared to follow the stream wherever it might lead.

"So much time you put in," says Polczinski. "It seemed to catch up with me this year. I'd get here at noon during the season, wouldn't get home till eight. Then lifting. Sixty, seventy hours a week. And then spring is really crazy. You know, in high school I had a three-point-nine GPA out of four-point-oh. But here, I'd study one hour for a midterm! I'd be so tired I'd go to the library, fall asleep, and wake up and think, 'Where the hell am I?' If I could tell the NCAA something, I'd say, 'Give us a mandatory day off, where we can't go *near* the stadium. Just let us be normal students for a day.' I talked with a buddy recently who's on the San Francisco 49ers, and he said I wouldn't believe how nice it is, how awesome, how much easier it is to be a pro."

Polczinski stops, reflects, starts again. "The coaches are so up and down—it's so hard for a player to stay on an even keel here. Everything changes all the time. You know what I mean, Rick?"

"Yes."

"Mind games just piss me off. I give one hundred percent. Don't jack me around."

"Sometimes you feel they don't give you credit for being an adult?" asks Aberman.

"Exactly! You're doing well, then you get knocked down—why embarrass you then? Why criticize? You can only kick a dog so many times before he'll turn and bite you."

Polczinski takes a longer pause this time. He looks at Aberman's clock, which is off by only two or ten hours, depending on one's point of view; at Albert Einstein looking down through his walrus mustache; at the Silly Putty in a plastic egg-half on the table. The room seems much smaller with the player in it; he is, after all, more than twice as heavy as the psychologist seated to his left. Polczinski looks into Aberman's face.

"I've never told you this, Rick," he says, "but you have helped me with my nerves, helped me figure things out." Again, the pause. "Just to talk about things. Really. Who else is there? Who else knows?"

16

It's dusk and the meeting hall at the Inn-Towner Motel at the west end of campus is full of tall, slender young women in nice dresses, heels, and heavily sprayed hair. There are balloons at tables and a bar at the back of the room, though none of the young women drink cocktails. They sip Diet Cokes and ginger ales, chatting with their mothers and fathers and the random little brothers and sisters that scurry between the tables like puppies. This is the women's basketball awards banquet, and it is a festive event; yet there is an underlying tone to the many cheery conversations that is somehow disconcerting, as though some item of daily business is continually being avoided.

Before the dinner, Joyce Rose, president of the Badger Cager Club, the women's basketball booster organization hosting the banquet (along with the Wisconsin Beef Council), introduces coach Mary Murphy by showing a video from Murphy's days as a star point guard at Northwestern a decade ago. Murphy, who is plainly not thrilled with the sight of her former self, flips off the tape after a minute or so and addresses the crowd. She thanks all the parents for their support "when things got tough" this year. There's no mention of what those things might have been. The squad finished with a disappointing 13–15 record overall, 7–11 in the Big Ten, running, as the coach describes it, "a helter-skelter, out-of-control offense." Implied is the notion that a stabilizing point guard could have helped the team greatly. Someone like Murphy herself, perhaps, in her prime. Or Amy Bauer.

But all was not gloomy this season. The seven conference wins were the most for UW in seven years. There were lots of team and individual records set. And six Lady Badgers made the All–Big Ten Academic team, Murphy announces. One of them, backup point guard Peggy Shreve, earned a 3.93 GPA in genetics. The announcement of this fact brings extra applause from the crowd. Murphy continues to give out awards, until it seems every member of the squad has walked to the front of the room several times. Most Valuable Rookies. Most Dedicated Athletes. Something called the Capitol Square Optimists Club Award. Then the team Most Valuable Player Award. Murphy gives out four of them.

There is a wrap-up slide show of the team in action, with music and narration. Remarkably, there is not a single shot, even in panorama, of the point guard who started twenty-three games for the team. There is no hint that the three-year starter who holds the UW season assist record of 141 and single-game record of 21 ever performed in Madison. Amy Bauer is a nonperson. The only glitch comes when the soundtrack says there were seven players on this year's conference All-Academic team. Nobody notices.

The banquet breaks up and Peggy Shreve, in a party dress with her left pinky in a cast (she broke the finger yesterday in a pickup game at the Shell), carefully reflects on former teammate and two-year apartment-mate, Bauer. "I'd like to tell everything I know," she says, looking around her. "But I have two more years here. I like Amy. I look up to her."

Murphy and some of the other women in attendance have gathered amidst the post-party cleanup and are chatting at the other side of the room. Shreve really needs to get going, she says. One question, then: Were there six players on the All-Academic team, as Murphy stated, or seven?

"There were seven," says Shreve. "Amy was on it, too."

RICK ABERMAN RUNS THROUGH THE STREETS OF MADISON, RECHARGING HIS battery. He just came from a long meeting with Al Fish in which the two discussed Aberman's contract with the school and his job in general. It struck the psychologist then, and he finds it mildly amusing now, that Fish, like almost everyone else in the athletic department, has no clear idea what exactly it is that Aberman does. It would be simpler, naturally, if Aberman just practiced on team members the usual psychobabbling, performance-enhancing blather that has become fashionable in sports management now that everyone is certain that, as Yogi Berra says, "Ninety percent of the game is half mental." The shrink as training tool. But that's not what Aberman is about. He could do those things—hypnotize, relax, "image"—but he won't. He considers himself a trainer, a healer, an expediter—not a cheerleader. Trainers massage injured bodies; he massages injured minds. An athlete should benefit afield from mental health off it, but that's not really the point; the point is that Rick Aberman cares about people as people, not athletes.

The discussion with Fish was pleasant, even though Aberman expressed to him the concerns he hears about the department becoming impersonal and corporate. Aberman, who is still considered only a half-time employee, also proposed that he become a full-time employee. He sees nearly one hundred athletes a year, out of approximately nine hundred under the department umbrella, and most of those he sees for more than one session. Becoming a full-time employee would mean that he could dedicate himself totally to the athletic department tasks at hand and would not have to spend time on his outside counseling work with family businesses, which he does to earn added income. After all, his UW salary is just $20,652, and he's often here seven days a week. Aberman suggests a full-time salary of $60,000. Fish said he could see Aberman as a full-time employee, but Aberman would have to do more than counseling; he would have to be the head of the "support program" and lecture on the evils of drug and alcohol usage and the benefits of proper nutrition, etc. And he could earn, say, $40,000, but not $60,000.

Aberman declined such a role, because he doesn't believe a counseling psychologist should also be a lecturer and rule-maker. Moreover, he understood Fish's not being comfortable with the $60,000 salary, since Fish himself only makes $67,500. But there's no harm in asking, is there? So they agreed to keep Aberman's job half-time for now, with the possibility of hiring a grad assistant in the future to help Aberman with the support items. For now, though, the status quo will be fine.

"Jeff," says the hockey secretary, Nancy Olson. "It's Solomon on the phone."

Jeff Sauer picks up the phone and hears a rundown on the status of Sean Hill from Hill's agent, Jeff Solomon. Hill is in Fredericton, New Brunswick, preparing to play a game tonight for the Montreal Canadiens' farm team against the Hartford Whalers' farm team. Fredericton, New Brunswick—basically, Hill is in nowhere-ville without friends or family or anchor, a child in an adult world. Even his contract got screwed up, because agent Solomon trusted the pro franchise and believed it would give Hill all the things it promised, even though nobody had signed the deal. Oh well, the contract is not too much worse than originally hoped for, and Hill is in the NHL, his dream since childhood. But there's something sad here, too.

Sauer hangs up. He talked to Hill yesterday when Hill called him via car phone while en route to Fredericton. Sauer asked him how his French was, since most of the higher-ups in the Montreal organization speak French as their first language. Though Hill took two years of French at UW—because he knew the Canadiens had his draft rights—he admitted, "It's tougher than I thought." Overall, he didn't sound too upbeat.

"I feel bad for Sean," says Sauer. "I feel bad for all these guys when they leave. They all will say they had it best when they were in college. Just the niceness of Nancy Olson saying hi every day. Now it's a business, a job."

Sauer shrugs. Who doesn't listen to the call of long cash? He recruits good players, makes them better, and watches as the best ones go off to seek fame and fortune. It's not much different from what happens in the other departments of the university, in a sense.

"I told him, 'Sean, you're a pro now, you have to wear a coat and tie. You have to grow up,'" says Sauer. "[Former UW player Chris] Chelios went to Montreal and got off the plane in shorts and a T-shirt, and the only way they knew it was him was the damned Wisconsin hockey bag going around the baggage carousel."

Sauer calculates for a moment. "Sean is about fifty-seven credits away from graduating, so I guess he could get out in, what, a year and a half if he came back and took a lot of courses? Education takes a backseat in these situations, of course." Sauer smiles, just thinking about his erstwhile defenseman. "He's an interesting, off-the-wall guy, a sensitive kid who gives the appearance of being crazy. But the last thing he did here was recruit these two brothers, Mark and Mike Strobel, great high school hockey players. He was with them on Saturday and Sunday, and Sunday they said they were coming here. They loved Sean."

Sauer laughs outright. "A week ago we had a team meeting, and I told the team that because of the new NCAA rules we're going from thirty-eight games a season to thirty-four. Hill looks at me and says, 'Coach, does that mean we're oh-and-four before we start?' "

ENDOWMENTS ARE WHAT MAKE THE WORLD GO ROUND. ENDOWMENTS FOR scholarships, for all sorts of positions in the athletic department—endowments are what you want so you don't have to beat the bushes every year trying to rustle up funds just to get you through the week. Get donors to put big chunks of money into trusts and then use the interest like a little self-generating cash machine. Endowments are the rage in college sport.

At least, endowments are the dream goals of John Swenson, the director of development for UW athletics, and his sidekick, assistant director Todd Kuckkahn. They are large (both over six feet three inches), outgoing young men who are in charge of shaking down alums and boosters for as much money as they can to keep the athletic department beast sated and calm. They offer clients the chance to make deferred or outright gifts to the athletic foundation, to fund charitable remainder trusts, annuity trusts, or "pooled income funds." They offer a kaleidoscope of money-giving schemes, so that a donor can pick the one that is most pleasing to him and give to his heart's content with the least amount of fuss and pain. Swenson and Kuckkahn are master handshakers who do everything but reach right into ex-Badgers' pockets to relieve the folks of excess collateral.

"Endowments," says Swenson, a dark-haired, squeaky-clean chap who looks like the perfect American MBA grad turned investment banker. "At Michigan they built the Center of Champions, a football facility with a hall of fame, banquet rooms, training room, weight room, conference room, lecture hall, and coaches' offices, and it cost between twelve and thirteen million dollars. They raised fifteen million, and they had to spend it on football, so what they did with the extra—they endowed *maintenance*. So if they need a new lightbulb or a roll of toilet paper? No problem, it's endowed."

Well, first things first here at Wisconsin. Swenson started two years ago in this job and, to be honest, he's still trying to figure it out. So, apparently, were the directors who preceded him, both of whom cleared out fast when they realized what a confusing world they had descended into. Swenson is the third chief UW fund-raiser in eighteen months. He knows why now.

"I came in really naïve," he says, looking out his foundation office window at the fog over Lake Mendota. "I thought it was pretty well tied together here. But this is how unique Wisconsin is: There are twenty-seven booster groups for athletics, all of which operate independently. They don't have to report to us at all. And yet we're supposed to direct and coordinate all fund-raising for the athletic department. So what have we got?" He turns and smiles at Kuckkahn, who smiles back from where he is standing by the window.

"We have chaos," says Swenson.

In the corner of the office away from the lake rests a shovel with its blade painted white and a plaque attached to the handle that reads McCLAIN ATHLETIC FACILITY GROUNDBREAKING CEREMONY, JULY 23, 1987. The horror. A hole was dug, and then money was dumped in. And the hole isn't filled yet.

"We have spinning wheels and tremendous duplication of efforts," says Swenson. "It's just tradition." Then, too, he adds, UW has booster clubs that seem to think the world ended with the advent of the Edsel. "Take the Mendota Gridiron Booster Club, the main football group that started twenty-six years ago. It started as a tavern thing, just pass the hat, give the coach a little extra incentive kind of thing. It was fifty dollars a year membership back then; today it's still fifty dollars a year. Other schools have booster clubs that cost a thousand dollars a year to join."

Nevertheless, Swenson affirms, he and Todd will continue to plug along, raising money from the myriad places it lurks, transferring it to the hands of Pat Richter and Al Fish once they get it. Indeed, just a week ago Swenson closed on a fairly unusual money-making deal. That was the day that an old man named Charlie Vogts died of cancer. Vogts was a lifelong Madison resident and UW alumnus who worked for the U.S. government in a clerical position and loved UW men's basketball. Swenson introduced himself to Vogts two years ago and slowly developed a friendship with the former World War II tank driver. Vogts already knew he had cancer, and as he grew weaker he found in Swenson a courteous and amiable pal with whom he could share his innermost thoughts.

Together Swenson and Vogts made plans for Vogts's passing from this earth; they visited funeral homes, picked out a casket, made all necessary arrangements for interment in advance. "He wanted a military funeral, very classy," says Swenson. "Six rifles—or seven, I guess, that fired twenty-one times." Before that final day, however, they also went over Vogts's financial situation with great care. "He took me through the house, showed me where his secret stash of jewels and bonds was. He had a checkbook hidden in the silverware drawer and a savings book in the Tupperware drawer. There were silver and coins in another drawer. His Bucky hat he wanted given to the Varsity Club at the Madison Inn off State Street."

All told, the quiet old man's estate came to about four hundred fifty thousand dollars, and this was where the UW foundation figured in. According to Swenson, Vogts had no family, except for a very old cousin living outside Chicago. "He met a girl during the war in Poland and asked his mother if he could marry her," says Swenson. "She said 'No,' and he never fell in love again." So, alone and dying, Vogts entrusted everything to the UW basketball program, with the personable Swenson acting as his financial representative. Ten days before he died Vogts even drew up and signed papers giving Swenson power of attorney over the estate. Swenson had virtually become the man's son. Vogts's cash—and Swenson estimates UW will get 91 percent of it—will soon endow three basketball scholarship positions in perpetuity.

"There's a fine line about closeness with a donor, I know," says Swenson. "Some people feel we went over the line on this one. I did get close to him, but he had no one else. And I liked him."

The money is out there, Swenson has learned. It's everywhere, as Al Fish has often commented; there are so many rich people in this country, it's astounding. It's just that so much of that money, if you can get your hands on it, comes with strings attached. The first person Swenson had to meet in his new job was Albert O. "Ab" Nicholas, a fabulously wealthy University of Wisconsin regent who through the years has been the biggest donor to the athletic department coffers. A former UW cager himself, Nicholas has very firm ideas on how things should be run, both on and off the court. "I met with him and for an hour and a half he blasted the university and basketball, how we had to get rid of Yoder, on and on," recalls Swenson. And then there was another big donor in Minocqua who told Swenson he wasn't going to give the ten thousand dollars he'd promised "unless we get rid of that 'goddamned bulldog chancellor.'"

Brother. Swenson shrugs at the lunacy. And yet, sometimes all those strings attached just make for easier dealmaking. "The easiest money I ever raised," he says, "came for the buyout of Don Morton and Ade Sponberg. I made one call to Chicago and the first person I got said, 'I'll go a quarter million.' All the other guys also gave instantly."

Go figure.

17

Rick Aberman is walking down State Street near the Badger Liquors store a few days after a last-gasp effort to reverse the sports cuts has failed. The store reminds him of a lesson he learned years ago. "In 1974 I used to picket Badger Liquors on Friday afternoons, protesting Gallo wine for the United Farm Workers. Then on Saturday we'd leaflet, because it was a highly visible thing to do. It was a good experience; we had study groups and things like that. But then one day the organizers, who were students from New York—Marxists, I think—went home. I felt abandoned. Actually, Gallo may have settled with the union, which was a victory. But for the people in the field it was a defeat. What do we do now? So then we got involved in the Menominee Indian problem, after William Kunstler came to town." Aberman looks back at the harmless little liquor store on the corner, the one that has been there for ages, and then smiles, "There are always causes."

Legal disturbances have nicked two UW athletes in the last twenty-four hours. After an argument with her roommate over an eight-hundred-dollar phone bill, Robin Threatt, the best player on the women's basketball team, was arrested on a tentative charge of domestic battery. Police said Threatt attacked her roomie, nineteen-year-old Tameeca Wilcoxin, punching her and kicking her in the stomach. Then, early Sunday morning senior linebacker Aaron Norvell, the son of athletic board member Merritt Norvell, was at a woman's apartment when the woman's estranged boyfriend returned, became enraged and cracked Norvell over the head with a vodka bottle. Norvell was treated for cuts and bruises on his face and head at Meriter Hospital, while Wilcoxin went to University Hospital for her treatment. Disputed phone bills, girlfriends, jealous lovers, violence—they're all part of the growing process, Aberman knows.

He remembers growing quickly himself when he first started as a practicing therapist. He worked in tandem with another therapist who had an office in New Glarus, a small farm town built to resemble a Swiss village, about thirty miles from Madison. New Glarus was not a Disneyland-type attraction, but a real place with many settlers of Swiss descent. One day Aberman got a call to come quick, there was an emergency with a family he had been counseling.

"What is it?" Aberman asked.

"The father lost his temper and tipped over the manure spreader," said his co-therapist.

Aberman drove to the town, wondering what the big deal was. "I had pictured a green Scott push-spreader that you used on your lawn," he recalls. "And when I got there, there was a huge machine tipped over. The point was, I'd never really been on a farm. And because of that, I'd missed that this was a real family crisis. For me it was all about culture, learning. And I remember it was deer season, too, and there were guns going off all the time as we talked to the family. For me it was very creepy. But you need to learn."

Aberman has been on many farms since, which has helped him in dealing with the troubled UW athletes who come from farming backgrounds. Just today he saw a Badger baseball player who was raised on a farm, who is feeling great stress because his family is moving to a nearby town, his sport is being cut, his girlfriend dropped him and, of all things, his dog just died. Moreover, the young man is distressed about the Persian Gulf War and the violence that has been wrought defending a purpose that is not clear to him.

"He gets on the mound and his mind is wandering, his grades are slipping, and he's just tremendously afraid of failing," says Aberman. "All the flux in his life is making him feel vulnerable, and he's never felt that way before. Things ending, people dying in the war, the dog dying, change—it has all made him ask the age-old question, Who am I? So many athletes are developmentally retarded because they've never asked that question. They've always been good at a sport and thus able to delay introspection.

"The ironic thing is in sport we *teach* dependency. Then we come down on athletes when they aren't independent. Sometimes I think the best thing that can happen to an athlete is to have a major injury, where he has to stop and figure out who he is outside his sport. It's traumatic, but it has to happen eventually."

What can Aberman do for the baseball player he's seeing now?

"I can help him by letting him know he's not going crazy," Aberman says. "Let him know he's growing up."

"Like, I just wanted to say, if you just had the dialogue a little, you know, earlier?" says a female student in a blue workshirt, baggy pants, and light-purple nails.

She is sitting at a table in a small classroom on the seventh floor of the Helen White Library, along with thirteen other students and the teacher of this creative writing class. Barry Baum looks at her and then at the female student whose paper is being discussed. Baum is wearing an orange Five-Star Basketball Camp sweatshirt and jeans. In front of him is the short story being critiqued. He didn't know quite what to make of this tale. "It reminded me of a diary," he says when his turn arrives. "And then it got softer as it went on. Uh, I don't know, is that right?"

His own offerings this semester, "The Formal" and "Waiting in the Smoke (For Her)," are far more accessible than some of his compatriots' fiction. His pieces are reminiscent of very early Woody Allen, with perhaps more innocence and a dash of Henny Youngman thrown in. From "The Formal" come these passages: "We were in Green Lake, Wisconsin, at the Woodbury Inn. This resort has a huge lake that sits on one side of the hotel as well as a ridiculously large amount of grass and more trees than there are in all of Queens. Nature is not for me. I get allergies when I *meet* people who have been to parks. . . . It's not that I'm bad looking; actually one girl on a blind date last year told me I had nice eyes. It made me feel so good, I paid for both of our dinners. I called her the next day and she told me she had met someone else. Since it was only twelve hours later, I couldn't imagine who she'd met. A few days later I saw her on the street holding hands with the waiter from our restaurant. . . . Gloria had dyed blond hair about shoulder length, dark blue eyes that were easy to stare into, a small nose, and a smile that could melt the stained-glass windows at Beth-El Synagogue on the Lower East Side. Most importantly, she was five-foot-two. This was extremely important because I'm five-seven. I am very conscious about height, namely mine. When I go to a bar I feel as if I'm wallet-sized and every other guy is an eight-by-ten glossy."

From "Waiting in the Smoke (For Her)" comes this: "She often had friends around who seemed to protect her from intruders like myself. Israeli Prime Minister Yitzhak Shamir is more accessible than this woman."

"My stories have to do with girls," Baum explained needlessly. "Somehow, it's just what I write about."

"What do you think, Robert?" asks the teacher. "You have that Buddha look about you."

A bored young man eating from a box of Triscuits looks up, shrugs, chews, swallows, and then begins to babble. After a time the teacher interrupts him, saying, "Defend it, Laura."

Laura, the author, says, "Well, I just wanted to make it funny."

"I didn't laugh much," says the student.

Baum's eyes go back and forth watching the debate. He is bemused, intrigued, baffled. A new short story entitled "Circle," about a doctor and a child, and the possibility of an adoption of, or by, the child or doctor, it seems, is next on the agenda. First to dissect it is the student with the purple nail polish.

She says, "I assume she, like, wanted to commit suicide?"

A VETERAN WOMEN'S SOCCER PLAYER, A SLENDER TWO-TIME ALL-AMERICA with blond hair and delicate features, sits in Aberman's office and kneads a wad of Silly Putty. A fifteen-letter athlete in high school, the player is an exceptional performer in virtually any sport, with the lateral movement and explosiveness of an elite male athlete. Her problems at UW began as a freshman, when she nearly quit school because of vague, unexplainable stress. She has been to see Rick Aberman often.

"The initial struggle?" asks Aberman now, reviewing the past.

"When I came here from Minnesota I'd never been away from

home, except to Florida," she says. "And then there were the ex-pectations my parents had of me. They only had two kids, me and my older sister. She was the scholar and I was the athlete. Maybe there was pressure because my parents didn't have a boy. We were a very enmeshed family."

Aberman nods at the phrase. It's one of his. "There are en-meshed families, as you know," he says. "And at the other end, disengaged families. Enmeshed families are ones where everybody is involved with every other member. The problems that occur are ones of differentiation, for each member to have the ability to live on his own. A disengaged family is one in which everyone is so individual-istic that it's not really like a family at all. Enmeshed families tend to be warm, loving families, but sometimes the enmeshment is ex-hibited under the guise of being love. It can be smothering, oppres-sive. A healthy family allows people to be together but separate."

The young woman nods. "I felt I couldn't be separate. My family wanted me to go, but wouldn't let me change. You know, 'Go out and grow up, but don't grow up.' I used to tell my parents everything. Now I'm beginning to realize maybe I shouldn't."

She looks down, stretching the putty. "I didn't know who I was. I was an athlete. Back as far as eighth grade I was already playing on the girls' varsity team, and so I never connected with my peer group. Being a good athlete can be a curse for a girl. You're known as a butch. People think you're a dyke, but then when you get closer to boys, you're a bitch."

"Coaches catered to you?"

"Oh yeah. If it was too cold out, they'd say, 'You don't have to practice.' "

The topic swings to the UW varsity team.

"Our team is very girly," she says. "Greg Ryan, our coach, will not recruit someone who's real masculine. So we have a very cute, cutesy, team. Also, because of him we were very religious, praying all the time. Greg would say something like, 'Please don't let us simply strive to defeat these people, but let us play to our best.' And I'd think, like, 'The point is, we're going to kick their asses!' I found the Jesus stuff eerie. Girls joined Athletes In Action. Girls put crosses on their cleats. And crosses on their hands. He let us know that this was the way he wanted things. And it split the team. It seemed like there was AIA and then the sinners, the heathens. I was kind of in the middle, and it felt so strange. I went to one AIA meeting as a freshman, and it was fine, but I just wasn't comfortable. I'm not a Christ-basher, but I thought religion had become a way to get ahead. I talked to Greg about it, and he said he was worried about my 'inner core,' and I was not taking the path my parents would want. I'm a Lutheran, a Christian, but on my own time. I feel religion should be private.

"The thing is, he could have benched me for not following along. He would have. Out East, coaches would say, 'Wisconsin is a Jesus team.' And the trouble was if we said something about it, we wouldn't play. And that's what we wanted to do—play. Because of all that I've learned to adjust, to finagle, to be more devious, I guess, to get what I want."

Now, though, she and Ryan have a tolerable relationship. He seems to have tempered his religious fervor somewhat and to be less of a crusader. Also, her skills have earned her a star's hands-off status. The only other problem she has, she admits, is simply the one that she feels most women athletes have at Wisconsin: "We're treated like shit here, Rick. We're not allowed in the good weight room. You kidding? You go in there and that fat blond guy will say, 'What are you doing! What sport are you in?' You say, 'Soccer,' and you feel so ungodly awful. He said to one girl who started to lift in there, 'You call that a workout?' One day I was just studying in the McClain study area, just minding my own business, and the football coaches asked me to leave. This guy said I was 'distracting' the football players. I thought that was really rude."

IT IS AFTERNOON NOW, AND ANOTHER YOUNG WOMAN IS SITTING ON THE shrink's couch. Her name is Heather Taggart, the senior star goaltender for the women's soccer team. She wears a sweatshirt and a miniskirt and her muscular legs are cut and bruised as though she has taken many falls on rough surfaces and been kicked repeatedly, which she has. Taggart, a biochemistry major, has a ready smile and a sunny disposition, except when she competes. Then she is a pit bull.

"My dream is to be an orthopedic surgeon," she tells Aberman. "Or a pediatrician and work with children. I've got the boards, the MCATs, on Saturday and I've been spending up to sixteen hours a week in the lab. Actually, that's been kind of fun. We've been going through the entire synthesis of a compound, some commercial compound that you would actually want to buy. I've been taking small, three-carbon compounds and combining them into a very expensive eleven-carbon compound. The thing I've been making is azulene, which costs about eighteen dollars a gram, and which is blue—incredibly, beautifully blue—so you know when you have it. Then, too, you're always trying out new things, to see if this works better than that. I mixed some sodium and potassium in an amalgam and then stirred in toluene, and if I wasn't careful, I could have blown out the side of the building."

She giggles and Aberman laughs quietly. They have talked off and on for a couple years. "You're very competitive," he says. "And now you've found ways to maximize that in a beneficial way. You're an achiever."

Taggart nods. "Like in soccer I look for a level of intensity from everyone—I want to lay it on the line. For ninety minutes show me everything you've got. I don't mind losing when people have shown they cared."

"Martin Smith's cross-country teams all have that same intensity."

"Yes, and that's why they're national champs," agrees Taggart. "Our team is not the kind of team that wins national championships. Girls will trap a ball that could have gone for a goal and they'll laugh and say, 'Bummer!' I can get nutmegged five times in a row in practice and I'll laugh, because it is funny. But in a game, it's not. A good portion of my teammates haven't figured out when to laugh and when to be serious."

"Is that because they're girls?"

"Sort of. But they've been athletes since they were little kids."

"Often girls have been socialized not to show that they care about things like that," says Aberman. "Boys have been socialized differently."

The dialogue shifts to analysis of Taggart's own expectations.

"How do your perfectionist qualities cause you problems?" asks Aberman.

"I ask a lot of myself. Socially, people think I'm too intense, they're afraid of me. They have a hard time separating me the person from me the athlete."

Aberman lets her ponder that for a while.

"The pressure I put on myself comes from me personally," she continues. "Why? I don't know. But if I have an exam and I'm not prepared, I'll say, 'Heather, stay up all night!' When I got a C on my first college exam, I cried and called home because I couldn't believe it. My dad, who's a chemist, was almost laughing at me. 'Relax,' he said."

"Your mother has talked to me about that quality in you," says Aberman. "It worries her. Mistakes eat at you."

"As I've matured, I think the one thing I've learned here—and if it's the only thing I've learned, that's good—is how to deal with failure, how to say, 'That's life.' Boy, I used to eat myself up over things." She hesitates, then goes on. "But I feel, I still do, that the people they let in this school, all of them, have the capability of getting four-point-ohs. It's all a big bunch of choices, and you make them. My grade-point now is a three-six, and it could be a three-eight, except for one semester when I screwed up."

Aberman smiles. "One semester I was seeing five kids with ulcers," he says. "How about you?"

"I've never had an ulcer," replies Taggart quickly, chuckling. She pushes her hair away from her face and returns to the notion of choices. "I was adopted by my dad at age four. And that was my own *choice*. My parents divorced when I was about two, and my dad had custody of my older sister and my mom had me, and I walked up to my dad, my biological father, and said, 'I want to be a Taggart.' I got a good deal out of it."

Aberman says nothing. The goalie is so tough that as a sophomore in high school at a U.S. Olympic development camp she stood in front of the coach and let him drop-kick balls at her at full force—from six yards away—and stopped every one of them.

"I was all-state in Nebraska in basketball and volleyball. But I was five feet four and a half and chubby," she says somberly. "I wasn't a good athlete."

"Heather!" Aberman laughs. "Think of what you're saying."

"I was too short and I couldn't jump. It's true!" She blushes. "Well okay. I do have good hand-eye coordination."

18

IT's FRIDAY AFTERNOON ON THE FIRST DAY OF BADGERFEST '91, AND AL FISH stands in the hallway outside his office, sipping an Old Style and reading a pamphlet called "The Norwegian Medical Journal." The tract contains such riotous definitions as *"varicose veins*—veins that are very close together," and *"rectum*—almost killed him," but it gets some howls from Fish all the same. BadgerFest '91 is a kind of loose-knit weekend series of events that celebrate spring sports at UW and is highlighted by the spring football game and the ensuing Fieldhouse polka-dancing/beer-guzzling hoedown known as Butch's Bologna Bash. Despite the bitter feelings of many folks regarding the sports cuts, almost all Wisconsinites can put down their grievances when a party is nigh. Fish is no different.

He has spent most of the day deciding what furnishings to put in at the brand-new UW golf course, University Ridge. "Everything from the refrigerator to the vent hood was bid on," he says proudly. "One shelf was $481, so I let that go"—and he's ready to take the edge off. He hands a beer to Jim Bakken and asks him if he's heard about a punk polka band that Fish checked out in Milwaukee not long ago. "Their big song was 'Blitzkrieg over Kenosha,'" says Fish. "It was unreal."

No, Bakken says. Never heard of it or them. "But have you heard of 'Da Yoopers'?" he asks. "A polka band from Michigan? They got a song called 'The Second Week of Deer Camp Is the Finest Week of All.' "

Over at the Fieldhouse the First Annual University of Wisconsin Athletic Hall of Fame ceremony is about to begin. Of the thirty-five men and women to be inducted into the hall, two of the oldest living inductees are seventy-one-year-old Gene Englund, a basketball center from 1938 through 1941 and an All-America and the MVP on UW's 1941 NCAA Championship team, and eighty-two-year-old Harold "Bud" Foster, a UW hoops All-America in 1930 and the coach of that NCAA title team in 1941. They both come from an era that seems so distant today as to be nearly out of sight. The Badgers haven't finished above .500 in the Big Ten since 1973–74 and haven't been to the NCAA tournament since 1947, when Foster was still the coach.

Sitting in the stands now Foster is stately and reserved, wearing a gray suit, a flattop, and hearing aids in both ears. He is the first person to acknowledge that nothing in college basketball is the way it used to be. "When we were Big Ten co-champions in '29, the jumpshot hadn't even come in," he says, with a wave of one of his long, bony hands. "I was the center at six-three. I'd be lucky to be a point guard now. Oh, it was different then. We'd go to Chicago to play Illinois or Purdue and we'd stay at the Morrison Hotel on Congress for a dollar fifty a night. Can't do that now."

He is, he admits, a little uncertain about modern times. "I don't care for the game much anymore," he says. "They all play the same, and nobody graduates." It's not clear whether he is aware that black players, in particular, have not done well in the UW academic mill; according to a survey printed in USA TODAY, UW had the fourth-worst record in Division I basketball for graduating its black players through the eighties. Foster coached several black players toward the end of his years at Wisconsin, and he recalls the difficulties they faced in the late fifties. "I remember we played down at Houston and SMU and we offered to leave them home, but they wanted to come along. They stayed in the hotel with us in Dallas, but they had to stay downstairs in a room off the dining area, and they couldn't leave by the front door. In Houston we had to sneak them in through the back door just to have our pregame meeting."

Englund is spry and outgoing, and he wanders the old arena

shaking hands and telling tales. "How did we win the NCAA championship?" he says. "We were lucky. At that time there weren't shenanigans going on in college basketball, which was good for a school like Wisconsin. There weren't athletic scholarships. Fees were $27.50 a semester. I'm from Kenosha, and nobody recruited me, nobody offered me anything."

To earn his meals Englund took a job "hopping tables" at Toby & Moon's Restaurant on State Street. To get walking-around cash he took a job turning on lights on the fronts of stores in downtown Madison. "I'd run down State Street, around the square, down to the railroad station, then back up the other side of the square, turning on light switches with my foot. It was about a three-mile circuit and I did it in forty-five, fifty minutes, seven days a week. Whenever practice was over I'd take off. It was a good job, paid fifteen dollars a month, and with that I'd pay my bills and have spending money left over. Remember, beer was only a nickel." He laughs at the notion. "I played nine years of pro ball, but there is no way in hell I could compete with these guys who are seven feet tall, can run like deer, and jump over the backboard."

SATURDAY, ELROY HIRSCH PACES BACK AND FORTH AT THE TWENTY-YARD LINE of the varsity football field, shaking hands with as many of the five thousand runners in this year's Crazylegs Run as he can reach. This is the tenth annual charity run that precedes the spring football game and is sponsored, naturally, by a beer company. This year the sponsor is Old Style, and a huge inflated can of Old Style is anchored at the thirty-yard line, and Old Style kegs are scattered about, providing free beer for any runner who has completed the course from the Capitol to Camp Randall's midfield stripe. Most of the runners wear blue Crazylegs Run T-shirts, with a likeness of Hirsch's face on the front and his back on the back, in football uniform, helmet under arm.

Hirsch pumps hands until he is weary, then downs the beer he's holding in his left hand and says, "Think I'll put a head on this." He wades through the runners standing four-deep at the beer spigots and gets another brew. In the stands, several thousand people bask in the sun, drinking beer as though it were water. "God, I hate this," Hirsch says, looking fondly at his golden Old Style.

He meanders into the still-arriving stream of runners. He grabs a man's leg and says, "How long you been sick?" Then he roars with laughter. "Here's one you can use at your next banquet," he tells a group, then launches enthusiastically into a tepid joke. People laugh and tell tales and file up to the beer kegs. It's now 10:45 A.M.

The spring football game is a dull, predictable affair pitting half the UW squad, "Rolling Red Thunder," against the other half, "White Lightning II." Of course, all coaches and staff have had T-shirts printed up with their team name inscribed—the football department seems compelled to spend money on everything it does. At halftime the scores of the two teams are reversed, so it's hard to say who won the 18–17 game at the end, and in truth, no one other than the fired-up assistant coaches seems to care.

Throughout the stadium the thousand or so onlookers (admission is free) seem as interested in soaking up the warm spring sunshine as in determining what this display might mean for the Badgers' football fortunes next fall. A few players are hurt—at least one with a severe knee injury—while coaches such as Scott Raridon become nearly orgasmic when a player tags another with a "big hit," and nothing much is accomplished by the event. Spring football is one of the more dubious parts of Division I programs that football coaches will tell you they absolutely cannot do without. The fact that the team will not play a real game for approximately five months after the spring skirmish never seems to matter; this is just the way it's done.

In his heart Alvarez knows the game is a worthless exercise. Did he learn anything from it? "No," he mutters postgame. "You just want to get it over without anybody getting hurt."

Perhaps the most interesting battle wound displayed by any of the players as they leave the field belongs to Aaron Norvell. He shows a nicely healing gash under his left eye from where the angry boyfriend slugged him with the vodka bottle a few nights ago.

The real treat of the day is the postgame fund-raising get-together in the Fieldhouse for ten thousand or so of UW's staunchest fans. Officially titled Butch's Badger Benefit, the hoedown is known to all as Butch's Bologna Bash, named after a former reserve UW basketball player from the forties named Palmer "Butch" Strickler. A businessman from New Glarus, the quaint little Swiss village, Strickler annually grinds up about three tons of animal flesh in the garage behind his home, turns it into sausage, and serves it as the principal bill of fare for the hungry bash attendees. One of Hirsch's best buddies, Strickler prides himself on being, as the press has often called him, "UW's biggest cheerleader." Though he may be that, he is also a relic from a bygone era and precisely the kind of good-hearted, well-meaning meddler that anchors UW athletics to the past.

At one time the festivities made a lot of money for the department—supposedly one year's take was two hundred ninety thousand dollars (though primitive bookkeeping makes all old department numbers suspect)—but now the bash seems to have less to do with revenue production and more to do with the old guys wandering around drinking beer, dancing polkas, talking about the '63 Rose Bowl, and slapping current players on the behinds. The raffle tickets, which have always been the prime source of income for the event, don't exactly fly off the tables anymore. Even Strickler, a man with small blue eyes, a red face, and hands that could crush a buck deer's skull, knows that things are not going like they used to. "Every year it seems there is a problem up here where they need money," he sighs. "The fact is, to turn this whole program around, we're gonna have to win some games."

But that is of no concern just now as the fans mingle throughout the Fieldhouse, eating, drinking, and yelling along with the UW cheerleaders who occasionally get on stage with the band to make noise. Butch himself mounts the stage and, holding the microphone like a walnut, says sadly to a hushed audience, "This is my last bash. We need somebody younger with new ideas. All I can say is thank you and good-bye." The moment would be brimming with poignancy were it not for the fact that Butch says this every year. The band sings, "Oh Butch We Love You," and soon the party is back in high gear.

Many of the UW athletes are here, milling about or working at the counters where people who have paid their fifteen dollars admission can drink all the beer they want and eat what is undoubtedly one of the unhealthiest meals ever laid out. The menu is a veritable paean to cholesterol, saturated fat, and lard: bologna, salami, sausage, bratwurst, ham, American cheese, Swiss cheese, potato salad, baked beans, mayonnaise, white bread, butter. No fruit, fresh vegetables, or whole grains in sight. But the beer flows like the Wisconsin River. Nobody gets carded. Nobody cares.

A wandering tuba band plays the Budweiser song, perking up

revelers wherever it goes. Mayor Paul Soglin, recently reelected over his questionable challengers, roams through the crowd, raffle tickets in hand. He is wearing a sport coat, a black shirt, and a multicolored floral tie and looks more like a Las Vegas enforcer than a mayor. He pauses with the rest of the crowd to listen to Barry Alvarez promise that "we'll do everything we can to get this program back where it belongs."

The Badger fans roar with approval, and moments later Butch Strickler gets back behind the mike to inform everyone that "bags with over six pounds of sausage or cheese" will be sold for five dollars at the exit gates after the party. People join arms and sing a somber rendition of "Varsity," rocking slowly back and forth in unison like tipsy bar pals.

Butch's Bologna Bash is finished for another year, and partyers stream into the cool night air, their bags of food glistening in the moonlight.

IT IS EARLY MAY AND SEVERAL VARSITY BASKETBALL PLAYERS LACE UP THEIR GYM shoes in the Fieldhouse locker room in preparation for some pickup games on the old floor. That the team needs all the practice it can muster is clear, because the two best players from last season are both seniors, team MVP and first-team All–Big Ten forward Patrick Tompkins and starting forward Willie Simms. They will be leaving school, though neither is graduating. Neither Tompkins nor Simms ever seemed to fit in very well with the UW student populace. Tompkins, with his homemade tattoos and great, glowering bulk, always seemed out of place amongst the smaller, fair-haired children of farmers, and the tall and skinny Simms always seemed somewhat angry and overwhelmed by his surroundings. That any black student at UW ever feels comfortable is a wonder; this academic year exactly 550 black undergraduate students are enrolled at UW out of a total student body of 43,536. Even counting the 239 black graduate students at the school, the percentage of black students is just 1.8 percent. That's pretty close to the racial mix UW has had for the last fifteen years. Before that, well, there were times when you could go for days without seeing a black face on campus.

The basketball team needs to practice, but it also needs to get itself in shape. Athletic young men typically have body fat ratios of somewhere around 12 percent; elite athletes can have ratios much lower than that, with players of the caliber of, say, Michael Jordan testing out at around 5 percent body fat. Skilled Division I basketball players should be wiry and strong and lean, and therefore it is a shock to see posted on the locker room wall the body fat ratios of the UW men's players.

Only ten of the seventeen players listed have ratios less than 12 percent, a level of fitness one would expect to find in most serious intramural basketball players. Patrick Tompkins is composed of 15.9 percent body fat, as is forward Jeff Peterson. Even skinny graduating starter John Ellenson has almost 12 percent blubber on him. Astoundingly, there were times last season when UW had five players on the floor with no one having less than 13 percent body fat. Taking the cake, however, is 6'1" sharpshooting junior guard Brian Good, who, in a remarkable arrangement of flab to bodyweight, has a full 17.6 percent body fat mixed into his slight 180.4 pounds. One wonders how the Badgers could ever hope to contend with the Indiana and Michigans and Minnesotas of the conference with a squad that is as physically unfit as this.

Still, the players are trying to beat the odds, and right now the varsity athletes, including Simms, who is hoping to play professionally somewhere, divide themselves among the gym rats already on the floor and start playing a four-on-four half-court game, shirts against skins. As pickup games will, this one degenerates into a fairly rough-and-tumble adventure. There is plenty of reaching and hacking and pushing, and no one concedes a layup. Being the tallest player and the best leaper, Simms receives his share of the slaps and elbows. Abruptly, he drops the ball, shoves junior guard Billy Douglass, a skin, and hisses, "Uh huh, you don't like fouls, do you?"

"Willie, come on, man," says Douglass, a white 6'4" sometime starter who made last year's Academic All–Big Ten team.

Simms has a look of rage in his eyes. Something has snapped inside him. He turns to another skin, a small black student who is not a member of the UW team, and walks toward him.

"You fucking *it*, dude?" Simms asks, his head tilted slightly. "You saying you it?" Simms pulls back his right fist. The kid backs up, silent, confused.

Simms runs at him and grabs him in a bear hug and attempts to punch him. Players on both teams rush in, trying to stop the fight.

"You it, huh?" Simms screams, his lip quivering, slamming the player to the floor, bodies tumbling, the terrified opponent's head banging frighteningly off the hardwood. "You it, yeah!" A player holds Simms, who swings and grazes the face of the player he has attacked. The smaller man is on his feet now, backing up, putting distance between himself and the furious Simms. The player hastily picks up his gear and leaves the gym.

Simms slowly decompresses, coming down to earth. He is all alone with his passion and his pain. Basketball is an intense game, but it's pretty much over for today.

SEAN HILL'S FATHER, ROBERT, A FORMER HOCKEY ALL-AMERICA AT THE University of Minnesota-Duluth, has been keeping fairly close tabs on his son since the youngster went off to seek his fame and fortune with the big boys. In a phone call from his home in Duluth, Robert tells of the latest development.

"Sean discovered a car he loves in Plattsburgh, New York, after playing three games in the minors," says Pop. "I'm not too happy about it—it's a 1977 Porsche. But he paid about twelve thousand dollars for the car, and I rejoiced at that. He was looking at a thirty-five-thousand-dollar Mitsubishi, and I was against that."

The father pauses to reflect on his hard-skating son. "Have you talked to Sean?" he asks. "You know what a goof he is. I'm a little dubious about his driving. He doesn't have a very good track record with cars." He sighs. "I've talked to him about that."

What more can a dad do?

RICK ABERMAN HAS BEEN DATING THE SAME WOMAN, KAREN PARKER, A TWENTY-seven-year-old former UW soccer player, for five years. They are close, but each has been following separate career paths. Karen is now an assistant soccer coach at Yale University, and she and Rick see each other only on holidays, during frenzied weekend trips made possible through the use of discounted airline tickets, and during the summer. It's not a particularly satisfying way to carry on a relationship, Aberman feels. But what can be done about the pulls of separate careers?

He is still perhaps closest in spirit to a former girlfriend named

Molly from his hometown in Minneapolis. They went together for more than a decade, from age ten to twenty-four, formative years, and had even planned to get married as far back as 1980. But that proposed union fell through for a variety of reasons; they drifted apart, and Molly married someone else last year and settled in Kansas City. In a month her first baby will be born. Aberman thinks of that and feels his life drifting away from him, feels the weariness of always investing in other people's dilemmas and concerns while letting his own garden wither and become overrun with weeds.

"I want kids and a family," he says, sitting in his small apartment and looking at the congealed remains of a pizza on his cluttered living room table. On his TV the Minnesota North Stars battle it out with the Edmonton Oilers in one of the final contests of an endless NHL season. On the wall is a calendar showing Nellie Fox in his batting stance. There are baseball cards scattered like leaves throughout the room. Around the corner in the tiny kitchen sits a bag of Kirby Puckett Brand pancake mix. On the refrigerator door are silly little baseball player magnet devices. A twelve-year-old boy would be happy in this abode.

"I'm tired of being alone," he says. "Maybe I should move back to Minneapolis. Madison is dead for me. All of the girls I could go out with are so young, they're all students—and what do we have in common? Madison is not a good place to be single and an adult."

It is an accident, really, that Aberman is even in Madison, and that his career has come to this point, with its successes and letdowns. Back in Minneapolis, Aberman was an unremarkable student who left barely a ripple on the athletic or academic scene. He played junior high football but soon quit because he was so skinny and the sport didn't suit his psychic needs. "I didn't like the football mentality, and I thought the coaches were jerks," he says. The cross-country coach wanted him to come out for that sport, but Aberman declined. He didn't want to stay after school, for reasons that are still vague to him but had mostly to do with the growing sense of alienation he felt from organized societal affairs. "Sport didn't bring out the best in me," he admits. "I went home, and I don't know what I did. Watched TV, I guess."

Because of his distaste for high school, he arranged to graduate early and then enrolled at Syracuse University. "I got there and was very excited, because now I could take the courses I wanted," he says.

"I was very independent and I knew I wanted to be a psychologist. So the first day I saw my adviser and he said, 'Here's what you will take.' I said, 'The hell I will.' He said, 'You have to take freshman English.' I said, 'I don't want to.' He said, 'You'll be the only one who doesn't.' I said, 'Okay.' He said, 'You'll never graduate from Syracuse.' And I said, 'I guess I won't.'"

Aberman left Syracuse in February and shortly enrolled at Wisconsin, where he found what he was looking for—a loosely defined major called "Broad Field Social Science" in the School of Education. He flourished, taking mostly courses he picked for himself, zipping through his master's program in developmental psychology and his Ph.D. studies in developmental and family therapy. He also found his guru and inspiration: the venerable and charismatic UW Medical School Professor of Psychiatry, Carl A. Whitaker. "I was never a lost soul," adds Aberman. "I just needed somebody to let me do what was best for me. I just needed somebody to understand."

He fumbles through a pile of old photographs that lie on the table. He laughs. Here is a snapshot of himself at the Baseball Hall of Fame in Cooperstown, New York, standing in front of Babe Ruth's locker, in running shorts and running shoes, shirtless, as though getting dressed. And here is a newer photo of his one-and-a-half-year-old nephew sitting on the hood of a car. This shot reminds him of the way humans so often live their lives, perplexed and unable to communicate with their fellow man. The nephew has a somewhat odd, even pained, look on his chubby face.

"He couldn't talk," recalls the psychologist. "But he was trying to tell us something the whole time we had him up there for the picture. Later, we realized it was, 'Hot.'"

TAMI HOLMQUIST LOOKS OVER THE EVER-EXPANDING PILE OF PAPERS SHE HAS IN her office. Next year's budget has been finalized at $16.5 million, but she knows nothing is ever final around here. "So many hidden costs," she says, shuffling a stack of budget numbers. "People say we need to raise a couple hundred thousand to be solvent, but that's not true. There are so many costs that are in the 'support areas,' things like the training room, the weight room, sports information, maintenance, that it's just hard to tell.

"Now I'm making the maintenance people start keeping track of their work on a time sheet, something we've never done. I'm doing it for two reasons. One, we've got some lazy people here; and two, they do a lot more work for football that doesn't show up anywhere than they do for the other sports. I'm just trying to find out how much each sport really spends."

She pulls out a sheet that is a request for reimbursement, done by her predecessor, the inscrutable Dick Schrock. Some numbers have been highlighted in orange marker and others have the word *omit* written next to them. Why? "That we don't know," says Holmquist. She is still struggling with old papers and strange calculations made by Schrock, the curse of cleaning up after an eccentric. Was any of the stuff he did unethical? She blushes.

"He kept some numbers off the books," she says. "He was underpaying the budget by at least $1 million in 1988–89. The extra money was coming from donations. The only people who really know what was going on here were . . ." She looks at her hands, then sighs in resignation. "I don't know."

She looks again at the orange-speckled paper and thinks about Schrock, a man she has never met. His personality is there in his work, passed along in accountant's code to another of the trade, waiting to be analyzed. "I think he meant well," Holmquist says after a time. "He was just trying to soften the blow, I think. If he was really devious, why didn't he take the whole thing by the throat, take the money and run? The opportunity was there in the past. Believe me."

She moves on to the file containing the figures for the recent Butch's Bologna Bash. The bash started in a bar called Rohde's in Madison years ago, with Strickler and his pals just sitting around drinking and scarfing down sausage before suddenly deciding to pass the hat for good-old football coach John Jardine and his Badger squad. Butch and company raised the whopping sum of seventy-five dollars that night, with Jardine, who was in attendance, contributing fifty dollars of the total. Holmquist wonders if the fest has really advanced beyond that original effort.

"I'm hoping, to tell you the truth, that we made *anything* on it this year," she says. Those hidden costs again. Plus, costs that are right out front.

"I saw a 1099 tax form—what people have to pay taxes on if they won something in the raffle," she says. "A person involved said, 'The air conditioner has a market value of fifteen hundred dollars, but we bought it for one thousand.' I said, 'We *bought* it?' That was the first I knew of it. We—the athletic department—bought the cars, all the things that were raffled. All of it. And I thought that with the free advertising, the dealers and merchants would give us the things. Also, I heard that the hats they gave out at the party were made by a company run by a member of the W Club, to help his business."

In the catacombs: administrative officer Al Fish and athletic director Pat Richter, architects of the effort to bring Wisconsin athletics into the late twentieth century, deep inside Camp Randall Stadium.

1

2

Chancellor Donna Shalala takes aim. Who else can claim to have been coached by both Bucky Badger and George Steinbrenner?

3

Assistant strength coach Steve Myrland and psychologist Rick Aberman share a moment in "Steve's" gym.

The trench coat gang. Al Fish, flanked by then director of development John Swenson and assistant director Todd Kuckkahn, signals he's at peace with the reporting efforts of Barry Baum.

4

At the 1991 women's basketball banquet: Joyce Rose, Badger Cager Club president; Donna Freitag, assistant coach; Mary Murphy, head coach.

6

Amy Bauer, the point guard who was made a nonperson by basketball coach Mary Murphy.

Hockey goalie Duane Derksen with injured teammate Doug Macdonald.

Going nowhere. Big Ten Freshman of the Year, quarterback Tony Lowery, running coach Don Morton's veer offense against Iowa, 1987.

9

Grim-faced on signing day, head football coach Barry Alvarez with recruiting coordinator Rob Ianello.

Tight collar: freshman football stud Jason Maniecki, from Wisconsin Dells.

10

A dying sport; a sport to die for. Fencer Jim Frueh stabs in anger.

Baseball players stand soberly while coach Steve Land
pleads for leniency from the seated Al Fish, Pat Richter,
and Roger Formisano.

12

13

Madison mayor Paul Soglin ponders the fate of his city,
baseball, and his Rotisserie team.

Crying time. Badger baseball players after the last game in
Wisconsin's 117-year baseball history.

Gymnasts Michelle Hernandez and Meredith Chang find something to smile about at the Red Gym.

Bucky, Kristin Sobocinski (#2), Liz Tortorello (#5), Samantha Scott (#9), Brigitte Lourey (#6), Lisa Hagan (#10), and Susan Wohlford (#11) prepare to sing the national anthem.

Milt Bruhn, the only coach to take Wisconsin to two Rose Bowls, with his dog, Brandi, shortly before the coach's death.

Elroy Hirsch (center) with three pals on a golf course.

The *Daily Cardinal* wise guys at a home football game: from left, Mike Bresnehan (in striped shirt), Andy Cohen, Barry Baum, and Rob Reischel.

21

Living on the porch,
fencers Tom Miller and
Jason Kerstein in their
spring home.

22

The only female
Bucky impersonator,
Liz Moeller, prepares
to enter character.

John Swenson contem-
plates the model of the
never-built, Frank Lloyd
Wright–designed conven-
tion center for Madison.

23

Basketball coach Steve Yoder awaits a recruit in front of a portentous sign.

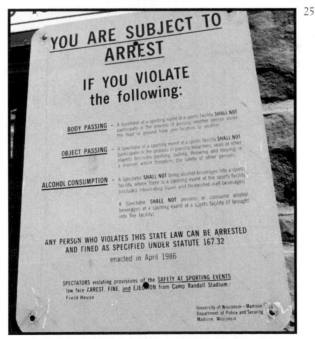

A sign at Camp Randall Stadium warns against bad behavior. Crackdowns on rowdy fans, combined with the decline of the football team, helped put the athletic department on the brink of bankruptcy.

Is there a quarterback in the house? Eighteen-year-old freshman Jay Macias (#16) is thrown into a starting role against the University of Iowa.

Hockey players Barry Richter and Chris Nelson with Rick Aberman on the sideline at a spring football practice.

Tony Lowery leaves the field
after the Wisconsin–Western
Illinois game under the appraising
eye of defensive coordinator
Dan McCarney.

Wisconsin's record holder in punt
return yardage, Thad McFadden,
a pen pal of Tony Lowery's.

30

Jenny Kraeger running free.

31

Distance runner
Heather Rawling.

32

Peter Tegen with
Suzy Favor: a runner
without obsessions.

Stephanie Herbst (#138), getting "intense" in a championship race, from a photo on the calendar celebrating ten years of Big Ten women's sports.

Stephanie Herbst in Milwaukee, four years later.

Rick Aberman with his mentor, psychiatrist Carl Whitaker.

35

36

Football players, including Duer Sharp (#36), Rafael Robinson (#25), Aaron Norvell (#48), and Todd Strop (#39), sing "Varsity" after the season-ending victory over Northwestern.

19

THE LITTLE MAN STANDS IN A DOORWAY ON THE EAST SIDE OF THE FIELD-house, looking out at the parking lot, looking down at his watch, looking out again at the asphalt dotted with motionless cars. Steve Yoder is waiting for a recruit, a high school junior who is very tall.

Where is the kid? Yoder is fifty-one years old and still he has to skip to the drumbeat of postadolescent boys who can help him keep his job. Standing not far from Yoder are two of his three assistants. One of them, Ray McCallum, played for Yoder at Ball State, back when Yoder was a two-time Mid-America Conference Coach of the Year. In 1983 the five-foot-nine-inch McCallum won the Naismith Hall of Fame Award as the nation's premier college basketball player under six feet tall. Those were better times for both men. Yoder is always on shaky ground at UW; thus, his assistants are never on firm footing, either.

"I want to get this kid to commit early," says Yoder, squinting into the distance. "If the kid commits, his word is good. It's the other fuckers out there you can't trust. The coaches. They'll tell the kid, 'You're weak. I'm gonna change your mind.'"

Yoder has heard about Willie Simms's recent blowup in the half-court game at the Fieldhouse. He thinks about his former player now. "A time bomb," he says. "A time bomb waiting to go off all season. I had to deal with that. Two of 'em. Tompkins, too."

Patrick Tompkins is officially the only UW basketball player to be named to the first-team all–Big Ten squad in twenty-three years. (A prior player, forward Cory Blackwell, was all–Big Ten in the early 1980s, but his name was stricken from the record books because of a car loan he received that was improperly guaranteed by a UW booster. Yoder was reprimanded for his failure to control the program better, and his salary was frozen for a year as a result.) Because of this, one would think his coach would be Tompkins' biggest booster. But there have been rumors that Yoder does not get along that well with his black players, particularly ones who are rough-and-tumble, like Tompkins, who hails from a tough part of Waukegan, Illinois.

"You take players, and when you talk to their high school coaches and administrators, they lie to you," continues Yoder. "They do it so they can say, 'I got this kid a scholarship.' So then a month goes by, and I see what I've really got." He looks at his watch one more time. Can his irritation make time stand still?

"Like the Stanford game in the NIT this year," he goes on. "The players didn't take Stanford seriously. [UW lost, 80–72.] Why? Because Stanford was white—they *can't* know how to play. It always happens." UW's appearance in the meaningless National Invitational Tournament this year—the sixty-four best college teams are already invited to the NCAA tournament—was only the second in Yoder's reign at the school.

Yoder sees a van entering the parking lot. Is this his recruit? "There's an old saying," he finishes. "You handle turds, your hands get messy."

It is, indeed, the recruit. The door to the van opens and a tall white kid with a short haircut steps out.

"See how we're at the mercy of these kids," Yoder says to McCallum, as the recruit spots them and starts to walk their way. "Now we'll have to go right to lunch."

JASON BOYKOFF, A TWENTY-YEAR-OLD MIDFIELDER AND FORMER CAPTAIN OF THE men's soccer team, has stopped in to see Rick Aberman. Boykoff is transferring to another university on the West Coast because he feels he has been treated shabbily here at UW. A slender young man with long brown hair and a gold hoop in his left ear, Boykoff had the unique distinction of breaking his right foot in an early game last fall and then, a minute later, while limping toward the ball, getting hit by a defender and dislocating his right shoulder. He had reconstructive surgery on each body part, and while convalescing, he realized that he did not mean that much to the team as damaged goods.

"You know, Rick, I've got screws in my foot," he says. "Enough so that my mom got me a gold card from the orthopedic institution that states that I have metal parts in my body, because I travel a lot and I set off those metal detectors in airports. I guess terrorists really want those cards." Aberman smiles and waits for the player to go on.

"After I was injured, only one of our four coaches visited me in the next four months, and that was only once. And he was an assistant. The head coach called three times from August to January, and one of the times was to get back my sweats and uniform. So after that I called around and got a full ride to the University of Portland. I'm really looking forward to it, to being appreciated, to going somewhere where they average five thousand fans a game, and there are only twenty-five hundred students in the school."

"Do you remember how we met?" asks Aberman.

Boykoff thinks for a moment. "That's right!" he says. "I was thrown out of McClain! I was bothering no one, just kicking a ball around by myself, and a guy like a building manager said, 'You gotta get out of here.' The only other person in the building was you, jogging. I forgot about that." The two laugh.

"I was so embarrassed," says Aberman.

"I was embarrassed, too," replies the athlete. "I guess there was a rule that you couldn't be in there without a coach. So then I realized, hey, this is ridiculous. I'm an athlete. I'm an adult. Who is this hurting? Why is there such a stupid rule? And then I started looking at our athletic department itself."

"Did getting thrown out mean anything symbolically to you?"

"Well, if I'd been tossing a football around, I don't think the guy would have said a thing. Respect, it has to start at the top. They're not really dedicated to soccer here. It's similar to baseball. That could have been us they got rid of."

Aberman wishes the young man well in his journey, and Boykoff, clad in shorts, T-shirt, and sandals, thanks the psychologist for helping him in his times of depression and doubt. "I'm leaving in August," he says. "There hasn't been much publicity. Coach, in the paper, said something like, 'Since we didn't have him last year, we aren't really losing anything.' It was ridiculous. I felt like saying— sorry to swear—'Fuck you!' Ah, who cares."

"I'm not sure our athletic director even knows you're leaving," says Aberman.

Boykoff nods. "Well, I do know Pat Richter," he says. "Not through soccer, but through life. Barry Richter and I were both born on September 11, 1970, in the same hospital in Madison. Our mothers even shared the same room for a while."

A quirk of fate. No more important than a million other trivial things. Less important, certainly, than the tattoo above Boykoff's right heel, the one of Bucky Badger in his red varsity sweater, kicking a soccer ball.

"That was my wild collegiate act," Boykoff says, looking down at the fierce little beast. "Ironic."

WHILE PREPARING FOR HIS DAILY JOG, ABERMAN IS APPROACHED BY A MALE athlete who says he would like to make an appointment to talk with him about some things. They set up a meeting time for later in the week. The athlete is Tony Lowery, the starting quarterback on the football team.

AT THE RED GYM, THE HUNDRED-YEAR-OLD REDBRICK TURRETED STRUCTURE that looks like a child's rendition of a primitive fort, some of the female gymnasts are hanging out, commiserating over their shared fate. Last night a number of the gymnasts went to a farewell party with the baseball players and fencers, all of them engaging in sarcastic toasting of the demise of their hopes and dreams. The highlight of the evening came as the revelers took turns throwing darts at a photo of Pat Richter.

Now, in the harsh light of day, dull melancholy has replaced the righteous anger of midnight. Senior Michelle Hernandez, in a long dress, spots for freshman Meredith Chang—all four feet ten and a half inches of her—who performs desultory exercises on the parallel bars. For Hernandez, it's all over; she'll graduate soon and pursue a career in elementary education. For the fiery little Chang, an honor roll student who came all the way from Honolulu to compete, the future is less certain. She has already received scholarship offers from Iowa, Cal-Berkeley, New Hampshire, Illinois, and other schools, but if she had wanted to go to those schools, she would have accepted one of their offers in high school. She could always stay at UW for three more years—the athletic department has promised to fulfill all scholarship promises for all athletes in the vanquished sports—but that would mean living in torment. Chang's whole life has been in gymnastics, and these college years will not come again. "I don't know what I'm going to do," she tells Hernandez between sets.

Rumor has it Shalala wants this rickety old building for more administrative offices. If that is true, there will be some interesting remodeling necessary. Above the gym on the top floor are such items as bricked-up fireplaces, exposed steel girders, and at least one huge trap door opening straight onto the floor exercise area twenty feet below.

The athletes hug one last time. School will be out in two weeks, and everyone will scatter with the wind.

"I do feel sorry for Pat Richter," Hernandez says before she goes. "He's definitely not going to be the hero. He came from a perfectly good corporate job to this godforsaken mess."

BARRY BAUM LIES ON HIS BED IN THE APARTMENT ON GORHAM STREET HE shares with six other male students. Baum's room is off the short hallway into the kitchen, which has two refrigerators and is itself connected to a fire exit, which is completely covered over with clothes, boxes, furniture, and golf bags. Baum is dispirited. "She blew me off big-time," he says. "I can't believe it."

"She" is a girl he thought was the love of his life. "I met her at the mailbox last week, and we schmoozed," he continues. "We go out Saturday, Sunday, Monday, Tuesday—by Friday it's all over. She toasts me, 'To new beginnings!' She says I'm the funniest guy she ever met, blah, blah, blah. Then she says, 'I just want to be friends.' What is it? What? What is it with women?"

Unlike the rooms in the rest of the house, Baum's is neat as well as sports-oriented. On the wall is a framed photo of Baum with former Knicks coach Stu Jackson. There is another photo of him in his Knicks ball boy uniform, shaking hands with Patrick Ewing. There is one with him and Larry King together at the CNN studio. And there is one in which Baum does not appear, taken as it was during an old Celtics-76ers game, showing Larry Bird and Julius Erving strangling each other. On his desk is a recent copy of the *Daily Cardinal* celebrating UW's invitation to the NIT. Baum's lead story on the back page begins, "Wisconsin received a bid—and it didn't have 'Farewell' after it."

Feeling down, Baum punishes himself some more, pulling from his drawer a column from the *Dubuque Telegraph-Herald* with a byline shared by him and his good friend and former *Daily Cardinal* writer who is now a stringer for the *Milwaukee Journal*, Andy Cohen. The story reads as though it were constructed by a robot after being translated from Swahili. "I wrote the story and Andy wrote a sidebar," sighs Baum. "And they combined them: first him, then me, then him. A debacle!"

The phone rings. It's a girl. Rebirth! Baum talks excitedly for a while and then hangs up, if not in ecstasy, at least with a lighter spirit.

"That was a girl named Katy," he says. "She's so gorgeous! She wants me to go to a toga party." What could be better?

"Uh, she's like my good friend," he admits. "A friend, a total friend. She tells me about all these other boys. But I like to go places with her so people know I can be with a beautiful girl."

He is buoyant once more; at any rate, he has talked with all his guy friends about women and the terrible things they can do to men's souls, and all his buddies, every last one of them, are mystified just as he is about this strange species. He thinks about journalism, the steadying influence in his life. Even that has raised some questions for him lately.

"If a player says, 'ain't,' I usually change it to 'is not.' Why embarrass him? That's the right thing to do, isn't it?" He squints as he ponders this. "I've changed Willie Simms's and Patrick Tompkins's words. Maybe—I don't know, would they care? It hasn't come up in journalism class. But since this is a college paper, you kind of hope the people speak correctly. I mean, they take the same freshman English course I do."

Now he is cheerful again. Just thinking about his column makes him confident. "I can do whatever I want," he exults. "I can write anything! Think of that. I love writing for the *Cardinal!*"

Well, enough about business. The toga party isn't until tomorrow, but right now it's Friday afternoon and, he has just remembered, there is a "crush party" to attend on the lawn of the Kappa Kappa Gamma sorority. Again, it's kind of a mixed blessing; every woman in Kappa and sister society Alpha Chi Omega has invited three men to the party—thus the "crush" of males—giving invitees bright orange cards which they need to show to get in. Someone has invited him ("She's more of a friend," Baum explains), and why shouldn't he go?

At the party music by the Doors blasts out of huge speakers near the stone house, while a swarm of young men mill about the front lawn, outnumbering the women in attendance by, it seems, ten to one. Many of the guys hang out around the grill where a cook is dishing out bratwurst as fast as he can singe them. There is no wild party atmosphere here because of the sexual ratio and because there is no beer available, only lemonade. Baum eats some potato chips and moves aimlessly through the crowd, trolling for romance, looking like the other males who are equally without plan.

A number of hockey players stand on the drive, talking with one another. Matt Buss is there, stuffing himself on brats. He is wearing a Wisconsin letter jacket, with a large white W on the breast. There are two bars on the W, indicating two years of lettering in a sport. The jacket isn't Buss's; it belongs to one of his teammates. Buss is gearing up for finals, he says, and hoping to do well. Has he been studying hard? He looks down. "I've been partying and drinking hard," he says. In fact, he has gone out drinking for thirty-three straight nights, a number that has significance because that's his jersey number. He still hasn't played in a game, but this act of self-destruction, he hopes, shows that he is one of the guys. He also knows that his own behavior is dangerously close to being out of control.

"They—the coaches—have told me to calm down," he admits. They have also told him to have a chat with Rick Aberman.

Doing crazy things, it is suggested to him, is one of the riskier parts of going to college, of growing up. Things like going fast in a car, and hoping you survive.

"Yeah," he agrees. "I was going a hundred on a motorcycle about an hour ago."

*   *   *

THE FOUR ATHLETES SIT IN THE RAY KUBLY ROOM OFF THE MAIN HALLWAY underneath Camp Randall Stadium. They are meeting with Ed Pollard, an academic counselor in the Student Affairs office who works primarily with athletes needing assistance in academic matters. Pollard is black, and because of that fact he quite often becomes a sounding board for black athletes at UW, which is the role he is performing just now. The four athletes—freshman gymnast Jennifer Redmond from Olympia Fields, Illinois, senior basketball player Gina Edmonds from West Nyack, New York, junior volleyball player Lisa Hagan from Louisville, Kentucky, and freshman hurdler Orlando Robinson from Milwaukee—have little in common except for the fact that they too are black and therefore share a rare cultural thread here on this pale campus. They have met not so much to accomplish anything but just to talk, to let Pollard know about the things that black athletes at UW simply think about.

Being different is not something that just happened, they all acknowledge.

"I went to a small, almost all-white prep school twenty minutes from home in Louisville, and it prepared me well academically," says Hagan, a tall All–Big Ten middle blocker. "But it might as well have been on another planet, compared to where I lived. Sometimes I stayed at the school until nine or ten at night. I became good friends with the janitor."

"I was in the honors program at my high school," says the petite Redmond, last year's Illinois state champion in the vault. "I was never very social in high school, because I spent all my youth in gymnastics."

"Now they check up on me, because I'm black," says Hagan. "They know when I miss a class. I cannot hide. I mean, even with my coat up, slouched down in my seat in a lecture room with five hundred students, I can't hide."

"The athletic board has a policy that you have to attend classes," interjects Pollard, a man with a huge belly who was once a lean basketball star at the University of Wyoming. "You miss too many . . ."

"But sometimes I get home from road trips at two-thirty A.M.!" complains Hagan. "I *can't* make it. Who cares if other students miss class? I'm an adult. Sometimes I feel like I'm back home with my mother."

Pollard asks Redmond what she plans to do now that her sport has been cut.

"I'm going to stay," she says. "And I'll tell you my reason. My parents said to me back in high school, 'Whatever you do, you will pay for your own education.' I want to prove I can do something on my own. I made a four-year commitment to Wisconsin. It made one to me."

Staying here, offers Hagan, may be a little dicey for the gymnast. "People are going to say to you, 'Wow, you're here on a scholarship and you do *nothing?*' "

"It's funny," says Robinson, a slender sprinter who specializes in the intermediate hurdles. "My roommate went to a great suburban school, and he's had a big problem adjusting. I've had a small problem. He's so homesick. But maybe that's because I'm from Wisconsin and he's from New York."

"I always heard that there were forty-three thousand students here, that this was the biggest party school in the U.S.A," says Hagan. "Then I get here and I think: 'Where are the black students?' Just eight hundred total? You pass them on the street and you *have* to wave. You have to."

"Before I got here I talked with my roommate on the phone, Meredith Chang," offers Redmond, the only black on the eleven-member women's gymnastics team. "She thought I was white. Until she saw my dad moving me in. It was a problem."

Hagan nods. "When I first talked to my roommate, we were both trying to figure out if the other was black or not, but neither of us wanted to ask. I think I may have described myself. But I assumed she was black, because she played basketball."

"I didn't see a black student until I started class," says Redmond. "It wore on my nerves. You just need that common focus."

Edmonds, the short and feisty basketball guard and one of this year's co-MVPs, agrees. "You just need to have somebody you can relate to. It's why we gravitate toward other blacks."

"But the black football players won't talk to the track athletes," states Robinson. "They're above us."

All the athletes agree.

"They put you through, like, a test," says Edmonds. "They talk about you—to see how you react."

"Like they said to me, 'There's Lisa, she'll only hang out with white people,' " says Hagan. "And I'm like, 'Well, yeah. If you're *nice*, maybe I'll talk to you. But I'm not gonna be lonely.' "

Edmonds believes black basketball players on the women's team are held to a different performance standard. [Coach Murphy] would have us pressing full-court, but when Amy Bauer and the others come out, the team drops back into a half-court defense," she says. "And, okay, I understand that when the black players are in there— all four of us—maybe we can do more, but we do get tired, too."

The athletes find more things in common, including the feeling that UW wants to be fair to them, but really doesn't know how.

"They're trying too hard," says Redmond.

"Right," adds Hagan. "Just come to me like I'm an athlete. Not black or white."

All of them have taken Afro-American studies courses taught by a white professor, an irony they find at once amusing and galling. "It's crazy, isn't it?" asks Hagan. "Actually, two of my three Afro professors are white." She smiles, recalling something else. "This girl in my Afro class, from a little Indian-named town in Wisconsin, said in class, 'I'm here because I just wanted to learn more about colored people.' Wow!"

This leads to a recounting of all the ways the athletes discovered they weren't on home turf any more.

"State Street!" says Redmond. "There was a man standing there in a sequined dress, singing. I thought, 'Where am I?' "

"Somebody skiing to class," says Edmonds.

"Traying down Bascom Hill."

"People playing broom ball."

"Ice fishing."

"Bike lanes."

"There is no crime," states Robinson. "I mean, there is *no crime*."

That can be a problem when a black person does do something illegal in Madison. Hagan recalls her good friend, a black male, getting taken in by police for questioning about a robbery. The suspect was black and drove a Ford Bronco, as did her friend. "Of course, he fit the description," she says of her friend. "They all look the same."

Robinson laughs at this. "And if you want a haircut?" he says. "Oh, man. I went to this barber shop and said, 'Can you cut my hair?' The lady said, 'Oh sure!' She took scissors and a comb, and when she's done I get up and, oh my God—I'm half bald! She just looks at me like there's no problem. She says, 'It will even out when you wash it.' "

QUARTERBACK TONY LOWERY LOOKS AT THE CLOCK ON RICK ABERMAN'S WALL in shock.

"Don't worry," says Aberman. "It's never right."

Lowery, a slender 6'3" senior from Columbus, Ohio, who was named the UPI Freshman of the Year in the Big Ten in 1987, relaxes a bit. He's a conscientious young man who prides himself on being punctual. Currently, he ranks fifth on the all-time UW passing yardage chart with 3,041 net yards, and he needs only 1,228 yards this coming season to pass leader Randy Wright. The record is a major goal for him and well within range; in 1990 Lowery passed for 1,757 total yards. He would like to set the record as an exclamation point for his own career and to show that a black quarterback can rise to the top.

"What do you do?" he asks Aberman cordially.

"I'm a little different from regular sports psychologists," Aberman answers, before explaining how his training in family therapy can help him assist athletes with their personal problems. Lowery nods. He started two years for the Badgers before taking a year off in 1989 out of frustration over the ineptness of Don Morton's veer offense and the fact that he was taking an extreme mental and physical beating in the predictable attack. He came back last year, had an up-and-down season, and suffered personally with the miserable 1–10 record.

"Last year I was stressed out," Lowery says. "I got cold sores, my face broke out. I never want to go through that again. It was a new coach for me, a new system of offense, and I made mistakes, but only normal ones. Coming into this past spring, Coach Alvarez and offensive coordinator Russ Jacques didn't say a thing to me. The quarterback job was wide open. So now that I've won the job—again— they're real buddy-buddy. Everything's happy. But now I'm wondering what will happen if I'm not doing good again."

"You can't control how they'll feel about you," offers Aberman. "Are you sensitive to their opinions?"

"I just want to be treated fairly. Really, what they did to me worked. I went into spring ball with an *attitude*. I was gonna have fun—if it worked, fine; if not, screw 'em. Now I want to get better. I want to take advantage of everything I can."

"You're not in crisis, you're looking to grow?"

Lowery thinks. "There are just a lot of pressures from my parents, fans, friends, coaches," he says.

Aberman asks about his family situation.

"I live with my mother when I'm home. My parents divorced when I was eleven. I knew what was going on, the constant arguing and fighting. My mom's a nurse, my dad's a supervisor at a Budweiser plant. My dad, I love him to death, but he was hardly ever home when I was a kid. The divorce made me grow up fast. Nobody has washed my clothes but me since then. My mom worked from three to eleven P.M., so I was a latchkey kid. Plus, I was an only child."

The stress of the family coming apart made it hard for Lowery to feel confident, he says. "I hated it when my mom and dad started arguing, because they'd always bring me in. I guess I'm a conflict avoider. I try to hide my feelings. I've only recently started to show my love to my mother. She was very close to her mother, who passed away in February, and she needs me more now. I had to do the eulogy at the funeral, and I thought I'd done all the crying I was going to do. But seeing my mother break down—and she's strong—well, I broke down."

Does any of this make sense to Aberman, Lowery asks. Of course it does. Performance, self-esteem, family harmony—they're all part of the same woven cloth, he explains.

"What parts are you of your mom and dad?" he asks.

Lowery considers this. He's warm like his mother, but sometimes he has a hard time getting close to people. "My dad's not close to anyone," he says. "Sometimes I want to be alone. Like after we lost to Northwestern, I'm coming out of the locker room, and now we're the worst team in America. This woman was there, the mother of a friend, trying to talk to me, and she thought I was being rude. Rude? I thought I was being polite. I guess because I'm in the media, people expect more of me. But I'm a shy person."

"Some people don't want to do well because of the limelight," says Aberman. "It makes them uncomfortable."

"Well, I'm comfortable with it," says Lowery. He reaches down and begins drinking from a plastic bottle filled with a thick pinkish liquid. It's a weight-gain solution; Lowery weighs only 185 pounds and he's tried almost everything under the sun to gain weight, so he won't get crushed in those collapsing pockets so common to the UW offense. He and the psychologist make an appointment for next Tuesday at 4 P.M.

Aberman sits in his chair for a few minutes after the quarterback has left. "All players want is a fair system," he says. "When coaches recruit, they play up the fairness aspect, and of course, most kids are brought up to believe life is fair. But college football isn't fair. It's a business. The coaches have a different agenda than the kids.

"Things are working for Tony right now because he got the quarterback job. Because there was nobody else. Because the coaches need him now. But midway through next season he could easily be on the bench. That's the hard part."

LATER IN THE DAY, AS PART OF HIS OUTSIDE CONSULTING WORK, ABERMAN SEES four cousins who run a family transportation business in Madison called Badger Bus Lines. The four have taken over for their parents, who formed the company, and now they are feuding over business and planning matters that may possibly spell the breakup of the company. As a last resort the men have agreed to seek joint group counseling with Aberman, to see if the conflict can be resolved through discussion rather than dissolution.

Aberman mostly listens to the four men, softly guiding them toward the real sources of their conflict. Amazingly, their problems have little to do with business, but with personal hurts and fears that in some cases go back to their relationships as small children. One man likes to take naps in the afternoon; it bothers him that one of the cousins is gung ho at that time of day. Another cousin has been resentful and difficult because he was not a good athlete as a boy, like at least one of the other cousins, and he hasn't gotten over that unfairness. He has a mixture of envy and anger built up in him that springs from his feeling that the others didn't appreciate his non-competitiveness back then, and they don't appreciate him now.

"I liked going to Curtis's house," he says, nodding at one of the cousins. "Because he had so many great toys. All the other kids had bats and balls. But if I went to Curtis's house, we'd play with trains and cars, which I liked."

After an hour the men leave, if not best friends, at least somewhat stunned by the simplicity of what keeps them apart.

Later Aberman says, "It's the same thing with sport as with these family businesses. The sport brings them into the office, but the solution usually doesn't lie in the game itself."

MILT BRUHN CALLS FOR HIS DOG, BRANDI, AND THE SMALL, SILKY-EARED MUTT skitters across the floor and jumps onto his lap. Bruhn smiles; his sweater, white mustache, and glasses give him a professorial look. The UW football coach from 1956 to 1966, Bruhn is an old man now, the son of a Minnesota blacksmith, and he finds simple pleasure in simple things: the birds outside his living room window here not far from Camp Randall, the small TV across the room, his dog nestled in his arms. Bruhn is more than just a former Wisconsin football coach; he is the only coach to have taken the Badgers to two Rose Bowls. Of course, UW lost both those games, in 1960 and 1963 (they lost their first one, too, back in 1952), but no matter; getting there was accomplishment enough.

"You know how we did it?" the sturdy man asks. And then he explains: First, Green Bay Packer coach Vince Lombardi let him copy the Packers' offense, because the Packers were eager to see college teams use pro offenses, which would help the Packers analyze talent for their NFL drafts. And second, says Bruhn, other Big Ten schools cheated so much that once those schools got caught and punished in the early sixties Bruhn's clean Badgers got a leg up.

"Vince called our entire staff up there to Green Bay and opened the books for us," he says. "A lot of athletic directors didn't want their schools to have anything to do with the pros. Our AD, Ivan Williamson, sure wasn't for it. So we had to sneak up there. I used to go up there for a week at a time and sleep right in the room with Lombardi at St. Norbert's. It was no accident both the Packers and Wisconsin were good in 1963."

Recruiting was always a problem, says Bruhn. "I'd go to small towns in Wisconsin, and the boys wouldn't think of coming here, they wanted to go to Iowa or wherever. I remember going to see Jim Grabowski, the great running back. He was lifting weights down in his basement. It was Fred Jacobi and I, and Grabowski said, 'Isn't there more you can do for me?' That's back when Illinois got them all, back when you had the hundred-dollar bills under the table. We couldn't do that here. Ivan Williamson was the purest of the pure. If I could have given them money, I don't know, maybe I would have. But I didn't have the chance."

What he did have was a sophisticated offense that could score points fast, as it did in the fourth quarter of that ill-fated 1963 Rose Bowl. Trailing Southern California, 42–14, with less than fifteen minutes to play, the Badgers rallied behind quarterback Ron Vander-Kelen and lost a squeaker, 42–37. Bruhn also had a remarkable athlete in Pat Richter, his star end, who in the Rose Bowl alone would catch 11 passes for 163 yards, setting a game record.

"Richter was a very intelligent player," recalls his old coach. "It didn't look like he was fast, but he had long legs and a knack for getting open. On our Seventy series he would signal to VanderKelen what he was going to do—he had six options, one of which was a fly pattern, and he'd put his hand on his fly if that's what he was going to run." Bruhn chuckles at this. He looks hale enough, but there is a table on wheels next to him full of medicine, a walker nearby, and a wheelchair by the TV. Bruhn has kidney dialysis treatments three times a week. He has diabetes, and his left foot is wrapped in a bandage because he has had all his toes removed due to poor circulation. Life isn't getting any easier, but talking about his boys makes the old leader vital with passion.

"We used Richter the way the Packers used [Max] McGee," he says. "Richter was making those signs all the time, like a third-base coach. I'd never done something like that with a player, but I knew I could do it with him. He had all the leadership qualities I needed, and he had a great pair of hands. I was on Woody Hayes's TV show one time, and he was talking about Wisconsin, and I remember he said, 'My, this Richter has a great pair of hands. Does he play the piano?' "

Bruhn was stunned even to have Richter on his team. "I didn't recruit Pat. I was told he was going to Kansas to play basketball. Then our basketball coach, John Erickson, said he was going to try to recruit him. On the first day of spring practice his freshman year, Richter tapped me on the shoulder and said, 'Is it okay if I try out for the team?' I don't know if I'd ever spoken to him about football."

Above all, what Bruhn noticed about his All-America receiver was how unflappable he was. "He was calm. He never showed emotion. And he's still that way today. And I could trust him. Vander-Kelen wanted to do things his own way. He drove me nuts—I never knew what he was going to do. Early on I told Pat, 'I'm gonna be all over Vandy, gonna get in his hide, because I plan to make him a quarterback. Just let me know when he's ready to go home to Green Bay.' Time goes by and then one day Pat comes up to me and says, 'Coach, he's ready to go to Green Bay.' And I eased off."

The old man laughs again, tickled by the image. "Oh, I had a good time through all those years," he says. Then he adds, "Really, though, I would rather have been the baseball coach. In baseball you can always get in there and take your cuts."

He thinks about that a moment, and then he remembers that, of course, baseball has been sent packing at the university. "It's a pity," he says. He pets Brandi slowly. Nothing stays the way it used to. Just the memories.

Five days later, at age seventy-eight, Milt Bruhn is dead.

20

GYMNAST LEA DECAROLIS, A JUNIOR FROM PENNSYLVANIA AND AN ALL–BIG
Ten Academic team member last season, talks to her teammate,
Michelle Hernandez. They are standing by the varsity baseball diamond on May 10, ready with the other thousand or so spectators to
watch the curtain come down on UW's affiliation with America's
game.

"So Chris Mills, one of the guys who plays Bucky at football
games, comes up to me," says DeCarolis. "And he's like, 'Lea, hi!
What are you doing next year?' And I'm like, 'Nothing.' And he says,
'What are you doing next year?' And I say, 'Being a regular college
student, I guess.' And he says, 'No. What you *doing* next year? You're
cheerleading! Right?' And I say, 'Wrong! That would be degrading.
And do you think I'd cheer for *this* athletic department?' "

The sun is shining brightly on Madison today, and people who
have never been to a college baseball game have decided to see this
one. The usually deserted stands at Guy Lowman Field are just
about filled, as the UW baseball players run onto the diamond for
the first game of a doubleheader against Purdue. Their uniforms look
different than they usually do, and that is because the players have
exchanged their red hats for black ones and their normally red spikes
have been painted over with black shoe polish. There is a funereal

sadness lingering in the air, which contrasts markedly with the balmy weather and the festive mood of the crowd. Outside the park a small plastic fish hangs from a noose; on the back of the fish is taped the word *Al*.

Richter and Fish, naturally, will not be here to see the last base-ball game played at UW after one hundred seventeen years as a school sport. There is too palpable a feeling here of betrayal, of anger, of a good thing gutted just because it doesn't have moneybags attached to it. Didn't Richter himself play in the most memorable game ever at this field, hitting a dramatic seventh-inning home run to give UW a stunning comeback 6–5 win over 1962 national cham-pion Michigan? With each warm-up throw arcing through the blue sky and each clank of the bat sending a ball skittering off brown dirt into green grass, people sense that getting rid of a game such as this just isn't right.

It's certain that Shalala won't wander over this way, either. The student senators and their brethren are here, and they're as combat-ive as ever. All of them are aware of the official statement Shalala made to the athletic teams, and hence, to all UW students, just two years ago: "I want to assure you that . . . I remain committed to retaining our entire array of sports programs and to maintaining them at a competitive level. I believe we are here to provide a first-class education and extraordinary competitive athletic opportu-nities to some of this country's finest young people. As I told the regents, an investment in these young people is an investment in the future of our state and country."

The game begins, and the Badgers show good teamwork and zest for a club that entered the day with a 15–35 record, worst in the Big Ten. While the players are working their way toward a 5–2 win, the crowd applauds their every move.

Midway through the game, runner Suzy Favor lopes over from the main campus, a mile or so away, and takes a seat in the stands. Clad in running shorts and T-shirt, she has come to pay respects because her fiancé, Mark Hamilton, whom she will marry in two weeks, is a baseball player. At 5'3" and 105 pounds, with the stride and stamina of a gazelle, she ran here so effortlessly that she is not even breathing hard. Until this setback, indeed, life itself had been going by pretty effortlessly for her. "I'm glad I'm in a sport where all you need is a pair of shoes and someplace to run," she says.

Her visibility as an attractive world-class athlete has recently gar-nered her a slew of endorsement contracts. Though she does not grad-uate for a week and technically is still an amateur athlete, she already has deals with Reebok, Blue Cross–Blue Shield, a Honda dealership, a poster company, and Wisconsin Manufactured Housing, the maker of prefab movable homes. The latter company has already featured her in a statewide TV commercial and put her running likeness on a billboard on Interstate 94, showing her zipping past a prefab house above the slogan, "Suzy Knows Manufactured Housing."

She is proud of her work, noting that all her earnings go into a trust fund, so that she can remain an amateur runner with Olympic aspirations. "The head of Manufactured Housing told me they re-ceived two thousand seven hundred calls because of the commercial, which ran for just about a month," she says. According to Manufac-tured Housing PR spokesman Chuck Collins, sales of the company's product went up 54 percent for the month of March while the commercial aired. Favor is truly favored. But what of these Badger baseball players?

They seem to lose their desire after a tear-jerking between-games ceremony, and they get mowed down in the second game, 1–0. The last thirteen batters fall in order, with a young man named John Vanden Heuvel taking the last official swing in University of Wis-consin baseball history, lining a ball to the Purdue centerfielder and into a suddenly fading past.

In the dugout the UW players pack their gear with a sense of disbelief. "It's hard to tell how it feels," says junior second baseman Tom O'Neil, his face grimy with infield dirt and tears. "These uni-forms—they'll probably sell them. I'd like to burn them."

Coach Steve Land looks out at the minimal furnishings that accompany this field. "It's a high school scoreboard," he says. "Look at it."

Land is having trouble talking about any of this any more. He's just about talked out. He's been affiliated with UW baseball for twenty-one years, and he sees more than a sport ending here today. "They said, 'Don't put any money into this field, if there's no return on it.' But if you look at college sport that way, you're looking at a . . . business. The beauty of this game is that it's not like college football. It's a sport." He's got nothing more to say. He's crying.

It's all over.

*   *   *

TONY LOWERY IS IN RICK ABERMAN'S OFFICE. HE HAS JUST FINISHED LIFTING weights, and his arms are nicely defined against his blue tank top, but he is as skinny as ever.

Aberman asks him what kind of student he is.

"Average," says Lowery. "But I hate studying, and I don't like my major."

"What is it?"

"Rural sociology. It's in the Ag School."

"What's rural sociology?"

"I've been in it a year, and I don't know. Mostly about farmers."

Aberman looks at the athlete with puzzlement.

"I got stuck in it when I didn't know what I wanted to do or be," says Lowery. "And soon it was too late."

"But why that?"

"It was an eligibility thing. I picked up more credits and a higher grade point by transferring into it. I don't blame anybody else for it. I wanted to be a criminal justice major, but I couldn't, because so many classes were late in the day, and I have to be done with everything by two P.M.

"I want to join the FBI or DEA, I've always wanted to be a cop. And right now it's a good thing for minorities to get into those fields. I wouldn't mind being a lawyer, but," he shrugs, "I hate studying."

"You left football for a year, didn't you?"

"Yes, I did. And when I came back everybody was so amazed. To me, it was like, so I took a year off. Why is this such a big deal? I had my own business that year, Golden Touch, a T-shirt distribution service. It's not as hard to start a business as people say. I've always been an entrepreneur."

Lowery was often outside Camp Randall on game days that fall, hawking his T-shirts while the Badgers were inside getting steam-rolled by their opponents. He missed the competition, but he didn't miss the humiliation.

"Ideally, I'd like to play football professionally for a while, be a part-time cop, then make enough money to start my own business," he says.

Aberman thinks for a while, and Lowery looks at him, waiting for the lead.

"When the coaches play mind games with you," says Aberman. "When they try to piss you off to motivate you—does that work?"

"It just makes me mad," snaps Lowery. "I take it personally. I may achieve what they want, but the relationship between us is over. That's what happened in spring ball. The relationship is over."

WHEN THE WEATHER IS NICE IN MADISON, YOU CAN LIVE OUTDOORS LIKE A modern-day pioneer, which is what fencer Jason Kerstein and his pal, fencing co-captain Tom Miller, have been doing for the last week. They have set up camp on the unroofed second-floor porch at their rented house at 16 S. Orchard Street, having brought out lawn chairs, a cooler, bug spray, a fan, blankets, and a TV for furnishings. They eat, sleep, and study here in a celebration of independence and balmy clime, giving their other four housemates more room to maneuver as well. Miller, a senior from Racine, majoring in international relations, has been sharing a bedroom with a woman fencer and her boyfriend for the last year, so this is a relief for him.

The two young men sit on their lawn chairs and watch kids play basketball on the playground across the street. Kerstein wears shorts, a shirt, and his fencing shoes, but Miller wears only gym shorts. His chest, stomach, and legs are badly sunburned from the times he has fallen asleep out here, but the peeling skin doesn't seem to bother him.

What bothers him is his sport of fencing's being tossed to the seas. "Our fencing team was very close," he says. "Men's and women's—we're family. There have been six marriages among fencers since the seventies. It's just great companionship. I can tell you this, Pat Richter is the biggest two-faced sonofabitch I've ever met. George Politis, the other co-captain, and I met with Richter all the time last year, and he went so far as to tell us to start looking for a house off-campus to use for practice, that maybe our alums could purchase, because Henry Mall [the fencing gym] was going to be torn down. We thought, 'Great!' He gave us hope. He made it sound like he would save us. But he knew."

Miller leans against the railing of the porch, squinting in the sun's rays, as Kerstein reclines, eyes shut to the world. Miller waves a letter from Richter stating that Miller and the other fencers can still use the athletic department facilities if they want, if they first "contact Duane Kleven, Associate Athletic Director for Men's Sports, to let him know of your interest so that appropriate arrangements can be made."

"Right," says Miller in disgust. "Right. I'll sure do that."

People got hurt in this deal, Miller wants it known. "Jim Frueh got shit on two years in a row. Last year there was so much competitive pressure on him. And this year . . ." Miller shakes his head.

"You know, Jim and I, we're not that close. Jim was very unsportsmanlike for a while. We had a fight in the gym, a lot of name-calling. Fencing is like a physical game of chess—once Jason hit me in the side of the head with his bellgard and broke my eardrum—but Jim would rip off his mask and come at you in a rage, punch you, whip you with his weapon, whatever. When he got stabbed, though, I was kind of amazed that they didn't tell me what was going on with him. Tony Gillem was falling asleep in the waiting room, so after an hour I just went looking for Jim in the hospital, going from room to room.

"When I found him it was one of the scariest moments of my life. The room was so big and he was alone. There were all these white sheets, and his eyes were slits and his body was gray. He looked dead. There were tubes in him, one in his chest, and he was hooked up to a breathing machine. It was awkward, because I wasn't his buddy, but he was all alone, and there was just this strange . . . focus . . . to it all. The first thing he said was, 'They put another fucking hole in me.' "

Back in Madison, Miller and Politis composed news stories for the student newspapers, which was always the way the papers got any information about the fencing team. "We gave them both the same story, with the facts about where he was staying and that," says Miller. "Then Tony Gillem talked to us and in an eloquent way informed us that the athletic department was not very receptive to bad press. He said that somebody there had said there better not be any more bad press about the incident. The *Cardinal* ran something, but I called the *Badger-Herald* and said don't run our story. They said they had the option to do what they wanted. But once I told them the athletic department didn't want it, they didn't run it."

In fact, the *Daily Cardinal* got no story at all from anyone involved with the fencing team. "Politis would call every week with the results of the fencing meets, which, frankly, we weren't very interested in," recalls the paper's sports editor, Mike Bresnehan. "But that week we got nothing." What the *Daily Cardinal* did get was an unexpected visit from a male student named Dana Bartholomew, who walked into the office on Thursday, five days after the event, and asked Bresnehan if he'd be interested in a story about a UW fencer who had nearly been killed at Notre Dame.

"That was the first I'd heard of it," says Bresnehan. "And I'd never seen Dana in my life. He told me the story and I said, 'Yeah, I'd like to see it,' and he sat down on the spot at a typewriter and wrote it. We have a rule that you can't get paid unless you've written at least three stories for the paper, so I didn't even pay him the six bucks. The only reason he knew about the story was because he was a friend of Frueh's." The article ran on Friday, March 8, six days after Frueh was stabbed.

Miller looks out at the kids shooting hoops. He says that he felt bad about squelching the news, about his role in the evasiveness, about more or less abandoning Frueh, but he felt he was assisting the entire team by his action. The depth of the news manipulation—an athletic department, a sports team, a newspaper all allegedly suppressing the news because of vested interests—did not seem wrong to him at the time. It was a turbulent time, he explains. These matters, he explains, are never as clear as they appear later. "At the time I was very worried about the cuts," he continues. "People were talking. I didn't want to piss anybody off."

He watches Kerstein leave the porch and go inside to change into his outfit for his night shift as a counterman at Cousin's Submarine Shop. Full scholarship athletes, like the football, basketball, and hockey players, are not allowed to have part-time jobs during the school year. Athletes in minor sports, however, are virtually compelled, out of economic necessity, to have them.

"Still, I don't have a lot of compassion for Jim," says Miller. "He didn't work all that hard, didn't try to be an All-America this year. It's hard to explain, really. The guy I feel the most compassion for is Jason." He sees Kerstein buttoning a white shirt. "Fencing is his life. Fencing is the only reason, I feel, that Jason's in college. He would have been captain. He would have been an All-America. He would have been on the All–Big Ten team three times. He could have been bigger than Jim."

Kerstein waves as he heads off to his job, turning down the sidewalk.

"Jason needs to find a new identity," says Miller.

21

SCHOOL'S OUT FOR SUMMER, AND THAT MEANS IT'S GOLF SEASON FOR ELROY Hirsch. Today's venue is a fund-raiser sponsored by the Mendota Gridiron Club, the football program's main booster group, at Nakoma Country Club in Madison. Hirsch is in mid-season form, grabbing an Old Style draft.

The day is gorgeous, and Hirsch, a decent golfer, is not even counting his strokes. "There's nothing I'd rather do than be on a golf course on a sunny day with three friends," he says quietly on number seven. A couple of holes later the sky darkens with scudding clouds, and it seems a summer shower might be on its way. Ol' Crazylegs sits back in the cart and stares into the distance. He knows how some people think of him: that he is a relic, a hanger-on, living on a tired, irrelevant reputation, that it's time for him to get out of the way before the modern age runs him down like a badger on the highway. But enthusiasm and heart still count for something. It can't all be bottom line and bean counting, can it? So many Wisconsin fans—old ones and young ones, babies even—who seem to love him. He sees their welcoming eyes wherever he goes.

"You know," he says almost to himself, "I'm sixty-eight. You look around, you wonder what you've done. Have you accomplished anything? You don't know how much longer you're going to live . . ."

He whips his head like a fighter clearing his senses. What is this melancholy? His white flattop ripples in the fresh breeze. He smiles. Hey, this is better than being in Iowa, ain't it? Better, as he often says, than a poke in the side with a sharp stick?

In another foursome, Barry Alvarez struggles along. He is suffering, has been suffering since last year's team went 1–10, despite playing Cal-Berkeley, Ball State, and Temple in its non-conference games. The team should have gone at least 3–8, he knows; with any kind of luck at all it could have beaten those three preseason dogs and that abysmal team from Northwestern and finished at 4–7. And the Michigan State game was there for the asking, a 14–9 loss that the Badgers should have walked away with. So make the record 5–6. And at 5–6, why, you're so close to .500 that you can feel the hot wind of luck carrying you all the way to 6–5, then 7–4, and at 7–4, hellfire, with the conference setup the way it is, you're in a bowl game! But what was the one distinction of last year's squad, the first college football team ever under Barry Alvarez's sole guidance? It was the worst scoring team in the entire U.S.A. Here he is, a highly paid head coach in one of the most prestigious conferences in the country, formerly the assistant head coach at legendary Notre Dame, and before that an assistant at respectable Iowa, and he's got a defense that can't attack, an offense that can't move, and an erratic, scatter-armed, half-witted quarterback who thinks he's some kind of clothing executive. It's enough to make a fellow dump his irons into the lake and sit on a log and cry.

In the shower Alvarez soaps himself as if trying to cleanse the ten losses from his soul. "This is supposed to be fun," he says of the outing. "But how can it be, when it's work? It's not fun when I get into a blue funk. And I'm in a blue funk." He towels off, adding, "All Elroy has to do is show up and have fun. He doesn't have to do dinner speeches."

Chuck Claflin, a member of the Mendota Gridiron Club and the vice president of the Wisconsin Alumni Association, sits near the bar with a bunch of boosters. There are no women here at this fund-raiser, whether by accident or design, probably mostly the latter. Claflin is a bit peeved with the attitude of fun-loving, lightweight UW boosters, much as Alvarez is.

"I don't think people here in Wisconsin know what it takes to have big-time sports," he states. "We're full of people who bought

season tickets for twenty years, and they think they're big boosters."
He snorts. "I saw a thing about the Bull Gators at Florida, and they
had seventy-seven members at a minimum of ten thousand dollars a
year. And the thousand-dollar members? The list looked like the
yellow pages! Our club, it's only fifty dollars. And you should see how
many give a thousand dollars—I bet it's less than a hundred."

Claflin would be embarrassed to know that it's actually a little
worse than he thinks. The Bull Gator Club of the University of
Florida, the main booster group for the football team, boasts 176
members as of this summer, all of whom have given at least ten
thousand dollars annually for a minimum of five years. The regular
Gator Boosters, the run-of-the-mill donors, number approximately
12,000 and combine with their big brethren to contribute about $8
million each year to the athletic department. The Mendota Gridiron
Club, which was founded by beer-drinking revelers years ago in a
Mendota tavern, boasts 800 members who contribute a little over
four hundred thousand dollars annually to the UW account.

Meanwhile, Alvarez, who has donned his red blazer, is dutifully
working the crowd like a campaigning politician. His eyes seem
slightly glazed over, but on the patio he tells some partyers as though
he means it, "It's a busy time, but it's a fun time."

Wayne Esser, the executive director of the Mendota Gridiron
Club, watches Alvarez with approval. Esser wears a gold pin on his
lapel that has cut-out letters stating, "I Know Barry Knows."

"We've never had a head coach work this hard to promote the
program," Esser says. "He's visible, he speaks well, he works a room
well."

A lot of the usual faces are in the crowd—Jim Bakken, Butch
Strickler, John Swenson, Todd Kuckkahn. Bakken entertains some
boosters with tales of his baseball exploits at UW. "Our coach,
Arthur 'Dynie' Mansfield, used to have the bus driver stop at a
roadside grocery store near the border whenever we'd be returning
from a road trip in Illinois or another state," he says. "He'd have an
assistant coach go in and buy him a couple, three pounds of colored
oleomargarine to bring home. Because he liked it."

The men chuckle. Being "Dairy Staters," they understand the
point of the tale: For years it was illegal to sell colored oleomargarine
in Wisconsin, and even the uncolored, lard-white oleo that could be
sold bore a prohibitive fifteen-cent-per-pound tax. After a while

stores sold uncolored margarine along with little tubs of yellow food coloring so people could mix their own non-butter solution, but to this day in Wisconsin it is illegal to serve colored margarine at a public eating place as a substitute for butter unless it is ordered by the customer. Cows do not give oleomargarine.

The official meeting begins, and Bakken gets things rolling by telling everyone that he "grew up just down the road," and then regaling the men with a joke about Ginger Rogers and Fred Astaire. This is not exactly cutting-edge material.

Alvarez at last takes the microphone and starts off with a tale about himself sitting on an airplane next to a beautiful young woman who breastfeeds her baby four times between Madison and Chicago. Alvarez asks her why, and she says, "Because it lubricates his throat, keeps his sinus passage clear, and also pops his ears." Alvarez stares at her and says, "Christ, and all these years I've been chewing gum!"

Well, all right, that gets them going.

"Last year you fellows raised four hundred and fifty thousand dollars," says the coach. "Guys, we cannot thank you enough."

Alvarez then tells everyone how it's going to be a tough road, but Wisconsin is going to be a monster on the gridiron some day soon, you just watch out. Nothing less than the Rose Bowl championship will satisfy him. He then introduces on-campus recruiting coordinator Rob Ianello, "the mouth from the South," who shows a video of highlights taken of the high school seniors who have signed with UW for next season. Ianello talks on and on as bad synthesizer music plays on the soundtrack along with poorly lit high school game films.

Finally Alvarez takes up the mike again and says of a wide receiver who has just smoked across the screen, "Recruiting coordinator Bernie Wyatt says he may be the best athlete he's ever recruited. His name is Lee DeRamus. He won a track meet by himself last week."

The men in the crowd make small noises of awe and appreciation. This is what they came for: Studs. Speeding bullets. Dreams of glory.

The fund-raiser is a success.

In the athletic department office later in the week Al Fish shows Steve Malchow and Mike Greene his new license plate for his car—a

University of Wisconsin plate with a small Bucky Badger on the left and the tag 4 UW in the middle.

"Wouldn't CUT 5–CAP 2 fit?" asks Malchow.

Fish ignores him. "We'll make fifty-to-sixty thousand dollars a year off these things," he says with a big grin. "And the beauty is"—he pauses for dramatic effect—"it's renewable annually!"

The marketing of the department continues at a fitful pace. There's money coming in for the track that didn't survive its warranty, but there's money going out for new carpeting in the most offensively floored offices. Then, too, a donor has pledged a quarter million dollars for a diving tower to be built in the SURF, the varsity swim team natatorium. "The problem is that to put the tower in, they'll have to raise the roof," says Fish. "The pool is deep enough, the deck is wide enough, but the ceiling's too low. This is what happens when a fourteen-million-dollar building is built for ten million." To raise the roof will cost an additional two hundred thousand dollars, which has ticked the donor off enough that he has withdrawn his pledge entirely.

Fish takes a drive out to the new UW-owned golf course, University Ridge, in Verona, to lighten his load and to see what today's golf fund-raiser has wrought. The course has just opened, and it is spectacular even in its infancy, benefitting from the natural kettle morraine sculpting of the land and the sweep and airiness of the rolling pastures over which the front nine was built. Of course, the university has had the land for the golf course for about, oh, forty years, but it took most of that time to pacify all the contentious parties who had a say in the layout, design, funding, revenue distribution, fee appropriation, hours of play, etc. If something is worth doing in Madison or at UW, it's worth protesting.

Fish, the man who calls golf "my wasted youth," beams as he looks down the fairways toward the glowing horizon. He is still an excellent player who is very much aware of the deal-making aspects of the game. "It's amazing how if you can hit a golf ball, people take what you say seriously," he says, gazing at the silos in the distance. "It's unbelievable bullshit, really."

Fish gets a cart, and on the number-eight tee he stops to meet with Pat Richter. Richter is stationed at the hole like a maître d', greeting each foursome that comes along and hitting a single shot toward the par-three green with them. He is nicely sunburned. Fish tells him the bad news about the diving tower.

"What was it supposed to cost?" asks Richter.

"Two forty," says Fish.

"Christ, so the top divers won't come here."

This is true, says Fish, unless the department raises more money, mollifies the original donor, and puts a skinny, expensive bubble in the roof of the Surf.

"Be like diving in a condom," says Richter, frowning.

Oh well, you can't miss what you never had.

Fish gets back into his cart and heads for the clubhouse. He feels chipper now, remembering how easy it is—despite all the set-backs—to raise money for a place such as UW.

"What is the University of Wisconsin, really?" he asks, speeding over the green grass. "It's more than a school, it's like . . . the Beatles. It's very emotional, from a seminal time in people's lives. It's like the bird bonding right after coming out of the egg. You're free! You bond with the first thing you see, whatever is around you." He spreads his arms wide, flapping them. Voilà! Hatchlings at UW see State Street, the Fieldhouse, Bucky Badger running amok with a bunch of cheerleaders in Camp Randall Stadium, sports teams, class-rooms, professors, parties. "So if you make a lot of money, recon-necting with that school makes you feel good. It's a white-hat organization."

He reflects on his own seminal bonding at his alma mater. Some-how, he didn't imprint on his surroundings as well as did the UW chick exiting the egg.

"Well, I do always like to have at least one Luther College T-shirt," he says defensively. "I give nominally to the place. Fifty dollars a year. Okay, I feel guilty."

THE FOOTBALL LOCKER ROOM IS A SPLENDID PLACE, THE KIND OF ROOM WHERE athletes can feel comfortable, not step on each other's toes, and still communally ponder their mission here at UW. For inspiration there are earnest if contorted slogans on the walls stating "W.I.N.—What's Important Now," "WIN! Whatever it takes. WIN!," and "How to Win on Game Day: Turnovers. Big Plays. Kicking Game. Mental Errors. Penalties. Lost Yardage Plays. Goal Line." And then there is the oddly evangelical "PHILOSOPHY: Trust . . . Commitment . . . Love . . . Belief." On the wall near the training room is a five-foot by three-foot painting of a defiant Bucky clutching a single red rose.

Though the largest number of players that can legally be put on scholarship on an NCAA football team is ninety-five (a number that will be dropping almost yearly as the NCAA attempts to reform the sport), the locker room boasts 143 double-doored red lockers in this vast, three-thousand-square-foot room. Each player's name is inscribed in white letters on a red plastic nameplate attached to one locker door, the player's uniform number inscribed on the other door. Red-carpeted benches line the base of the lockers, and five-foot by seven-foot mirrors frame the ends of each aisle. The main walkway through the locker area is sixteen feet wide, and the aisles themselves are almost twelve feet wide, so that no player need bump another at any time. Indeed, an athlete could lie down and sleep on the carpeted floor without another player even needing to step over him. Two-foot-high stereo speakers are mounted in all four corners of the room, and near the front entrance there are 156 cubby-lockers with combination locks on them. Another sign on the wall urges the player to TAKE PRIDE IN THE BEST LOCKER ROOM FACILITY IN THE NATION.

Rick Aberman looks at the splendor of the facility and wonders.

"A lot of people here think that stuff translates into wins," he says. "But when you depend on stuff, you're in trouble. You don't know what winning is all about. You'll get your butt kicked by people who do know how to win. It's not the external things that make you great; it's the internal things. You need that inner strength, the things you can control, because you can't always control the external things. That's the problem I'm always dealing with—people whose whole definition of themselves is what they have, not what they are."

He nods at one of the equipment men who walks by, pushing a cart of laundry. It seems enough towels are cleaned here to outfit an entire hotel chain.

"It can be dangerous," Aberman continues. "It can be misdirection. Players say, 'My God, I have all this, and I still can't win?' It's disconcerting. For world-class athletes, it's fine. But we don't have that yet in the football program. They used to say, 'We need the McClain facility to be competitive.' But we've gotten worse."

THE HALLWAY SMELLS LIKE HAY. IN THE GYMNASIUM, WHICH HAS A TARPAULIN spread over the folding chairs to be used for the upcoming graduation ceremony, a student class sits in the bleachers and throws paper airplanes out onto the floor, the distance of each flight being measured by a teacher with a yardstick.

It's the last day of school at Wisconsin Dells High School, and Jason Maniecki, the "man" of Barry Alvarez's dreams, sneaks down the hallway, carrying a loaded squirt gun. Maniecki, clad in baggy, patterned shorts, a striped shirt, and gym shoes, passes a trophy case where there is a photo of him next to a wrestling trophy which was recently presented to him. The trophy reads:

WIAA Class B Heavyweight Champion
1989–90   33–0
1990–91   34–0

Maniecki, who was also a star shot-putter and discus thrower on the Wisconsin Dells track team, as well as Most Valuable Offensive and Defensive Player on the football team, looks right and left, and proceeds cautiously. Suddenly another student with a huge machine gun leaps from a doorway and nails Maniecki with a burst of water, soaking his left shoulder. "Gotcha, Minnie!" shouts the student. Maniecki laughs loudly. Not only is he a star athlete, but he's good-natured, too. He has a 3.15 GPA and scored an excellent 25 on his ACT college entrance exam. He would be any football coach's dream, but he's gift-wrapped for Wisconsin, a sign that maybe the Badgers' gridiron fortunes will be improving.

Maniecki sits on a chair in an empty classroom, his squirt gun at his side, looking at the water splotch spreading over his shirt. "I wouldn't have considered playing for Don Morton," he says in a deep voice with more than a trace of Eastern European accent. Born and raised in Poland, he has been in this country for only seven years, having come over after his mother left their hometown of Rabka, remarried, and eventually became the owner of the sixty-three-room Shamrock Motel in the heart of the Dells' amusement area. (Jason is the night desk clerk and fix-it man at the motel, and, of course, the muscle guy when the heavy stuff needs lugging or rowdy guests need tossing. "I do everything but bathrooms," he says.)

"Morton was, like, he didn't know who you were," he continues. "These guys knew who I was." Maniecki had offers from a lot of big-name schools, including Notre Dame ("They didn't know who you were," he says. "You had to wear a name tag"). But in his short time in this country, he had already "imprinted" on Wisconsin, the state and the university. He went to most of UW's home games last year and says, "It didn't bother me that they went one and ten. They were always in it, until the fourth quarter."

The Dells are everything that is hideous and wonderful about American tourist areas—a town that has capitalized on the natural beauty of an area (in this case, river rapids, cliffs, and pine forests) by adding fast-food joints, T-shirt shops, go-cart tracks, fireworks stands, bars, miniature-golf courses, motels, a dog track, and indescribably tacky things such as giant Pepsi cans and Bill Nehring's Dungeon of Horrors, and labeling it "family amusement." The Shamrock Motel is directly across the street from Noah's Ark, a mammoth water slide park part-owned by the parents of Jen Waterman, a forward on the UW women's basketball team. Jason sometimes goes there to cool off after his chores, and last summer he just happened to bump into Alvarez, who had driven the sixty miles north from Madison and was throwing back a beer at the Triangle Bar. "A complete accident," says Maniecki quickly. "No recruiting violation."

In the Dells it is normal to have parents who work in the tourist industry, so Jason's role at the Shamrock is not an unusual one among his peers. But none of the Dells kids had to learn English in the fifth grade, as Maniecki did.

"I started with picture books," he says. "The word that comes to mind is *refrigerator*—I could never say it." He pronounces it *re-FRISHerator*. His mom dug up a photo of Jason one day, showing him at age two back in Poland, in a three-point stance. "And they don't even have football!" laughs the young man. But he was made for the sport, it's clear. He'd like to play pro ball, he says, but above all he will graduate first. "I want to go into business, start a motel chain across the country, and call it the Shamrock."

He feels he knows the important things that folks look for in motels, and he knows why motels can quickly go belly up. "The biggest problem is when there is no personality, no human factor. No guests like dealing with machines, with cut-and-dried rules. We're reasonable at the Shamrock. For instance, if people talk to us, we'll let them stay in the pool after hours."

He furrows his brow, then corrects himself. "Actually, clean is the number one thing. If it's not clean, they'll never come back."

Neither, of course, will the naked drunk come back, the one Jason found sleeping in the baby pool one night. Or the lady who smuggled her dog into her room. "Dogs make a mess and nobody likes the smell," he says. But there's always something going on at a motel, and the business has taught Jason how to do hard work and look for the benefit he will reap down the road.

After school he heads home to do his chores. In no time he's fiddling with a large bottle of liquid drain cleaner at the Shamrock, pouring and probing, working on a clogged pipe in a guest's room. He's not doing a bathroom, but it's darned close. He can't wait for college football to start.

22

DISCOVERING WHAT HE FELT WAS A SEVENTY-SIX-CENT MISTAKE IN THE FINANCE charge on his Visa card, Barry Baum called the Citibank 800-number in Hagerstown, Maryland, and asked for assistance. The woman who answered his question was, as he says, "not nice," so he asked her what was wrong. One thing led to another, and they ended up talking for nearly a half hour about everything under the sun. She was twenty-two and her first name was Angie, but it was against the rules to give out her last name, she said. Nothing was wrong, she added, she'd just been in a bad mood. Now she was in a good mood.

A certain rapid neuron-firing occurred in the young reporter's head. He was already in Washington, D.C., for a summer internship as a writer for *USA TODAY*'s *Baseball Weekly*, and, let's see, Hagerstown was, according to his map, only about fifty, sixty miles up Route 70 toward Pennsylvania.

Baum called the 800-number the next day to talk to the young woman. Somebody else answered. Could he speak to the twenty-two-year-old woman named Angie he'd spoken with yesterday? he asked. Get real, said the new voice, there are five hundred people working here, mostly women, nobody knows anybody, there might be two hundred Angies here. Through persistence, humor, and the ability to use his notebook-like mind to describe the girl to his listener—

she has a sister who's eighteen, a 1990 Celica—Baum eventually found the right woman.

"We talked again, and this was looking pretty good," he says. "I told her I was twenty-two—well, I will be in a month. And I liked the fact that she was only five feet tall." He was concerned about a couple of factors, however. "She has a very tough Pennsylvania accent. Ever heard Bill Conlin of the *Philadelphia Inquirer* talk?" And, of course, there was the fact that he hadn't seen her. "I didn't ask her how much she weighed," he says. "But she said she liked to go to the beach and tan, so I got a hint there. And I don't like real short hair, so I said, 'Your hair's real short, huh?' She said no, which was good."

So he asked her for a date. And she accepted. She'd drive down sometimes, she said, and they'd hook up.

"I still don't know her last name," Baum muses. "But she knows everything about me. She knows I spent almost five hundred dollars on my Visa card this year. She knows what restaurants I've eaten at. She knows I bought a new car radio." He thinks for a moment. "I wonder if she could push a button and make twenty percent disappear?"

Cupid fires his arrows through all media. This could be the romance Baum has been waiting for.

THE PARKING LOT IS HUGE FOR A HIGH SCHOOL, BUT THIS IS MONTEBELLO, California, part of the east Los Angeles urban sprawl, and a kid is nothing if he doesn't have a car. There are hundreds of cars in the parking lot, some covered with toilet paper. Tomorrow is commencement for the seniors here at Schurr High School, and the pranks have already begun. In front of the school a low-riding Volkswagen bug, cherry-red and throbbing, inches toward the main drag.

Seventeen-year-old Jay Macias, 6'1" and 195 pounds, dark-haired with handsome Hispanic features, walks between classes in the courtyard area that lies in the middle of the school's four main buildings.

Macias is a quarterback, and he has accepted a scholarship to the University of Wisconsin, where much is already expected of him, though he is unaware of it. There is much that he does not know. The first time he flew in an airplane was when he took a commercial flight to Madison in late April to visit the campus and watch the spring game. It was also the first time he had been out of California.

"I saw things I'd never seen before," he says. "Horse buggies. Streams. They told me beforehand that the freshman dorm was near a lake, and when I was flying, I looked down and saw a *million* lakes. We don't have lakes around here. I was real nervous. I saw things I've only seen on TV."

But that is also why he is going to Wisconsin: to change, to grow. "I'm an adventurer," he says. "For some reason I feel like I have to get out of here."

With an enrollment that is mostly Hispanic, Asian, and African-American, the high school suffers from some racial tension and the other problems that plague public schools everywhere. But as Macias says, "It's still cool to be an athlete here," which is why, he feels, he probably has stayed on the straight and narrow path rather than getting involved in drugs or gangs. "My parents divorced when I was five and my mom lives in San Diego," he says. "Now I live just with my dad; he's a truck driver for Clearwater Trucking. My older brothers are on their own, and my younger sister, Regina, lives with my mom. My brother Nick, who's twenty-nine, was a middle linebacker who played with John Elway at Granada Hills High School. He was good, and he could have gone to college, but nobody pushed him with his grades. That's one mistake my dad didn't make with me."

Macias was recruited by UCLA and Southern California, but Wisconsin plucked him away when both those schools dragged their feet on their scholarship offers. "I could have done better in school," Macias admits. "But I have a *B, C* average and I got a seven hundred exactly on the SAT." He smiles sheepishly; a seven hundred is the NCAA minimum needed to avoid having to sit out a year of eligibility.

"Wisconsin is very good academically," he continues. "I know I'm really going to have to adjust, but I've got to get a degree. A linebacker can wipe me out at anytime. The coaches told me that if I get a degree from Wisconsin, I can get a job anywhere."

Macias sits on a bench under the cloudless sky. He is wearing shorts, high-top basketball shoes, and a green T-shirt. One of the school counselors, Peter Fong, walks up and says hello. Fong knows that Macias is making a bold move.

"We had one kid, Israel Rosales, who went to Harvard in the late seventies," says Fong. "He was a Senate page. But we've never had a football player go to the Big Ten. We've never even had a student go to the Big Ten." He looks down on the young man who once threw a ninety-seven-yard touchdown pass to win a game. "He'll do well," he says. "He's not a partyer."

Macias is a quiet, easygoing fellow who is young for his class; he won't turn eighteen until August, when he'll be preparing to play a dangerous sport with some athletes who will be almost twenty-three. But Macias doesn't need much to get his juices going. As a fifteen-year-old sophomore third-string QB, he was suddenly called upon to enter a game after the starter went down with an injury. "Players were yelling my name, but I didn't know what was happening—I was listening to a guy tell a joke on the bench," he says. "And I wanted to hear the end of it." He went in and proceeded to lead Schurr from a 14–0 deficit to a 15–14 win, throwing a scoring pass with less than a minute left and then kicking the clinching extra point. "I was also the punter," he adds.

The key word for Macias is *opportunity*. "Around here there aren't too many people who are successful. I want to experience a new lifestyle," he says, watching the students laugh and yell as they form their cliques, flirt, and strut. "The only thing against going to Wisconsin is the family thing. My dad lives to watch me play. But he said, 'You're a big boy. Don't ever say, "I should have gone." ' "

One of Macias's English teachers, Tim O'Brien, walks by.

"Drop me a line, Jay," he says. "Go get 'em!"

Though Macias's grandparents were born in Mexico, Jay himself is American through and through. "I've thought a lot about Jim Plunkett," he says of the former Heisman Trophy–winning Stanford quarterback of Mexican descent. "I'm proud of my Mexican roots, but if they want me to speak Spanish up there, Sorry, fellas. I don't know any."

Wisconsin should have no trouble getting used to the affable young man; he is the one who will have to adapt to a foreign land without a relative or pal within two thousand miles. When Macias first arrived in Madison, he was relieved to see a Burger King; he had feared the fast-food chain didn't exist in that strange land. Then he saw a parked car with its windows rolled down. Macias said to his host, center Brian Patterson, "Uh, what's going on?" He pointed at the car.

"There's no crime in Madison," Patterson answered.

Macias still has never touched snow—never seen it, except on film. But the culture of Wisconsin is stranger than anything that falls out of the sky. He visited a dorm on his recruiting trip and was forced to step out of the way as a student ran down the hall, pulling a rope that was held by another student sitting on a cafeteria tray. Macias was amazed. "He pulled him real fast down the hall, whipped around a corner, and the guy flew out the window," he says.

It was the young Californian's first look at spring traying.

BARRY BAUM'S STILL WAITING FOR LOVE. LAST FRIDAY NIGHT HE SPENT SEVERAL hours on the corner of 36th Street and Avenue N in Washington, D.C., where his mystery date was supposed to meet him. Time went by and she didn't show. Baum saw a car like hers go past and had a moment of terror; the woman at the wheel was, as he puts it, "a hundred-and-eighty pounder." Thankfully, it was not his date.

After an hour a homeless man approached Baum and asked for money. Baum told him he didn't have any, which was basically true, and then told the vagrant why he was waiting on the corner, the whole giddy, fantastic, hopeless tale. The two struck up a conversation and whiled away the time chatting about women and bad luck. Cars came and went, but no date. Finally, the bum told Baum, "Listen, you go back up to your apartment. If she shows, I'll send her up."

Baum left, but the girl never arrived. He called her at the 800-number the next day, and she claimed she couldn't make it the night before because she "had to help a friend." She said she tried to leave a message on Baum's phone machine, but that something didn't work. Baum accepted her apology and made a date for the following week.

TO: Alan Fish
FROM: Tami Holmquist
RE: Athletic Department Concerns, Etc.

I would just like to say for the record that a lot of thought was put into writing this memo. . . . My job as Business Manager has become a very unpleasant one. . . . As I see it, the major problem is a lack of leadership and direction from the administration of this organization—from the

very top down. We have not cleaned house enough, we
have not identified who is responsible for what, we have
not put forth guidelines as far as what is acceptable and
what is not, and we have not been consistent in adminis-
tering our programs. I'd like to see this change, I really
would. . . .

Tami Holmquist stops at the Irish Waters Bar on University
Avenue after work to drink an iced tea and calm her frazzled nerves.
She gave her memo to Fish, and she hasn't heard back from him yet.
But she's not sure how much more she can take of this organization;
it seems more like a charity with delusions of grandeur than a business. A month ago head athletic department fund-raiser John Swenson quit to take a job at Taliesin, the Frank Lloyd Wright museum
and foundation, and Todd Kuckkahn was promoted to take his place.
Last week, Kuckkahn quit the post. Both men cited, according to
Holmquist, "a lack of direction in the department" as their reasons
for shoving off.

She slowly stirs her tea. She feels alone, overwhelmed by idiots
and poseurs. "I remember the acceptance letter I sent to Pat, saying
I thought this was the perfect job for me," she says. "And now a year
later I am thinking this is the worst decision I ever made." What is
she supposed to do, she asks, about a guy on the payroll who does
nothing and at long last has been given notice, but still gets paid for
a whole year? "Twelve months," she says. "Forty-eight thousand
dollars salary, plus fifteen thousand in fringe benefits, plus a car?"

And the budget that was supposed to reflect hard times? It's
bigger than last year's, with five fewer sports. Women's golf has
increased its expenditures by 41 percent. Men's soccer is up 50
percent, and men's basketball has increased its travel expenses alone
from $112,000 in 1990–91 to $156,000 for 1991–92. Everything is up,
up, up, and fencing—poor, little extinct fencing—cost just $37,540
for the men and $18,660 for the women last year.

And Barry Alvarez and Scott Raridon have continued to make
Holmquist's life unpleasant with their demands and insouciance.
Raridon was stopped by the police for driving while intoxicated—in
a UW car. He also was caught by a night watchman naked with a girl
in the weight room late at night. He seems to have been involved
somehow in the falsifying of names on plane ticket receipts to St.

Louis for a strength coach convention. Steve Myrland's name was written on one of the receipts, though Myrland told Tami that he did not go to the convention and, in fact, knew nothing about it. Raridon said he and assistant strength coach John Dettman went to the convention, but when Myrland called the convention center to check the records, the place said nobody from the University of Wisconsin had shown up. "To this point I don't really know what happened," says Holmquist.

The old-fashioned fund-raising wingdings that supposedly are vital to the athletic department's morale and inner fiber and wallet, Holmquist has concluded, are really just bad habits run amok. "Butch's Bologna Bash barely made twenty-one thousand dollars, after all the talk of making hundreds of thousands," says Holmquist, adding that the hidden costs might even put the whole deal in the red. "And the alumni golf outing to Las Vegas ended up costing us twenty-eight thousand."

"The other thorn in my side is Jim Bakken. And Pat will lay down and die before he deals with him. He was hired by Pat to take care of marketing and promotions, but all he wants to do is run around in Pat's shadow and play golf. During the day he draws little claws. His big idea last year was to paint claws on the road all the way from the airport to Camp Randall so the other team could see them the whole time. But he couldn't get the backing from the rest of us."

Holmquist considers having another iced tea, but decides one is her limit and heads for the comfort of home.

LAST NIGHT BARRY BAUM FINALLY MET HIS MYSTERY GIRLFRIEND. IT WAS HIS worst nightmare come true.

The young woman was shaped like a tackling dummy, with a face straight from a bulldog show and the personality of a witch. "Her glasses were thicker than . . . I mean, her eyes were four inches wide," says Baum now, still not fully recovered. "She looked like Art Buch-wald."

To avoid seeing anyone he might know, Baum took the woman from Visa for a quick meal at a bland restaurant ("I paid with American Express just to get on her nerves," he says) and then to a movie far from his neighborhood. To his chagrin he promptly walked into three former classmates from UW, all women, at the theater.

After the show he said good-night to his blind date, without even a handshake, and went to his room, asking himself what part of his life he had lived wrong, why God had chosen him for heightened suffering.

"It was a horrifying experience," he says now. "You cannot believe. I don't want to talk about it, really."

23

THE WOMEN ON THE UW VOLLEYBALL TEAM ARE DISMAYED. THEIR HEAD coach and much beloved instructor/cheerleader/friend Steve Lowe has fallen ill with lung cancer. It all happened fast; he went to the hospital on July 27 with what was believed to be pneumonia, and then the cancer was discovered, and now Lowe, a vibrant and energetic thirty-five-year-old who has never smoked, has been bedridden for over two weeks.

Practice for the Big Ten champion volleyball team is being run by Lowe's three assistant coaches, Margie Fitzpatrick, Liz Hert, and Andrea Riddick, until Lowe returns; Lowe has no doubt he'll be back coaching his team, even if it takes him a little time to regain his energy.

"My gut feeling is that I'll have to come back slowly," he told sports editor Bill Brophy of the *Wisconsin State Journal* from his bed at Meriter Hospital, his words muffled by the oxygen mask over his mouth. "I'd like to get out of the hospital by next week and then go to a couple of practices a week. I'm short of breath, so I'll have a hard time being real verbal at practice, so I'll be observing more. But as the year goes on, I hope to be more involved."

Until that time, his assistants are bringing videotapes of each practice to the hospital for Lowe, last season's Big Ten Volleyball

Coach of the Year, to analyze and critique. Lowe is an optimist whose enthusiasm for competition rubs off on his players to the point that they no longer feel bound by their physical limitations. He took over a program in 1986 that had just finished with a 7–24 record and five straight losing seasons, and he turned it on its head. The last two years the team has gone a combined 54–19, with last fall's team finishing with a 16–2 Big Ten record as well as leading the conference in attendance. Last season's team set an NCAA tournament single-game attendance record by drawing a crowd of nearly eleven thousand to its first-round match with Illinois. Lowe never played sports in college, and his interest in coaching volleyball comes more from his impassioned desire to see people take chances and be the best they can be than it does from any blind love for the game itself.

In a chapter of a book entitled *The Science of Coaching Volleyball*, Lowe and his co-authors—psychologists Thom McKenzie of San Diego State University and Martin Gipson of the University of the Pacific—write lovingly of the benefits of confident athletes' striving for lofty goals under the eye of an encouraging coach. Under the heading "Risk Taking" the authors write "Players must be willing to attempt a tough serve, to call for a set at match point, both of which are the signs of a confident player. But for players to do this, they must be rewarded for taking risks even if the outcome is not always positive. For example, if a player attempts to serve 'tough,' to go for an ace, and nets instead, that player should be rewarded for taking the risk, not yelled at for missing the serve. . . . Coaches who punish based on the outcome limit player risk-taking because players, like anyone else, will avoid doing what they have been punished for doing."

Clearly, Steve Lowe is a player's coach, quite likely the best coach in the entire UW athletic department.

Barry Baum has shifted his sights to the volleyball team since returning from his stint at *Baseball Weekly* and beginning a new school year. The football team's exploits have become old news to him, even down to the players' and coaches' loathing of him, and he has found that he enjoys the excitement of following a team that actually wins more games than it loses. Moreover, he has found the volleyball scenery to his liking, taking a specific interest in long-haired, five-foot eight-inch, doe-eyed All–Big Ten senior setter Liz Tortorello. He also is fascinated by blond second-team All–Big Ten digger Susan Wohlford, who at five feet seven is the shortest member of the team and one of the few to wear full makeup during games.

Everything is strictly professional between him and the athletes, he is quick to point out. The word *platonic* was invented for his relationship with these women; in fact, they barely acknowledge him at all, except to throw him a few quotes when he comes calling. But as Baum points out, where there is journalism, there is hope.

Baum makes a note to himself that he should take a trip to Meriter Hospital to do an interview with Steve Lowe. The women on the team adore the man.

It's Media Day for the 1991 football team, and the squad members wander the bright confines of Camp Randall Stadium, waiting for the official team photo to be taken and for any of the few assembled members of the media to interview them. Barry Alvarez is the grand orchestra leader here, the emperor of all that he sees.

The freshmen came in six days ago, and as the publicity department handout proudly proclaims, the Badger youngsters have been "Rated in the Top 30" of national recruiting classes, by some unnamed talent appraisers. Alvarez is moderately happy with what he has seen of the freshmen thus far; he's pleased with Jason Maniecki and Jay Macias, at any rate: Maniecki is "two seventy-five, ten percent body fat, cut, could play"; Macias "is a talent; he can air it out." Maybe it's just hype, but Alvarez says, "Those two kids are probably the biggest leaders."

He's less upbeat about the team as a whole, however. "It's like we got the death penalty," he says grimly, out of earshot of his players. "Of the players who sat down with us on picture day last year, fifty-two are gone. They were walk-ons, seniors, and guys who quit, who came to me and said, 'I'm just not good enough.' That's the quality of some of these players they gave scholarships to. Brother!"

It's a common lament for new coaches: It ain't me, it's the empty storeroom. Sometimes it's true. Who knows? Don Morton no doubt said the same thing, and Hilles before him, and McClain before him. Alvarez has already told the local writers to have patience, that this is a young team. He himself will maintain the stiff upper lip and wear a big smile below it.

"It's not easy," he says. "But if I'm not up, then my assistants and kids will get down, and then, hell, you don't have a chance. I know human nature. When you're down, people are gonna kick you."

He turns and looks out at his players, many of whom look like giants with their helmets and shoulder pads on. "The scrutiny here—man, it's tough. At Notre Dame they don't air things in public, they keep things to themselves. Here, everything's public knowledge. Nothing is sacred."

And why should it be sacred? thinks *Wisconsin State Journal* columnist Vic Feuerherd, sitting in the stands, smoking a cigarette.

"I've only been around this four years, so I don't carry as much baggage as some guys," Feuerherd says, watching Alvarez lead his troops into formation. "Even though I've lived here twenty-one years, I've got enough New York in me to be cynical and jaded. I mean, shouldn't a school with a sixteen-million-dollar sports program hire bright people? Is that asking too much? Who do they get, a bunch of Iowa guys and Jim Bakken?"

Even by crusty journalist standards the mustachioed, gray-haired Feuerherd is a raging cynic, though his columns quite often belie his attitude, leaning more toward evenhandedness than outrage. (Notable exception: Feuerherd's relentless savaging of Don Morton, a personal target.) Not so his spoken words. "All I want is for somebody to give me a sign that my time for the next three and a half months is well spent. Not just this crap. A pass, a run, a draw, a punt. A bad punt at that."

He scowls and fires up another Kool. He has his shirt off, soaking up the sun. He should be happy; a lot of people have far worse jobs. He watches as below him players who didn't get into shape over the summer run two-hundred-yard sprints under Scott Raridon's command, then collapse and roll in exhaustion.

"What a stupid game," says Feuerherd in disgust. "My son is nine years old and he's four-feet-nine, ninety-five pounds, big and solid, and one day an assistant saw him and said, 'You'll be a good offensive lineman.' 'No, I won't, sir,' he said." Feuerherd beams and puffs a thin jet of smoke into the air. "That's my kid."

The writer smiles thinly. Then he thinks of Wisconsin's first three games this year, the non-conference slots that every coach likes to fill with cupcakes. UW has shamelessly filled them with dainty cherry tarts: Western Illinois, Iowa State, Eastern Michigan. At least one writer has called this lineup the easiest Division I pre-conference schedule in the land. The things a coach will do for the almighty W. Feuerherd exhales a blast of smoke.

"Western Illinois starts off against Washburn," he says. (Washburn is a glorified community college in Kansas.) "Then Western plays Wisconsin. Western might not be looking ahead, but after the Badgers they've got . . . St. Ambrose."

Poor Feuerherd. He needs to get his facts straight. After Wisconsin, Western Illinois doesn't play St. Ambrose; it plays Northwood Institute.

MARY GRINAKER, THE NEW ASSISTANT WOMEN'S TRACK COACH, TAKES SOME time to chat with Laura Graf, a weight room assistant for Steve Myrland. Both women were outstanding athletes during their careers at UW in the late seventies and early eighties, Grinaker as a Big Ten champion pentathlete and Graf as a national champion in the eight-person shell, and they know the abuses athletes sometimes perpetrate on themselves in attempts to excel at their sport. They look at the large calendar on Myrland's office wall at the side of the weight room and nod knowingly.

The calendar was produced by the Big Ten conference to celebrate the first ten years of women's NCAA sports, and for the month of August it features a photo of cross-country runners jockeying for position at the start of a championship race. In the middle of the photo is former UW runner Stephanie Herbst, her legs like sticks, her arms like wire hangers.

"The mind-set of an anorexic is that you can do anything," says Grinaker, looking at Herbst's bony frame. "They'll use anything from diuretics to laxatives to lose weight. They'll restrict their water intake, eat the same meal of white iceberg lettuce with lemon juice again and again. Or only cold cereal. One runner I knew ate a cupful of Grape-Nuts a day with watered-down skim milk.

"I always think of Cory Kneuer, a pentathlete when I was here. She was a great natural athlete who got weird. She won the pentathlon her freshman year, and then she started getting real thin. We watched her. She'd only eat the raisins out of a box of Raisin Bran. She started baking cookies all the time, she'd be up in the middle of the night baking plates of them."

Kneuer is now Cory Everson, the wife of former UW strength coach Jeff Everson, and a bodybuilder who has reformed her body through weight lifting and other tactics to become a six-time Ms. Olympia winner. Called by *Ironman* magazine "undoubtedly the most popular female bodybuilder ever," she played the part of "a bone-crushing lesbian assassin who gives new meaning to the term 'killer thighs' " (*Entertainment Weekly*) in Jean-Claude Van Damme's 1991 martial arts movie, *Double Impact*. Grinaker remembers her from the old days as simply a bright college talent who was dangerously thin. Everson, who has published a fitness book and was the star of ESPN's *Bodyshaping* series, has lost some of the spooky muscle mass she once carried, but for a while she bore no resemblance whatsoever to the slender young woman who lettered in four sports at Wisconsin.

Is it likely any woman could get as big as Cory was without using some kind of muscle-building drug? "No," says Grinaker. (In a newspaper report, Cory has flatly denied using any such drugs.) The whole issue of eating and training and obsession with perfection is, for many female athletes, "a thin line," says Grinaker.

"So many women with eating disorders are so smart," says Graf. "They know everything about their disorder. Everything. They talk about it."

The trouble is, at some point the disorder causes the athlete to break down either mentally or physically, says Graf, who was the women's crew coach at the Naval Academy until coming here. "There was a girl here when I was an athlete, Katie Ishmael. She got hit by a car one day and just kept running, that's how crazy she was. She used to be stocky, but she metamorphosed herself into an anorexic distance runner. I lost a friend because she became so compulsive. I talked to her mother a while ago and she said, 'She's working in Vail, and she's put on weight.' I worry about her.

"The trouble is, you may be sick, but you're scoring points for a track team in Division I, in the Big Ten," says Grinaker. "I saw this woman in a UW uniform at the outdoor track meet in Columbus last spring, and she was dying. I mean it. You can't believe it. My thought was, 'Get her right into a hospital!' "

BARRY BAUM AND MIKE BRESNEHAN, THE SPORTS EDITOR AT THE *DAILY CAR-dinal*, dig into a greasy pizza at Rozino's on Fairchild Street, two blocks from the Capitol. Between bites they remind each other of the contempt and lack of respect they elicit from people.

"I went up to defensive line coach Dan McCarney for the first time last year," says Baum. "I said, 'Hi, I'm from the *Daily Cardinal.*' He says, 'Oh, the *Daily Communist.*' "

Bresnehan grunts in acknowledgment. "Remember when we went to Roy Firestone's show on ESPN?"

"Oh yeah!" cries Baum. "I wrote to him, then wrote a second letter. And he never wrote back, so I called him at home. He was very nice and said, 'Come to the show.' So we went out to L.A. for spring break, right?"

Bresnehan nods. They stayed at Bresnehan's parents' house in Encino. "You gave him a Bleacher Creature T-shirt."

"With Yoder on the back," says Baum. "So we get there and he walks right past me."

"Didn't say a word."

"He didn't *look* at me. He gets behind his desk and starts watching himself on video, an old show."

The two scribes grow silent for a spell, continuing to eat.

"We're gonna go to Lexington for the volleyball game, right?" says Baum. "We're driving nine and a half hours each way, thirty-eighty dollars a night for the room. The *Cardinal* should pay."

"Who knows?" says Bresnehan. "Last year we drove down and stayed at a Motel 6."

"Did the *Cardinal* pay?"

"No."

"Why not?"

"I don't know. As a freshman I went to Detroit and St. Paul to cover the hockey team in the NCAAs, by Greyhound. And there was a strike going on, too, so there were guys around with guns. I paid half-fare for the bus ride and then I had to buy scalped tickets for thirty-five dollars with my own money to see the games. Then I had to sneak into the locker room. I slept on the floor of another writer's room, and I missed three days of school."

"Money?" asks Baum.

Bresnehan shakes his head. "Nothing."

*　　*　　*

IT'S HOT TODAY EVEN AT TWILIGHT, AND BAUM TAKES REFUGE BRIEFLY IN THE cool darkness of Jingles' Bar, just across the street from the athletic department. He slugs down an ice water and reflects on what he knows.

"Jerzy Radz, I hear, got a job at Wayne State as the fencing coach. Which is nice. And a gymnast got a scholarship to somewhere."

He asks the bartender for a refill. Jingles is basically a quonset hut with an ice machine and a bar; it's almost empty now, but on game days it can be so full of people that fans get squeezed out the front door and into the street like filling from a doughnut. There are photos of various UW football players on the walls, including a shot of the current bartender, 1989 team co-captain Tim Knoeck. The former linebacker serves Baum his water.

"Oh, man, I got a great class this year!" says Baum suddenly with great enthusiasm. "Women's Studies 103: 'Women and Their Bodies.'" He considers that good news again, still proud of the way he was able to beat so many applicants at registration for the class.

"It's a science requirement. I need it," he explains. "Well, I need a science requirement. It'll probably be all feminists, girls with pigtails under the arms. But there's a lecture and then discussion groups. I can just see it. 'When you bring a girl home. should you give her vodka or Jack Daniel's?' Today's lecture: 'Crotches.'"

He drains his water. Gotta go; a deadline beckons.

WASHINGTON POST SPORTS COLUMNIST LEONARD SHAPIRO WAS A STUDENT AT UW from 1964 to 1968, where he wrote for the *Daily Cardinal* and was the paper's sports editor in 1966 and 1967.

"We literally had bomb-throwers on our staff back then," Shapiro says from his desk at the *Post*. "One kid who covered crew for me was Leo Burt—he was actually on the crew team. [Burt was one of the bombers who, along with Karlton Armstrong, was convicted of setting the blast that blew up the physics building, killing researcher Robert Fassnacht.] I got a call from the FBI after I went to Portland and was covering crew myself, and they said, 'If you see Leo at any of these regattas, give us a call.' Sure, I'm gonna turn my buddy in. I think they're still looking for him."

The paper was a crucible in which many talented young people forged their journalistic skills and not just their rebelliousness, Shapiro adds. "Rita Kempley was there; she's a star with CBS News now. Ellen Alt went to the *Wall Street Journal*. Steve Klein is the sports editor of the East Lansing paper. One guy, Neal Ulevich, was a great photographer who won a Pulitzer Prize in Southeast Asia in the early seventies. Jeff Greenfield, the political guy on ABC News, he was the editor of the *Cardinal* around '65. And Dave Wolff, who wrote *Foul: The Connie Hawkins Story*, was the sports editor in 1964.

"It was just a great experience," says Shapiro. "I'd spend fifty hours a week on the *Cardinal*. We were all very close. Hell, I married my sports editor, Diane Seidler. She was one of the first women sports editors anywhere. She'd go to the press box with her knitting—it drove Jim Mott [the former SID] nuts."

Shapiro himself played one year of baseball at UW—as a "bad, too fat catcher"—before getting serious about reporting. He started off covering fencing as a sophomore, and then moved on to football. "The team was just awful," he notes. "I remember after a big loss [football coach John] Coatta was crying and I was next to him, and he said, 'Tell 'em, Len! Tell 'em, Len! Every week it's the same thing. Tell 'em, Len!'

"I think the biggest problem was the cold, trying to get great athletes to Madison. And then it wasn't a great place for black athletes to show up. Basketball star Jumpin' Joe Franklin was dating a white girl, and it was a big problem. Mostly, the football and basketball people just never recruited right. They just never did it."

Shapiro met Barry Baum during a visit to the alma mater last year, and he was struck by the youngster's pluck and friendliness. "He's a talented young kid," says the veteran newspaperman. "And he's aggressive, he works his ass off. I think he's got the bug. He reminds me of a lot of people we had on the *Cardinal*."

Shapiro laughs. "He reminds me of me."

24

It's ten-thirty in the morning and the women's volleyball team is part way through a three-hour practice. Interim coach Margie Fitzpatrick looks at the women diving for balls and swatting spikes, and she thinks of the vagaries of fate. "Steve's absence has affected them personally," she says. "But on the court, I don't know."

Assistant coach Andrea Riddick watches, too. There is a decided look and personality to this team, just as there is to any sports team in which certain physical, mental, and cultural characteristics are expected and rewarded. In general, the players are tall, long-legged, long-haired, outgoing, and attractive. Only one of the twelve, Arlisa Hagen, is black, and she is fetching enough and tall enough at six feet one inch to be a runway model; she has lately been receiving inquiries about her availability for high-fashion work. Of the fifteen women, coaches included, ten are blondes or at least "summer blondes."

"Fewer blondes than last year, actually," notes Riddick with a grin. But the team is very focused and rigid in its expectation of itself. At times it seems less a collection of separate individuals than a single, undifferentiated organism. And it very much gets its strength from the lingering dynamism of Steve Lowe.

"We're going to go see him in the hospital as soon as practice is over," says Fitzpatrick. "He has to know what's going on."

*   *   *

IN THE ATHLETIC DEPARTMENT OFFICE A SMALL LUNCHTIME PIZZA PARTY IS
under way to bid farewell to assistant sports information director,
Greg Elkin, who is taking the job as the basketball SID at Indiana
University. Everyone knows what that means; Elkin will be working
in a high-profile, big-money, ultramodern, and lavish program run by
one of the great tyrants or geniuses in all of college sport. For Elkin
it is clearly the latter. "I talked to Bobby Knight for forty minutes,"
he says of Indiana's legendary basketball coach. "Bobby Knight."

Joel Maturi, the humble and hardworking, if largely unnoticed,
associate athletic director, is ready to walk down the hall to the
gathering, but first he checks out something in the massive NCAA
rules book. The book could pass for the combined works of Dosto-
evski, but it is a tome without literary value that Maturi must constantly wade through in his role as NCAA rules compliance official
for the department. A former coach and athletic director at Edge-
wood Catholic High School in Madison, Maturi believes in the sanc-
tity of sport, the forgiveness of beneficent coaches, and the power of
money to corrupt. Just now he is trying to determine whether it
would be possible for Amy Bauer to play golf at UW, a sport in which
she is proficient and might be interested in playing, and still maintain the scholarship she was awarded for playing basketball.

"This book," he says in anguish. "Ever looked at it? It's quite a
document." That is about as critical as Maturi usually gets.

He flips through pages of tiny print. "I don't believe she could
play golf and have her scholarship honored," he says, scanning paragraph after paragraph, "because that would technically be a golf
scholarship, and we don't give those."

He stops near the middle of the book, his finger pointing to
figure 15–2 under "Grant-in-Aid Limitations," and follows with his
finger a flow chart from football to basketball on down to "all other
sports," and from there through various bylaws, headings, and sub-
headings until he turns to a new page, then another, and comes to
something labeled Section 15.5.6.1, "Multiple Sports Participants."

Does the barely comprehensible verbiage below apply? Maybe.
But how can you tell for sure until the NCAA has come after you
with a big-time investigation?

Maturi sighs deeply.

In the party room, Steve Malchow, Mike Greene, Tami Holmquist, Jim Bakken, assistant SID Julie Kluge, and Pat Richter all hoist Cokes and eat pizza slices and wish Elkin good luck. Bakken is less interested in Elkin's leaving than he is in getting closer to Knight somehow, a man he refers to as "the General." He takes Elkin aside for a moment. "How does the General hit the golf ball?" he asks.

Richter gets Elkin's attention and tells him about the time a few years back when Richter was doing TV color commentary with Gary Bender at an Indiana basketball game. The volcanic Knight was upset with center Kent Benson "and reached up and grabbed him by the neck—Benson's six feet ten—and then hit him on the butt so hard you could hear it in the stands. Then," Richter pauses for effect, "he did it to the SID." Everyone laughs, and Richter shakes Elkin's hand and departs.

Bakken buttonholes Elkin again. "Remember," he says. "I want the General for the Friday before the game. A fund-raiser. Fifty bucks a head." That Knight doesn't do things like that, especially for enemy schools, or that Elkin might not care to help Wisconsin once he's with a rival program, seems to escape Bakken.

"What about me with white hair and a pillow under my sweater?" says Elkin, trying to make a joke of the matter.

"Nope," insists Bakken. "I want the General." And he slaps Elkin on the arm to reinforce the deal.

BARRY BAUM, FOR PERHAPS THE FIRST TIME IN HIS BUDDING JOURNALISM CAREER, is at a loss for words. Steve Lowe is dead.

Lowe died last night and now Baum is here in the third-floor women's sports information office, and Liz Tortorello, Susan Wohlford, and middle blocker Jeanette Simenson have walked in, and they're all crying, and he is overwhelmed with their grief and is feeling as though he understands getting the facts and having a strong opinion and making jokes about people's petty failings and vanity, but that no one ever prepared him for something like this.

He had called Meriter Hospital last night at five to see about maybe visiting Lowe for a story. "He was in 'fair' condition when I called," says Baum. "And then he just died. How can that happen? How can that happen?" At 8 P.M. Baum went to the hospital, hoping to sniff out facts, but what he found instead was a dark and deserted sixth-floor cancer ward. Steve Lowe's bed was empty. He finally tracked down two nurses, but they had nothing to say to him.

Here right now in front of him is the truth of the matter. He tries to talk to the women, but he can't. He leaves and goes back to the *Daily Cardinal* office.

"Liz, she's pretty," he says. "But for one of the first times, I didn't look. Steve Lowe was such an inspiration for them. They all came to play for *him*."

Baum calls Rick Aberman and asks him about the situation, about death, and the loss of a loved one and what it means to athletes, to anyone. Aberman tells him people react in different ways to such loss. Baum sits at his computer terminal, shaken, thinking about things that haven't threatened his little world before. He has never written an obituary before. What a gift it is, he thinks once again, to be a writer.

For nine hours he stays in the *Daily Cardinal* office, thinking, making calls, writing about a man he never met. His column appears the next day, as students are completing registration and reveling in the crisp late-summer weather. Baum's story is a good piece, the best thing to appear on the man in any of the Madison papers.

> There was a coach who for five years at Wisconsin dealt with blocks and sets and digs. But Steve Lowe also dealt with Liz Tortorello and Susan Wohlford and Jeanette Si-menson and Sara Wilson. These seniors played three years for him and prayed, begged, for a fourth.
>
> On August 22, cancer took their volleyball coach away from them . . .
>
> Susan Wohlford remembered a frightening experience.
>
> "My sophomore year we were at Iowa and I had an ap-pendicitis attack," she said. "Steve and his parents stayed with me all night at the hospital. When the team contin-ued on to Illinois, his parents stayed with me.
>
> "The whole team is so close—our parents, his parents, his kids. That's the way he builds his teams." . . .

Baum quoted Tortorello, too, from an interview he had with her three days earlier. And then he summed it all up:

Steve Lowe brought Wisconsin volleyball to a level it
had never reached before. He leaves the Fieldhouse a winner."

Sunday at the Cress Funeral Home a closed casket holding Steve
Lowe's mortal remains rests at the front of a large room. On the
casket is an arrangement of red and white flowers saying, "Go Badgers." People stream in from the sweltering afternoon sun, pay their
respects to the family, look at the collected photographs of Lowe and
his team, and then move on. Al Fish stands near the back; like many
other athletic department members, he barely knew Lowe, but what
he knew he liked. "He was a stable, reasonable guy," says Fish. "In
Big Ten sports? Hard to find."

Martin Gipson, professor of psychology at the University of the
Pacific and Lowe's coauthor for the coaching book, has flown in to
pay tribute to his friend. "Did you know that Steve worked for two
and a half years at a hospital for the criminally insane in Iowa?" he
says. "He did. He was teaching the inmates how to be good sports,
not violent, to use sports for development of social skills. Even for
those people."

Gipson smiles at the thought. "Steve never played volleyball, but
he was very competitive. He was using his training in psychology to
be a coach. He believed you should enjoy sports, not just yell and
scream."

Barry Baum studies the photos, looking uncomfortable in a white
shirt and tie. He doesn't really belong here; he's not looking for a
story. He simply felt compelled to stop by.

He seeks out Margie Fitzpatrick. "I'm so sorry," he says. And
then he goes.

JENNY KRAEGER HAS RUN AND RUN UNTIL SHE HAS BROKEN DOWN. WHILE
training for this summer's Olympic Festival and other preliminary
events that might lead to a berth on the 1992 U.S. Olympic squad,
Kraeger developed a stress fracture in her left femur. The femur, or
thigh bone, is one of the densest bones in the body and it takes a
tremendous amount of pounding to break it. "Usually runners get
stress fractures in their feet or lower legs," notes Kraeger correctly.
But if you run to escape the thought of imperfection, and if you

don't eat properly—and her friends say Kraeger eats like a bird—you can combine stress and poor nutrition and break just about anything you want.

Kraeger continues to run in the pool and ride a stationary bike for hours on end, for the thought of not running is loathsome to her. "I love the things I see and think about when I run—the lakes, the change in seasons, the paths," she says. "I always get creative ideas when I run. Great things."

She just goes too far. Kraeger's former soccer teammate Heather Taggart recalls driving to a mall "about eight miles from campus, and I'd see Jenny running by. And she was coming *back* from somewhere." Taggart, the pre-med student, says, "She arrived her first year and you didn't notice so much, then the next year she came back and everybody noticed. She looked deathly." Taggart shivers with the thought. Then a look of cynicism crosses her face. "But people say she's okay to compete."

Pediatrician Greg Landry, the principal diagnosing physician for the athletic department, has in fact been worried about Kraeger for some time. "Many runners are at risk for anorexia nervosa," he says. "Many exhibit habits consistent with the disease. It is possible to weigh ninety-eight pounds and still perform athletically; it is difficult to tell just by looking. But Jenny, uh . . . we have been concerned about her, with her thinness. And we have confronted her. I'd better leave it at that."

But Kraeger is blithe about her physical condition. As she sits on the stairs inside Camp Randall, she smiles as members of the women's soccer team walk in the door. They stroll past Kraeger, calling her name, rubbing her blond hair as they head up the steps. Kraeger rotates her ankles. Loud crackles and pops issue forth. "I'll probably be arthritic at fifty," she laughs.

If she acknowledges any problem at all, it is the way she handled her early career in running. Her dad was a soccer coach, and she was always a jock, and when she was a fifteen-year-old sophomore in high school she went to the state championship in the two-mile run. "First place could have gone to anybody," she recalls. "But I was too uptight. I finished sixteenth or seventeenth. I was so nervous, so scared, and I felt so much pressure, and my coach didn't help at all. The pressure just built and built and my coach was just trying to do some psychological thing on me. I needed somebody to take the time to boost my confidence, somebody," she pauses briefly, "just to tell me it wasn't life or death."

After that, she says, everybody urged her to keep running competitively, despite her fears and insecurity. "My dad wanted me to continue, everybody did," she says. "But I didn't want to. It wasn't making me happy. So I just did it for fun. I stayed in shape."

And then she came to Wisconsin, where she switched sports from soccer to long-distance running, and found the leader she needed, head women's track coach Peter Tegen. "Peter helped me so much," she says. "He had this strategy: 'Don't worry about it. I'll take care of everything. If it works, great. If not, shit happens.' His exact words."

Clad in green running shorts and a white T-shirt that hangs on her like a sheet on a scarecrow, Kraeger rubs her left leg. "It's been six weeks and it's almost calcified," she says cheerily. When, she is asked, should a runner cut back on training and attempt to be, well, normal?

"When is it too much?" she responds, furrowing her brow. "When you feel run down."

And what might the right weight be for her as an athlete?

"Oh," she says. "I don't even think about it."

She pops her ankle two, three more times, with loud cracks. It is startling: there is just so little of her.

OVER IN STEVE MYRLAND'S WEIGHT ROOM RUNNER HEATHER RAWLING IS doing bench presses with sixty-five pounds on an Olympic bar. She wears red running shorts and a white sleeveless jersey, and her arms look like fishing rods. She is so gaunt that other lifters who see her stop in their tracks.

Mary Grinaker sits in Myrland's office with Laura Graf and thinks about the dilemma the athlete produces for a coach. "Peter says Heather is a lot more muscular this year than last," says Grinaker with a cringe. "Jenny is so full of energy, so bouncy, that everybody likes her. But Heather, I don't think I've seen her smile since I got here. She just has this tunnel vision. Her whole life is running. If someone told her she'd lose five seconds if she didn't eat for a week, she'd do it."

Graf looks at Grinaker, a woman who earned her master's degree in exercise science from Smith College, who coached five runners to NCAA Division III national championships there, who has talked about the eating disorders that were so rampant at that women's college that maids actually quit their jobs rather than continue to empty waste baskets full of vomit. "Why don't you say something to Peter?" she says.

"It's not my place," Grinaker answers. "He knows. And I'm the assistant coach."

They talk about other matters, then Graf says again, "Couldn't you say something to Peter?"

"In time. I haven't been here long enough."

Grinaker explains the mind-set of her boss. "Peter doesn't believe in psychology. He believes in everybody using their own inner strength. He's very German."

The assistant coach, who is herself tall, hollow-eyed, and thin, admits she has not eaten today. There was a day last week when she ate four Life Saver Holes. There are grapes and nuts on Graf's desk right now, but Grinaker doesn't want any.

RICK ABERMAN HAS HAD A SESSION WITH FIVE VOLLEYBALL PLAYERS, BUT IT WAS cut short when a sixth member of the team did not appear. Ironically, in the short time the women met with the psychologist, there was no talk about Steve Lowe's untimely death. "They didn't even mention his name," says Aberman. "This was about a teammate of theirs who is bulimic."

That team members have not swamped him with anguished requests for meetings to deal with the death of their coach is precisely what Aberman expected. He has said all along that the loss will be handled in its own way and its own time by each volleyball player. If someone needs help getting through the mourning process, fine, he will be there in his office to assist. But he was against any mandatory group therapy session, knowing that sometimes do-gooderism can create worse problems than already exist.

"What was interesting about this session," says Aberman, "was that the bulimic was supposed to be there, and she didn't show. She had told them about her problem, so they saw that as her way of seeking help. She sees herself as fat, but she's just big-boned. The group is going to come again tomorrow, and really there are two issues here: the player's sickness, and the support system around her. I said to the women who came, 'Aren't you a little angry that she didn't show up?' The trainer told me that as it gets closer to the regular season competition, the players are getting antsy because they want this woman back. They lost their opener in Kentucky without her."

Aberman cuts across a crowded street, dodging a tractor that is rumbling toward one of the many construction pits that dot this part of campus.

"One player is concerned because her own sister was bulimic," Aberman continued. "Each player brings her own situation to the problem. They're supposed to all come in tomorrow, but they also need to learn that there are limits to what they can do for the bulimic player. If she doesn't want treatment, there isn't much they can do, other than let her know they're pissed at her."

AT SATURDAY'S "HIGH-AND-HARD" PRESEASON FOOTBALL SCRIMMAGE, DONNA Shalala wanders through Camp Randall Stadium, led by her dog, Bucky, who strains at his leash. High-and-hard means that there will be full-tilt blocking, line play, and pass-rushing, but no tackling in the game. "We can't tackle," explains assistant coach John Dettman. "We're too thin in numbers." How many players are here today? "A hundred and five," he says. Almost five full teams for both offense and defense. Not enough.

Shalala watches the scrimmage with interest. "I'm not concerned about the team, but I know Pat is," she says. "I still believe in excellence, that we should do it at the highest level. But I'm not anxious." She looks at Alvarez on the sideline. "I actually like him," she whispers, pointing at the coach.

Shalala is a perfect companion for a dog that won't sit still. "We really don't allow dogs on campus," she says. "Only the CEO can allow dogs into university buildings. Who's that? Me. This is what you call managing by walking around. People just stop me and try to calm me down. You know, at games I'm supposed to sit up there." She turns and points high up in the stands. "I'm supposed to be in the two center boxes on top. But I like to be outside, it's hard for me to sit still. I move around the stands and I like to talk to team members' families, to the fans. People stop you when you walk around, and you get a pretty good feel for what's happening not only in the program but at your entire school."

It works especially well when you're walking a big red dog on a red leash. When Shalala first started her peregrinations on campus, a person leaned out of a building and shouted, "Hey, Bucky! Tell your master to fire Don Morton!"

"Who the heck is that?" Shalala says, as number 33, sophomore running back Brent Moss, a two-time prep All-America from Racine, bolts past her and her pooch for a long sideline run. "He is fast!" Indeed, he is. He was also a Proposition 48 academic casualty last season and has yet to play in a game for the Badgers. A good kid, Moss is nevertheless here at UW only as a result of the football team's need to win. (Several Division I conferences will not even accept Prop 48 athletes.)

Shalala thinks wistfully of her own postgraduate days at Syracuse, where she saw her first live college football game. "It was Floyd Little and Larry Csonka," she says. "The other team would kick off and Floyd would run all the way to the other end. I didn't know there was such a thing as stopping in between."

Sports takes up so much of the public's interest in a large university, she adds, that it's hard sometimes to remember how many other matters there are for a chancellor to address. "Holding on to talented faculty, that's the biggest job," she says. "By far." But even the students get sucked into the sports soap opera, letting its fervor replace more relevant educational dramas.

"I heard one student's tires were slit last spring because he voted for the sports cuts," she says almost sadly, looking down at Bucky. "It wasn't a good time for student politics."

25

JENNY KRAEGER STANDS IN THE PRESS BOX AT BREESE STEVENS SOCCER FIELD videotaping the UW women's soccer team as it plays Creighton University. The day is hot, humid, and almost cloudless, and yellow-jacket bees, which are actually small wasps, swarm wherever there is food or drink. The insects are ravenous for winter supplies, and several of them dart close to Kraeger's head as she sucks on a green lollipop, her lunch for today. Kraeger is dressed in black running shorts and a blue T-shirt that says RUN FOR THE MONEY on it. Her black running shoes are worn and salt-stained.

She waves the pests away from her sucker and focuses on the game below, which she is taping for her former coach. In the stands are a number of other UW athletes, including veteran hockey players Doug Macdonald and Duane Derksen and a half dozen freshmen hockey skaters and volleyball players Liz Tortorello and Jeanette Simenson. They all have come to cheer for their friends. Al Fish is also in the stands; having just turned forty, he wears one of his birthday presents—a T-shirt with dozens of different kinds of fish on it.

Abruptly there is a frightening collision between several players in a scramble for a loose ball. A Creighton woman goes down, and she doesn't move. Time goes by. "She's probably tired," says Kraeger. But after fifteen minutes, it appears there must be more to it than that. The player still has not moved. An ambulance drives onto the field, and attendants wearing rubber gloves strap the player to a wooden stretcher and place her in the back of the vehicle. The ambulance drives off, leaving deep tracks in the green and soggy turf.

The hockey players are impressed; this is not a game for sissies, either. As the game resumes it becomes clear that UW has two stellar players who are shoulders above any of the other players on either team. One is Kari Maijala, the quick and athletic forward, and the other is Heather Taggart, the badgerlike goaltender. Maijala makes a perfect corner kick to set up a header for a goal by one of her teammates, and Taggart, her green thigh-length jersey drenched in sweat, her hands covered by large black gloves, stops every shot that comes her way and kicks like an NFL punter.

In the press box, women's sports information director Tam Flarup smiles at Taggart's play. She'll nominate All-America Taggart for the national award for the most valuable soccer player in Division I, as she did last year, says Flarup, but she knows it's hard to promote a player who does all the little things so well. "She's got about a 3.5 grade point average," says Flarup, "but it's so hard for goalies to get recognition, because they have so few stats."

She swats at a yellowjacket.

"I saw a workman at the stadium, all alone, drinking coffee and eating a piece of cake, and there were four bees around him," she says. "I wonder what we'll do when we have fifty thousand people there for the football game on Saturday, drinking Cokes."

Academic advisor Ed Pollard, who is at the game sitting in the bleachers with his wife, has a response to that question, one that is tempered by experience.

"They'll probably hand out rat traps," he says.

THE HELMETED AND PADDED FOOTBALL PLAYERS RUN THROUGH THEIR DRILLS with an intensity that springs from the knowledge that the season opener against Western Illinois is just four days away. Team physician Greg Landry, a trim, balding man in his late thirties and a former quarterback at Butler University, reclines on the grassy slope at the edge of the practice field and watches the players crash into each other like red and white pool balls. The worst football injury

Landry ever has heard of occurred on the football field at Camp Randall in the spring of 1979, when Wisconsin tight end Jay Seiler died from head injuries sustained while making a tackle in practice. But the gradations and variety of injuries and illnesses that beset UW's athletes range from Seiler's tragedy down to things as minor as scrapes and ingrown hairs. In between, however, lies a huge, teeming sea of ailments.

Landry is just one of the seven doctors and dentists available to UW athletes at any time, professionals with expertise in everything from orthopedic surgery to allergy control. Diagnosing and treating the sports injuries is sometimes the easiest part of his job, notes Landry; the hard part is dealing with the egos and expectations and psychological blind spots of the athletes and their coaches.

"The biggest decisions we have to make, Dr. Jim Keene and I, is determining when a player can and cannot play," he says as the team runs through a seven-on-seven dummy drill. "Most of the coaches have been very good about it. But some are more difficult. I don't know why. I honestly don't. It puzzles me."

The coaches who are most receptive to the doctors' opinions, Landry says, "are the ones in sports that have the most contact with us—football, hockey, and basketball." Landry travels to all games with the football team and to many games with the basketball and hockey squads. "Barry Alvarez has been great with us. But there are those sports that are just a bitch. I'd rather not say which and jeopardize an already tenuous relationship."

One of the largest issues of modern sports medicine, continues Landry, is the increasing prevalence of eating disorders, particularly "where thinness is an important part of competition." The sports most affected, he notes, are track, cross-country, and wrestling. "But universally, it's more a women's problem. Wrestlers generally don't get into eating problems year-round. But there are male anorexics who got started in the sport of wrestling. In some ways they're more psychologically ill than the women who have the problem."

Landry shakes his head while looking at the blocking drills, marveling at the size of the athletes down on the field; even lowly Wisconsin has a number of linemen who stand over 6'6" tall or who weigh over 300 pounds. "There are a lot of similarities between eating disorders and [steroid] abuse," he notes. "They both can be psychological addictions. But steroid use is less a problem here than it was before. In the early eighties, I'd say from talking with other physicians that steroids were used by at least thirty percent of the linemen. At least. Now, well, we're guessing there are only a handful of steroid users on the team."

But what happens with women who become severely bulimic (binging and purging) or anorexic, says Landry, is "that they lose control over their behavior. And it can be life-threatening. Many of the sick athletes can function well for a long time, but eventually their performance will decline. Most of them will confide in someone that they are out of control."

Landry is a thoughtful man, and he knows that this is delicate, uncertain terrain, that what may seem clear-cut to an observer may be anything but clear-cut to the person or people involved. "A lot of female runners, and some males, are . . . on the edge," he says. "One of the most challenging aspects of my job is diagnosing the ones who are over the edge. Some of the best runners are very thin, and very close to that edge. The fact is that the thinner you are, the less weight you have to carry. It's simple physics. Up to a point. To tell you the truth, I don't think we know or will ever be able to get at the true percentage of girls it affects."

Landry feels that the relationship between women athletes and their sometimes charismatic male coaches can be a tinderbox for emotional fires and unhealthy behavior. "At the highest level of competition so much is under a microscope," he says, "that some athletes don't know who to trust. That enmeshment, that codependent relationship, puts the athlete at risk. It's not a well-studied thing, but it may be why so many track athletes have eating disorders."

And the solution? "At some point along the line young people must think for themselves," says the doctor. "Here we hope a teammate will tell the trainer or Rick Aberman and then, ultimately, confront the person, much the way you would with an alcoholic. Nothing is going to happen until somebody brings it up."

Is Jenny Kraeger anorexic?

Landry rises and brushes the grass from his hands. "Why don't you ask her?" he says.

STEVE MYRLAND, THE WEIGHT COACH WHO WOULD BE A NOVELIST, HAS STRONG feelings about Peter Tegen and his role with UW athletes. "Peter is a genius," he says. "No doubt. But I wish he were teaching men instead of women, because he can get his athletes to the edge, and sometimes the women too easily go over it. The men tend not to. Peter is the ultimate guru, and I don't like that. The only time I ever have trouble in here, with people not putting weights away and just kind of being pains, is with the two track teams."

Myrland sees the abnormal bodies on some of the athletes as well, both the steroid users and those who have eating disorders, and he often wonders what is going on in the athletes' minds. "The first person with an apparent eating disorder I knew of was Cory Kneuer," he says. "She was one of the most gifted athletes I've ever seen. She is just genetically engineered for sport. I remember people saying she was anorexic, and I'd never heard the word. I said to Jeff Everson [then the UW strength coach who eventually would marry Kneuer], 'What's that mean?' Jeff said, 'She won't eat.'"

It appears that Cory went from one mesmerizing male figure to another when she changed allegiances from Tegen to Everson. Everson was long rumored to have some kind of involvement in steroid use, and his shaping of his wife from a wiry athlete into the frighteningly over-muscled, big-busted Ms. Olympia has also been said to be a result of his control over her. Myrland, however, has another problem with the Eversons.

In 1985 he saw an article in *Ironman* magazine about the body-building husband-and-wife team and was stunned to see his own name listed as the author of the piece. He was even more stunned when he complained to the publisher of the magazine, Perry Rader, and was told by Rader that he must be the writer since Rader had sent him a check for a hundred dollars and Myrland had cashed it. Myrland got a copy of the canceled check and found that someone had forged his name and signed it over to the "Jeffrey M. Everson Account." The check was then stamped for deposit into the "Samson and Delilah" account, that being the name of one of Everson's business accounts.

Myrland tried to get the police to prosecute Everson for the crime, but Everson had moved to California and was beyond local jurisdiction. Everson had been fired as UW's head strength coach in 1983 as a result of being found guilty of misconduct in a public office and having a private interest in a public contract (he scammed the weight room out of equipment), and was sentenced to three years' probation and forced to repay $3,593 to the Wisconsin Department of Health and Social Services. There was nothing Myrland could do without spending a lot of money to build his case, and he didn't have a lot of money.

Myrland still gets furious when he thinks of the fraud, largely because the story itself is so poorly written and, as he says, "I take writing seriously." Then, too, the article is embarrassingly complimentary toward the Eversons, calling them "the most powerfully athletic couple in bodybuilding today," as well as a pair that will not "subject themselves to all of the drugs and dieting necessary to win big today." Cory herself states that "you shouldn't have to become a steroid bulked up bull or an anorectic whippet to win." And the fortuitous pairing of the two bodybuilders is described as a miraculous event that "produced a number of things beyond the eventual National Pairs Championship. It was also the beginning of a romantic relationship leading to wedding cake and wedding bells. If it all sounds a little fantasylike, well, it is!"

Myrland can be a bit of a curmudgeon, and as he puts the article back in his files, he grumbles with rekindled anger. Somehow, he just doesn't seem to get along with other strength coaches.

ADE SPONBERG IS A DECENT ENOUGH MAN; HE JUST WASN'T CUT OUT FOR THE pressures of operating an athletic department under duress. The former athletic director at North Dakota State, Sponberg became the AD at Wisconsin in May 1987, and was canned, or rather, "resigned by mutual agreement with the chancellor," in November 1989. He lives back in Fargo, North Dakota, now, where he works as an agent with the Lutheran Brotherhood, a financial services company with the religious backing of the Lutheran Church. He is happier now than during his two years in Madison, saying of his firing, "I was done a favor, although at the time, I didn't know it."

The problems in the athletic department weren't caused by him or Don Morton or anybody in their circle, he insists. "The problem wasn't the veer offense. No, no, no. And it wasn't Dick Schrock. Oh, no! They just tied the can to him. They blamed Dick for the seven-hundred-thousand-dollar accounting error, and I never understood that." The problem, says the former AD, is that you can't get anything done in the Wisconsin athletic department because of inertia, meddling by do-gooders, and that peculiar, high-minded combative-ness so entrenched in the university, city, and state. The direction the department is headed at any given moment, he says, "all depends on which of the five factions you're dealing with at the time." And they are? "The university administration, the faculty, the ticket-buying public, the W Club boosters, the student body, and the athletic board." He thinks for a moment. "That's six factions, actually, not to mention the coaches."

Sponberg was a convenient, and perhaps culpable, scapegoat, though it's hard to see what he could have done quickly at the school since, as he notes, "The first budget I inherited, we were already nearly one and a half million dollars in the red." He got out before anything turned really ugly, and his biggest concern toward the end was not for himself but for his good friend and fellow Lutheran from North Dakota State, Don Morton. "I used to tell people, 'This program killed Dave McClain and John Jardine,'" he says. "'And if you're not careful, you'll kill Don Morton, too.'"

Sponberg was pleased when, at least physically, Morton made it out in one piece.

BEFORE THE ATHLETIC BOARD'S FIRST MEETING OF THE YEAR, A GATHERING THAT will focus on the budget, Rick Aberman studies a letter that was sent to him by Kip Marvin, one of the administrative assistants to Pat Richter. The letter deals with Aberman's own little budget and is wonderfully bizarre in that its sole purpose is to courteously inform Aberman that the paltry one-percent raise he was promised in an earlier letter was a mistake.

"I am afraid I have made somewhat of an embarrassing blunder," Marvin begins, before explaining that Aberman cannot get the annual salary raise to $41,717.00 he was promised, because it is above the maximum pay range for his position as designated by the Un-classified Staff Compensation instructions, whatever they are. "The maximum of your range is what you are presently at: $41,304.00," Marvin continues. "Unfortunately, this is where your salary must remain. I should not have notified you that you were getting an increase. I am sorry if this causes you any inconvenience."

Aberman does a little figuring. His raise was to have been $413 annually, but since he gets only half pay, or $20,652, that would have been just a $206.50 raise. Since he pays about 30 percent in taxes, that figures out to a net yearly increase of $144.55. Broken down into twenty-six paychecks, that would be approximately $5.56 every two weeks. On a weekly basis his raise would have given him new purchasing power of $2.78 every seven days. He tries to think of something that costs $2.78. A six-pack of beer—domestic, of course. A small box of cereal. Shampoo. The cheapest socks imaginable. A quality bratwurst.

He'll just do without, he decides. Just pull the belt in another notch.

On his way into the meeting, Bill Brophy of the *Wisconsin State Journal* comments to Al Fish on the large claw prints that have been painted on the blacktop leading down the driveway and into the football department at Camp Randall. "Very nice Badger paws," he says. "Now we know what Bakken's been doing."

Fish says nothing, having other matters on his mind just now. Tami Holmquist has made her official report to the board that the athletic department can project a net savings of about $762,000 for the 1991–92 budget by having cut the five sports and capped the crew teams' budgets. Board member and physics professor Jerry Kulcinski, who was vehemently against the cuts last spring, stands up and proclaims that Holmquist's figures are wrong by more than $350,000.

"It's just not right to say we are saving $762,000 by cutting those sports," says Kulcinski, holding up his own figures. "We're saving between $300,000 and $500,000. That's enough. Why do we say we're saving so much more than we're actually saving?"

It's a good question, and one that might point to the desire of the department to put on a tough, results-oriented front for critics, or simply to the subtleties of creative accounting. Whatever, Fish comes into the lobby during a break and says to one of the reporters who is reading over Kulcinski's impenetrable numbers, "Let me see that." He studies the sheet, muttering all the while about "the rocket scientist" who created it. He calls Holmquist over and together they pore over the figures.

"This is creative lying," says Fish, finally. "What kind of rocket would he send up? A Scud." He looks proudly at Holmquist. "But we have our Patriot." He taps the blushing accountant on the back and reenters the meeting.

＊　　　＊　　　＊

DON MORTON HASN'T LEFT MADISON, AND THAT HAS MADE HIS DAILY LIFE strange indeed. He sits in his new home in a rolling subdivision and does very little at all. He has all the money given him by the athletic department in the buyout of his contract and he has his wife, Sue, and his two children, Stephanie—a student at Michigan State—and Josh—a senior at Madison Memorial High School—and he has his memories of eleven years as a head coach at various universities, but he has little else. He works from home as associate general agent with the Tollefson Insurance Agency of the Lutheran Brotherhood—part of Sponberg's group—but that is a fairly uneventful undertaking, and when he talks of the business it is usually without great enthusiasm.

The Mortons were going to move after he was fired, or rather, "reassigned to another position within the university," then bought out, but they didn't for the sole reason that seventeen-year-old Josh was set to be the starting quarterback at Memorial High, and moving somewhere and forcing him to start his football career over didn't seem fair. There had been enough athletic uprooting for one family already, they all decided, and so Don Morton is a hostage in a city he despises, a man under virtual house arrest of his own design. He doesn't go near campus, he doesn't frequent restaurants or malls where UW boosters might congregate, he doesn't get involved in the main business of this community, which is the business of the state university. His bitterness toward the University of Wisconsin, Donna Shalala, and the athletic department has dimmed some in the twenty-one months since he was axed, but it hasn't faded from sight.

"Ab Nicholas, after only my ninth Big Ten game, was calling for my scalp," says the forty-four-year-old Morton with disgust. It is Friday at dusk, and Don and Sue are driving in the family Cadillac to Beloit, where the Madison Memorial Spartans will soon be playing the Beloit High School Purple Knights. "Ab Nicholas is a typical, ill-informed, wealthy booster. I mean, here it was only my second season! They really think there that if you call the right plays on third down, everything will be fine, people will come back and fill the stadium." Morton pulls into the outside lane to pass a car with the license plate BADGR, and Sue says to the auto in mock derision, "Hey, you're going the wrong way. Your team's back there!"

Morton has lapsed into one of his silences, one of those abrupt moments of introspection that must have been disconcerting to at least some of his former coaches and players. A minute later, as though a gear has properly engaged, he is back on track. "That [1963] Rose Bowl was almost the worst thing that ever happened to Wisconsin," he says. "I have a little problem with a place when the highlight of your football history is a game you lost. In 1981 Wisconsin finished third in the conference, and that's the best it's done in twenty-nine years!"

The point, he states, is that he never got a chance to do anything at Wisconsin, because for once in its history the school acted fast and fired someone: him. Which was asinine. "I wouldn't do a thing different," he says of his own performance as coach. "Nothing. I just wouldn't have taken the job. It's funny, because Donna said to me, 'You just don't have very good press relations.' Well. And there you are, bleeding in the middle of sharks." He nods his head angrily. "They'll blame it on me for a long time to come."

Morton thinks of the people he worked with at UW, and the ones he feels stabbed him in the back. He doesn't read any local papers now, only the *Chicago Tribune* and the *Wall Street Journal.* And he doesn't listen to anything that has to do with UW football on radio or TV or from friends, unless it might be word that the team has failed in some way, which pleases him a lot. He thinks of Elroy Hirsch, the man who ostensibly hired him back in 1986.

"Elroy, he drinks," says Morton with something close to real venom. "Then he gets sentimental. He's a fun guy, but there's not a lot of depth there. I remember when Elroy and Otto Breitenbach came to Tulsa to interview me. They sat down and Elroy fell asleep on the couch. He dozed off a little bit, and Otto conducted the interview. But I remember when Elroy walked in the house, and it was a beautiful place with a pool in the back, and he looked at me and said, 'Why would you leave here?' "

Morton wonders the same thing now, since it seems likely his shot at big-time head-coaching is over; after all, who wants to hire a coach who was sent packing by a program as dismal as UW's? "There are not a lot of intellectual giants in coaching," Morton says, just spewing anger now. "I mean, how hard is it to coach? You have to have good players and teach them a system, but that's about it. Had Dave McClain taken Wisconsin about as far as it could go? Probably."

Morton guides the big car into a parking area near Beloit High

School, and he and Sue join up with Sue's parents, who have driven in from Michigan to visit. Josh Morton, who is described in the newspapers as being 6'1", 185 pounds, in the game programs as 6'0", 166 pounds, and is really 5'11", 162 pounds, has shown an uncanny knack for keeping his relatively small and slow team in games until he can find a way to beat the opponent. As one would expect of a coach's son, he has good mechanics as a thrower and the ability to read defenses quickly. He also has the motivation that comes from wanting to silence his father's critics. In a recent article in the *Wisconsin State Journal* the young Morton said, "I can remember the week before my dad was fired, sitting up until midnight every night waiting for him to come home, confused, worried, upset about what I'd seen on the news or read in the paper. I couldn't study, couldn't sleep, couldn't eat, couldn't concentrate on my football . . . nothing. I was a wreck. It was terrible—it was just terrible." Then, too, there were those times when he'd drop back to pass, get knocked down, and have an opponent hiss into his earhole, "Your dad sucks!"

The teams warm up, and Don Morton mostly watches Beloit, checking them out, the way a coach sizes up an opponent. At times he stares off into the deep purple sky, beyond the few hundred people in the enemy bleachers. "Twenty-five years from now I wonder if football will even exist," he says after a time. "It's not really supported at the high school level. It's expensive. And it's hard. It's a hard sport."

The game begins and Beloit takes an early 6–0 lead. Josh Morton connects on a few nice passes, but Memorial looks out of synch and rather, well, high schoolish. In the second quarter Memorial kicks a field goal and adds a touchdown on a long fumble return to take a 10–6 lead into halftime, and it seems they may be able to win this game simply by avoiding major mistakes.

The Purple Knights come out hungry in the second half, however, and score twice to move out to a 21–10 lead. Then it is late in the fourth quarter and Josh Morton is rolling. He hits an out pattern and then a nice crossing route to his tight end. He throws a TD pass to make the score 21–16, and promptly bootlegs around left end for a two-point conversion, making the score 21–18 with less than three minutes left. Don has been quiet the whole game and doesn't get worked up now, but he does say calmly, "Last week Memorial went eighty yards in forty seconds." Led, of course, by his son.

Memorial kicks off, holds Beloit on downs, and gets the ball back with 1:42 on the clock. Now the green-and-white-clad Memorial cheerleaders are going wild, and the parents and student rooters in the stands are waving their pompons and stamping their feet. A field goal will tie the game; a touchdown will win it. "I wonder why I used to think this was fun," says Sue, grim-faced with a mother's determination and fear. Don looks at the offense taking the field. "You know what I miss?" he says. "Working with black kids. I don't have any contact with black people now."

Josh completes a pass, then gets nowhere on the next two plays. On fourth and sixth, he completes another pass for the critical first down. Memorial is still far from paydirt, but the quarterback seems in control now, and the shrieking fans are hoping for a miracle, the kind they see on TV football highlight films all the time, the kind that make people forget that this is not a scripted performance, just a bunch of young kids trying to do a difficult thing.

Morton drops back and eludes one rusher. He sidesteps another, rolling toward the sideline, then scrambling back toward the center of the field, his skinny legs pumping as defenders swarm around him. He winds up and heaves a bomb to a receiver running a post route, and the ball seems to hang in the air forever. A Beloit defensive back intercepts it and falls to the field in joy. Beloit takes one snap and the clock runs out, and the game is over.

The Mortons walk slowly toward the parking lot with the rest of the people, through the grassy area where the players make their way toward the locker room. Josh comes off the field and approaches his parents. He has a towel stuck in through his face mask so that it covers his eyes. He lifts it every now and then as he talks quietly to his mom and dad, but he puts it back quickly because he is crying the hardest tears of a boy's life—those of a high school quarterback who has just lost a big game. Don Morton says little, though it is clear he understands his redheaded son's anguish and sends him silent support. Sue pats her boy on the back and watches him walk slowly off with his teammates to the bus. She hurts for Josh, though she is also very proud of him. "You don't want to say the wrong thing to him," she says. "But what are you supposed to say?"

Don Morton shrugs. On the way back to Madison he says firmly, "We will move as soon as Josh is out of high school."

26

WISCONSIN OPENS ITS FOOTBALL SEASON TODAY AGAINST WESTERN ILLINOIS, A
Division I-AA school with an enrollment of approximately thirty
thousand fewer students than UW, no historical rivalry with the
Badgers (indeed, the two schools have never played each other on
the gridiron), and a mediocre football team to boot. For Wisconsin
it's what is known in the business as "a bought W." Even though
Western Illinois is currently 1–0, its 42–3 victory last week against
Division II Washburn doesn't mean a whole lot. Wisconsin's season
opener was originally scheduled to be played at Kansas State, a
school that, while not a power, is at least a Division I foe, but Alvarez
ducked out of that contest as soon as he was named coach.

The only downside to a game like this is that if you lose, you not
only look bad, you look stupid. And as the student reporters for the
Daily Cardinal look on in cynical silence from their press box seats, it
appears UW is going to qualify for both those handles. Western Illinois takes the lead early in the second quarter with a 13-play, 77-yard
drive for a touchdown. The Leathernecks then capitalize on a center
snap that sails directly through the Wisconsin punter's hands, hits
him in the face mask, and bounces to a Western Illinois player; Western scores on the next play on a long pass over All-America cornerback
Troy Vincent, and suddenly the score is 13–0, patsies.

Tony Lowery does not look very sharp at quarterback for the Badgers, missing open receivers, even bouncing a pass to freshman wide receiver Lee DeRamus on one play. Still, UW claws back to just a 13–10 deficit at halftime, and then the 42,861 fans who have showed up for this atrocity get to do what they do best, which is party. Some middle-aged guy wearing a fraternity cap and a white tuxedo with the words YOU'VE SAID IT ALL embroidered on the back marries a formal-gowned woman at midfield, and then he and the bride and Bucky Badger and all the cheerleaders and most of the people in the stands dance a quick jig before everyone joins in a solemn rendition of "Varsity."

What this has to do with a football game is anybody's guess, but it seems to sober up the UW team. In the second half the squad finally acts like the Big Ten team it is and steps on the Leathernecks for a 31–13 victory. The Fifth Quarter festivities are fervent because of the win and the opening-day enthusiasm, but mostly just because, well, because this is Wisconsin. The newlyweds come back onto the field and lead the stands in a rollicking polka as the band finally plays the Budweiser song and the students go berserk.

The ecstasy trickles down to young Jason Maniecki, who played about a dozen plays on the defensive line and has found college life generally to his liking. "My brother was here on Wednesday," he says outside the locker room, "and he took my dirty clothes home and my mom sent all clean ones back." He beams. Already dressed, he looks as though he is being strangled by the skinny black tie around his thick neck; he cannot quite get the ends of his shirt collar to meet.

"It was fun!" he says of the game. "It was just like the coaches said it would be, just like in practice. But it's a lot faster than high school." And school itself? "School is school. A lot of reading, but everything is going great, putting itself into place."

The big young man rotates his neck inside its cloth prison. Then he smiles the smile of a little kid. "And there's no parents to tell you what to do!"

Upstairs above the locker room, in the foyer that looks out over the McClain indoor field, Barry Alvarez is even feeling chipper. He has just doubled his total number of victories as a head coach and that has made him magnanimous, even to the little people who nip at his ankles. Barry Baum has approached him warily and, buffered by the presence of two other writers, has carefully asked Alvarez how it was that Troy Vincent, UW's Jim Thorpe Award candidate as the best defense back in America, got beat on that long TD pass in the first half. Alvarez sees who it is in front of him and smiles like a grandfather confronting his mischievous but good-hearted nephew.

"Let me teach you a little something," he says to Baum. Then he takes a note pad and diagrams the scoring play for the reporter, showing how a linebacker actually should have stayed with the WIU receiver and that Vincent did not have coverage responsibility in the deep outside third, but only looked like he was getting beaten because he was closest to the play. Baum nods and takes all this in.

Earlier in the week he had been told by new *Daily Cardinal* writer Kareem Hardison, a former football player, that some of the players were still mad about the crap Baum wrote about the team. "Kareem said he was talking with linebacker Gary Casper and that Casper said that if he ever saw me, he'd knock me down," Baum had noted fatalistically a few days ago. "So it doesn't look good."

But now Alvarez has left for other business, and the writer tilts his head. Who cares about a linebacker and his petty grievances? Baum has just been talking civilly with the *coach*.

"That was really nice," he says in amazement.

NCAA EXECUTIVE DIRECTOR DICK SCHULTZ, A SLENDER, TIRED-LOOKING man with pale blue eyes, listens to Merritt Norvell as the athletic board member asks him, "What will the NCAA be in 2000?"

Schultz, who flies his own plane, is making one of his trademark whistle-stops at another of the 802 schools that hold membership in the National Collegiate Athletic Association. Among the small group he is addressing in this informal gathering in the National W Club room are Al Fish, Roger Formisano, Cheryl Marra, Jeff Sauer, Duane Kleven, Peter Tegen, and Jim Bakken. Schultz is a man under great stress, as he has been since he replaced the autocratic, conservative, and ultra-secretive Walter Byers as head of the organization in 1987.

The NCAA has always claimed that it is nothing more than a group of people serving its member organizations in any way those members see fit, but more and more the NCAA is perceived as a bureaucracy unto itself, manipulating athletic departments and athletes alike for TV and tournament revenue and the greater glory of the bureaucrats themselves. Schultz would like to humanize the

NCAA and sweeten its dark image while retaining control of the big-time sports programs that the NCAA needs to exist. It is a tough task, one that shows its toll in his hangdog face.

"Well," he begins. "Division I is where the problem lies, because some Division I basketball schools have athletic budgets at one million dollars, while some have budgets of twenty-five million. We've got apples, oranges, and grapefruit in the same basket." This, he says, means that something must be done in the next few years about revenue-sharing from NCAA TV income or else more and more schools will be running headlong into budget crunches such as Wisconsin's.

Schultz then adds that by the year 2000 he'd like to see athletes "be identical to the student body. I think we've brought them in and spoiled them, tutoring them and all that, athletic dorms. I want to see a simpler, more homogenized organization." He smiles wanly. "It all goes back to the level playing field theory. But don't get me started on that, because I don't know if it exists."

Norvell says, "What about a corporation running an athletic department?"

"From a management standpoint, universities can pretty much do what they want," says Schultz. "I don't see that happening, though."

Schultz sees from the looks on the dozen or so faces in front of him that people are beginning to tune him out, that he is just another naysayer, telling everyone what they can't do to solve their problems. But he wants them to know he appreciates their distress. "I have suggested to others that athletic departments be part of the university budgets just the way the chemistry departments are," he says. "So that a shortfall would be handled just like anything else in the university proper, or if there's a profit, the same thing." He looks at his group. This is a nice, reasonable idea, but he doesn't have to tell anyone here that it has about as much chance of happening as a badger sprouting wings. The universities don't want any more of a burden than they already have; if there's a shortfall in the athletic department, well then, make the football team win more games. That's the collegiate way.

"Virtually all university academic departments lose money," says Formisano. "But very few departments are held as accountable as the athletic department."

Schultz says nothing, but simply nods in agreement.

"We recently cut five sports," says Fish after a time. "More schools say they're going to do it. We had to do it because of our deficit. What do you think is going to happen around the nation?"

"Unfortunately, you're going to see more programs dropped," Schultz responds. "That's how it's going."

Outside Camp Randall on this fine Saturday morning vendors are selling T-shirts that say on the front What's the Difference Between a Cheesehead and a Dickhead? and on the back, The Illinois State Line. There is no love lost between Wisconsinites and Illinoisans, perhaps because of the Packers–Chicago Bears NFL rivalry, or perhaps the perception by the bordering states that the other is full of a) slow-witted farmhands, or b) urban terrorists on welfare.

Wisconsin doesn't take much to the neighboring state of Iowa, either, seeing in its rural dullness what Wisconsin might be if all its lakes were drained and every hill leveled and turned into a hog run. Even Rick Aberman marvels at the phenomenon that is Iowa. "The state is just below Minnesota," he says. "And they all talk with Southern accents. Iowa football coach Hayden Fry always talks about coming up to Wes-consin. You see people in yellow and black everywhere. Very strange."

Today's football game is with the Iowa football team that does not wear yellow and black, however; it is with scarlet-and-gold-clad weak sister and Big Eight member Iowa State. Still, it's a game that everybody says Wisconsin must win to prove that good times have returned under savior Barry.

In the press box Dick Schultz says hello to Shalala as she comes zipping by with State Attorney General Jim Doyle in tow. The game begins and Iowa State kicks a field goal to take a 3–0 lead. Then Tony Lowery leads the Badgers on a solid fifteen-play, 75-yard drive just before the half, capping it off with a 10-yard touchdown pass to UW tight end Mike Roan, for a 7–3 lead.

"Haven't seen a drive like that in seven years!" says Doyle excitedly to the NCAA chief as both look down on the gridiron. One thing that few people in the press box have noticed is the latest Al Fish revenue-producing coup: four training equipment carts on the Badger sidelines with big advertising boards on the sides. One cart proclaims that WOLX ALL OLDIES ALL THE TIME 94.9FM SUPPORTS WISCONSIN; another states that Fontana Sports does the same; another says Hardee's is behind UW; and the last says Famous Footwear backs the Badgers. The word *Wisconsin*, in all cases, is slightly larger than the sponsor's name. Fish knows when something is on the right side of the law.

Schultz actually likes Wisconsin, appreciates its charm and quirky good humor. He himself was a coach at the University of Iowa in baseball and basketball, and he remembers coming to Camp Randall years ago when the UW football team, as he says, "was in the depths of a losing streak. They beat Iowa that day, and with fifty-five seconds left, the fans poured onto the field. I mean, they *packed* the field. The game was called, and when they finally cleared the field, it was the strangest sight." He turns to his listener to make sure this is being appreciated. "There must have been two hundred shoes out there. People's shoes. They came off and nobody could bend down to pick them up."

Shalala zooms about during the halftime, a small radio around her waist, earphones in her ears, asking people, "What do you think the attendance is? Do you know?" For the record, it is 50,710—no sellout certainly, but not bad.

The game resumes and Wisconsin holds on to win, 7–6, deflecting a point-blank Iowa State field goal with fifteen seconds left in the contest, winning a game, as Vic Feuerherd will write for his paper, "it normally loses." Of course, Wisconsin normally loses most games, no matter what.

With a 2–0 team on its hands, the UW students feel such joy that the Fifth Quarter celebration takes on a particularly zesty tone. Aberman even decides to stay for the ritual, something he has not done in years. As the band plays "If You Want to Be a Badger," the students turn their backs in unison and give the finger to the adults on the other side. Then the band spins around, roars into "Tequila," and the thousands of students turn and make little hand claps in unison and then "surf" on top of their bleacher seats.

"This is amazing to me," says Aberman in awe, as the band leads the stadium through faster and faster verses of the "Chicken Dance," as stupid a song as has ever been foisted on an audience. "Look at the students! I mean, did they see a video at registration? How do they know what to do?"

The students wave their hands in the air, flap their wings, and shake their tailfeathers at hyper speed, until it looks as though the section has suffered a direct hit of nerve gas. The whole affair is a shameless, primitive ritual that seems to speak directly to some need within the revelers. There was a time a few years back when the band was ordered to stop playing the Bud song at games, because engineers were worried that the seismic forces of seventy-five thousand people all stomping in unison could crumble the stadium. Now, with the stands a third empty, there is less concern; still, a viewer like Rick Aberman is most impressed with the collective energy of this display.

"I've always said they should let the students in for free," he declares on the way out.

In the locker room, amidst the joy, young Jay Macias is not overwhelmed. He has not played in a college football game yet, but he thinks he should have. "Jeez, Tony just wasn't seeing things today," he says, shaking his head in frustration. "I thought for a minute they were going to me. But they didn't." He raises his eyebrows in a what's-happening-here? expression. "Man, I can see so many openings, so many things out there."

Jason Maniecki is not thrilled by the events of today, either; he didn't play a down, and he's twitching with unused energy.

"We had that four-man front," he snarls testily. "Just two tackles and two ends. I hope we get rid of that shit."

IN AN INTEROFFICE MEMO PAT RICHTER HAS ANNOUNCED TO HIS STAFF THAT Vince Sweeney, the former head of the licensing program for the university, will be taking over Jim Bakken's post as the director of marketing and promotions for the athletic department.

Bakken will be kicked sideways into the newly created post of director of community affairs. And what is that? "One of Jim's primary objectives will be to develop and implement a statewide Badger support network that is available to assist us in broadening our base of fan interest in athletic and special events," Richter writes. "In addition, Jim will be responsible for overseeing, coordinating, and improving upon revenue-generating activities already in place." If that isn't clear enough, Bakken also "will now pick up all golf . . . activities . . ." That part, at least, is understandable.

So great has been the in-house water-cooler questioning of just what it is that Bakken does for his paycheck that Rick Aberman finally decided he would stop all the rumors in the only decent way and simply ask Bakken himself. Aberman stopped by Bakken's office and after a bit of small talk, simply asked, "Jim, what do you do here?" Bakken, remarkably, was overjoyed at the question. Nobody had ever asked him that, he said. He proceeded to describe his responsibilities in detail. Aberman thanked him and walked away still uncertain of what Bakken's precise role was, but convinced, as Richter had noted in detail in his memo, that Bakken did indeed do *something*.

It's hot tonight, swelteringly hot, and Aberman strolls across campus to the Student Union on the south shore of Lake Mendota. He orders a sixteen-ounce Labatt's and a box of popcorn at the bar and takes a seat at the Rathskeller, near the terrace that looks out over the dark water. At the table next to him is former student senate president Mike Verveer and his friends Joel Zwiefelhoffer, still an undergraduate and current senator, and graduate law student Brian Finley. Verveer graduated last May and is currently doing charity work for the Jesuit Volunteer Corps in Milwaukee, helping unemployed poor people find jobs. At the commencement ceremony last spring Verveer was one of only two students that Shalala hugged after they received their diplomas. The other was Dave Gassman—the senator whose tires were slashed over his sports vote.

Verveer and Aberman have met before, and they strike up a conversation now.

"Did you see a lot of athletes whose sports were cut?" Verveer asks.

"Some, not too many," says Aberman. "Not as many as people suspect."

"A lot of those kids were really hurting," continues Verveer. "You must have a really hard job."

Aberman shrugs. "Kids are pretty flexible."

He looks at Verveer's red-and-white-striped Wisconsin rugby shirt and tells the young man he must be a supporter of the sports teams.

Verveer looks at his shirt. "I bought it freshman year," he says. "Why? Because I was a freshman."

Verveer is in town today to attend the football game, something he hasn't done in a while.

"Why did you quit going to games?" Aberman asks.

"Because they weren't any fun, and because of the Gestapo."

It is well known that in the early- and mid-eighties, drinking, partying, and rowdy behavior had gotten so out of hand at Camp Randall that the authorities had to do something to restore order. Incidents of body-passing (passing a person hand-over-hand from the bottom of the bleachers to the top), bottle-throwing, and the dumping of objects—including entire bleacher benches—over the top of the stadium had increased to the point that it was just a matter of time before someone was severely injured or killed during the pranks. There were times when the football game on the field was the least entertaining and least watched part of the action inside the stadium.

The Indiana game in 1986, attended by almost 79,000 people, put matters over the top, with 13 fans being arrested and 177 being ejected from Camp Randall for illegal behavior. Something had to be done. Professor Donald Peterson, the chairman of the university's crowd control committee, wrote a paper advocating increased use of police "patdowns," and crowd-scanning video cameras, as well as basic no-nonsense enforcement of all pertinent laws. "We will pull no punches," Peterson told the press. "If there are some who are guilty, we'll make examples of them."

Sure enough, the police got tough at exactly the same time the UW football program was going down the tubes, and the two events combined to create the now infamous half-empty stadium dilemma—bad teams, no fun, no fans, no revenue.

"I'll tell you why I quit going to games," interjects Finley. "It's because in 1986 I was arrested in the stands, put in handcuffs, and taken to a mobile trailer outside the stadium and charged with—this is what it said—'Inciting the crowd with a beach ball.' What happened was I grabbed a Miller Beer ball as it came by, and I palmed it and was waving it around. The football team was getting killed, like 30–0, and all of a sudden these fans tackled me, trying to get the ball, and it just flew away. Then two sheriff's deputies came and grabbed me, and the people grabbed me back, and the cops handcuffed me. Everybody started chanting, 'Use your gun! Use your gun!' So the cops lead me out, they write up the ticket, and I didn't go back to a game until 1990."

"Why then?" asks Aberman, fascinated.

"I guess because of Alvarez coming," says Finley, thinking. "And I'm a Big Brother, have been for six years, and I started taking my Little Brother, a fourteen-year-old kid, to the games."

The young men leave and Aberman is left alone at his table, sipping his beer and studying the students around him. He looks down at the old wooden table and examines the carved initials and messages gouged into the surface. He laughs out loud when he sees the large letters *MULA* just where he had set his popcorn bowl.

"MULA," he says. "It stands for Madison Union Labor Association. We started that, what, fifteen years ago?" He laughs again, dusting kernels out of the grooves.

"The first thing we did was strike," he says, finishing his beer. "How can you have a labor association and not strike?"

LAURIE IRWIN IS KNOWN AROUND THE ATHLETIC DEPARTMENT AS BUCKY'S Mom. That's because in her role as promotion coordinator for women's sports she is responsible not only for the smooth functioning of the cheerleader and pompon squads, but also for the day-to-day handling of the proud school mascot itself, Buckingham U. Badger. There are a number of Bucky outfits, and Irwin has to make sure they are always accounted for and do not fall into the hands of desecrators or pranksters or rival schools' mascots. She also oversees five students who play Bucky on a rotating basis, including one woman, a fairly new development.

"Bucky's head used to be fiberglass and mounted on shoulder pads," says Irwin from behind the desk in her small office. "It was too big for girls, so Chancellor Shalala bought us a foam one that's lighter, at her own expense."

The basic criteria for being a Bucky, says Irwin, are that you have to be at least five feet eight inches, you have to like people, you have to be able to handle having your head enclosed in a small space, you have to be able to work long stretches of time without talking, you can't trample small children, and you have to respond with great enthusiasm to the action around you.

"I've got one here," she says, dumping a huge velveteen head with a large black nose onto the floor. "People love Bucky," she continues, tilting the head so that the overhead light illuminates what looks like a nasty, dark place where one would not want to put one's own cranium. "Little kids come right up and say, 'I love you' to Bucky. And Bucky is in great demand—all the public schools want Bucky to come by. He goes to fund-raisers, parades, athletic events, dinners, and sometimes we'll charge forty dollars an hour. He doesn't endorse things, but he's seen as a state symbol. He goes to the Cow Chip Parade in Prairie du Sac, places like that, any place we think it's good for us."

Sometimes, Irwin admits, things can get a little out of hand with the mascot. "Things do go wrong," she says. "A kid was at President Shaw's, and the kid had been drinking; he threw up and passed out inside the Bucky. And another Bucky was on the ice at the Coliseum and he crashed into the glass and knocked himself out. We hauled him off. Another head got stolen and we found it on Abraham Lincoln's lap in front of Bascom Hall. Probably the worst thing that happened was at the Fieldhouse when a drunk woman grabbed a Bucky through his costume by the balls. She was very drunk. The guy could barely make it down the steps after that."

As far as the cheerleaders and pompon gang goes, well, Irwin has her doubts about the need for those groups. "We have eight male cheerleaders, eight female cheerleaders, eighteen pompon girls, and a total of thirty-nine people involved," says Irwin. "Men see these pretty young women in short skirts, and they think they can do anything. They put their hands under the skirts; they're almost always drunk. And I've had girls who didn't know how to handle being in compromising positions, like when they're in the stands and a guy says, 'Sit on my lap and I'll give you a hundred dollars.'

"This is my fourth year being in charge, and before that the squads just did whatever they wanted," Irwin says. She sighs deeply and opens a folded piece of paper on her desk. "It's hard to know exactly what they are supposed to do. I mean, listen to this letter."

The missive is addressed to Pat Richter and it comes from a married female UW fan from Arena, Wisconsin. It says, in part:

> In nearly every routine, the pompon women are performing some sexually explicit, "come-on" moves, such as pelvic bumps, hip grinds, holding their arms out and swaying their breasts, then folding their arms over their chests as if in humility. What these movements are quite clearly stat-

ing is sexual in nature, some movements a distinct part of the sex act. Even when they stand at rest between numbers, they must have one hip pointed out and one leg placed in a certain pose as if they're goddesses . . . it is appalling that some men can be seen only getting the binoculars or video recorder out when the pompon women perform . . . JUST WHAT ARE WE DOING HERE?

Irwin refolds the letter. "I'd love to try a game without them," she says. "I really would. People say it's part of the tradition to have them. What tradition? Girls dancing to music in little skirts?"

27

THE RACE WAS THE ULTIMATE TEST OF WILLS. THE UNIVERSITY OF WISCONsin's Stephanie Herbst battled with the pack for the first ten laps, and then by the 6,000-meter mark she took the lead, narrowly, just a few steps ahead of two other runners and twenty-one-year-old Kathy Ormsby, a junior from North Carolina State who six weeks earlier had set the U.S. collegiate women's record at this distance, 10,000 meters.

Herbst was a twenty-year-old sophomore who had won the 1985 Big Ten cross-country championship the previous fall and also had won the NCAA indoor 3,000-meter crown three months before this race. Now in June she was moving toward her biggest moment ever at the 1986 NCAA championships at Indiana University, and her mind was focused like, she would think later, a deranged person's.

Fighting her own raging demons, Herbst was unaware of the psychic meltdown occurring just in back of her. That was where Ormsby, the valedictorian of her high school class, a pre-med major and dean's list student at N.C. State and the favorite in this race, was short-circuiting. At the far turn, instead of following Herbst around the curve, Ormsby ran straight ahead and off the track, ducking to go underneath a railing that bordered the oval. As she ducked, the skinny, 5'8", 108-pound runner almost bumped into UW coach Peter Tegen.

"I thought she was running directly toward me," Tegen said later. "I thought she may have confused me for her coach; I was wearing red and white, the same colors as N.C. State. There were eight and a half laps to go. I know that because I was supposed to give a signal to Stephanie Herbst then. I missed giving it because I was watching Ormsby."

He couldn't watch her for long, however, because Ormsby quickly ran beyond the stands and disappeared. Out of sight of everyone now, she ran across a softball diamond, climbed over a seven-foot fence, and ran down a Bloomington street to a bridge over the White River from which she threw herself headlong into the void. Tegen would remember his last glimpse of Ormsby as she left the world of high-pressure intercollegiate distance running behind. "It was eerie," he told *Sports Illustrated*. "Her eyes were focused straight ahead. She didn't look left or right."

She didn't because the pain and pressure and struggle to do everything perfectly had suddenly become too much, and her only goal now was to kill herself, to end the torment. A well-liked young woman, Ormsby was described by her physics professor at N.C. State as being "sweet, courteous, diligent, sensible . . . the model student-athlete." She botched her attempt at self-destruction, however, falling thirty-five feet before landing on soggy turf near the river's edge, breaking a rib, puncturing a lung, and fracturing vertebrae in her spine. She survived, but the spinal injury left her paralyzed from the waist down.

Oblivious to the fact that her chief competitor was no longer on the track, Herbst opened a hundred-meter lead on her nearest follower and won the race in an NCAA-record time of 32:32:75. She didn't laugh or jump for joy when it was over; she smiled slightly and then went about her business. She didn't know what had happened to Ormsby until Tegen told her later, and the news, when she heard it, didn't shock her; she described Ormsby's attempted suicide to one writer as "a typical situation," to another as "not really so unusual." She was, in fact, peeved at reporters who tried to get her thoughts on the incident as she prepared the next day for her 5,000-meter race. "I was appalled that I had to deal with this thing now," she said. Couldn't people figure it out, anyway? Kathy Ormsby had just broken down. Like you pull a hamstring. A casualty of the sport. And couldn't people see that there but for the grace of God went Stephanie Herbst herself?

Herbst smiles now, the way she seldom did back then. She is twenty-five and a marketing representative for IBM in Milwaukee, working out of a fourteenth-floor office in the company building on Wisconsin Avenue when she is not on the road, dealing with clients. She remembers those old UW days, not so very distant days, actually, with varying degrees of horror and fascination and regret. She was not completely sane then, she realizes, but she was a fearsome competitor, and she was doing what she felt she had to do. She was more like Kathy Ormsby than anybody knew.

"My big fault," she says, lowering her huge, deep brown eyes to think about this, "was that I was too intense. I've noticed that even here at IBM, that I'm pretty intense. I drove myself until I *hated* the sport. The intensity had driven me up a wall. I was living and dying for the run."

Intense, and variations of the word, pop into Herbst's description of her UW days so frequently that one wonders if she ever relaxed. Back then she ran fifteen miles a day, seven days a week, and if there was something she could do to get thinner or run faster, she'd do it. "If there were a drug that could have made me go faster, of course I would have taken it," she says, no longer smiling. "It's like an alcoholic who needs to drink; the consequences of losing were so severe. I never took steroids, but it wasn't that I *wouldn't* take them, it was just that I didn't think they'd work for me."

At times goaded, at times delicately encouraged, but always inspired onward by Tegen, Herbst ran with a group of female UW athletes who would carry their school to the Big Ten and national cross-country championship two years in a row. Some of the runners were stable young women, but others, such as Herbst, were lost in a world where exercise, thinness, competitiveness, self-doubt, and stress coalesced to form a dark hole from which suicide could look like a viable way out.

Herbst had already written a short story entitled "All Alone" for her sophomore English class at UW. In the story, a boy who is a great runner wins a big race, receives a gold medal, and then instead of returning to his waiting family, kills himself. "That was even before I won any big events," says Herbst, who subconsciously was dealing with her own problems, giving them symbolic form. "Somebody told me later that you always give out warning signals before suicide, and this could have been my warning. I made the runner a boy, to keep my distance, I guess. My teacher picked up on it, though. She said to me, '*You're* a distance runner. Are you unhappy?' I said no. I sent the story to my dad, and he never said anything to me about it."

Herbst looks up. There is something in the insensitivity or fearfulness or blindness her father displayed by not responding to her fiction that still bothers her. Orphaned at age two when her parents were killed in a plane crash, Herbst and her younger sister were raised by their father's sister and her husband in Chaska, Minnesota. Stephanie's original last name was Boll; she wears her real mother's engagement and wedding rings on her right hand. "I'd be at home from school and my parents would order pizza, and I'd ask for an individual pizza with no cheese, no meat, no topping at all," she says coldly. "And they'd get so upset. 'Why are you doing this!' They could not understand. I mean I was *splurging*—I was eating grain."

For weeks on end Herbst would eat nothing but lettuce with a few chopped vegetables and maybe a little vinegar. No breakfast at all. Maybe a crouton or two occasionally on the salad, but nothing else. Water to drink. She would put raw carrots out on her desk at night to nibble on, but she wouldn't eat them because she might gain weight. "It made me happy," she explains. "It felt good: I'm getting lighter and my competition is getting heavier."

She stands five feet seven inches tall, and in time she was down to ninety-five pounds. Kathy Ormsby had nothing on Herbst in the weight department. Herbst was also a very good student; she would graduate in 1988 with a double major in product management and marketing and administrative management. She looks now at the current Big Ten women's sports calendar, the one that shows her sepulchral form in the midst of twenty or so cross-country racers. "If I was looking at this picture back then, my first thought would be, 'Yeah, I can beat these girls. They're too heavy, they're wearing gloves.' Sure it was cold out, but so what? They're not tough."

She studies the photo longer and then remarks, "I'm very thin, but I don't look that intense. If I could have been thinner than that, I would have. But your body fights it."

She did all this, she says, simply because she wanted to win, and because she wanted "someone to believe in me." That person, to a large extent, became Peter Tegen, whose every word and gesture she clung to like a timid child clinging to the hand of its mother. She loved Tegen for his assistance and enthusiasm. "Peter is a phenomenal coach," she says. "Very focused, very intense. I really wanted to please him. I didn't have a lot of confidence at the beginning, but then Peter encouraged me and told me, 'You can do better.' I got down to under eight percent body fat, and I can't tell you the intensity I had. I thought about winning all the time. If I could put in an extra two miles, I would. Peter was a little concerned about my weight, but he likes lean runners."

She thinks for a moment, looking out the window of her office above Lake Michigan. "I don't know what you know about high-intensity distance races," says Herbst, who was a four-time state cross-country champion in high school in Minnesota. "But it can be sleeting, slush inside your shoes, and you don't care. You're running and you have no bladder control, no bowel control, you're going to the bathroom in your pants. You start at this wide line with all the other runners and then there's this very narrow gate maybe four hundred feet ahead, and it's very intense. It's so easy to give up. But the winners don't even know it's sleeting."

And UW had its share of winners who were close to mental detonation. "One of my teammates, Laurie Walters, was very intense," says Herbst. "She eventually lost it. It started slowly, she just began doing strange things, had these weird quirks. She had to have on just the right shoe at the right time, had to wear certain jeans at a certain time; she took all the shampoo from the showers when we would just arrive for five days in a motel room. She even took the shampoo out of the wall dispensers. I had quirks, too. If I saw colors, I had to pick blue or gold right away, because they were winning colors. I had to think about winning every minute.

"And then there was Katie Ishmael, who was really intense. Katie got hit by a car while on a run, and instead of going to the hospital, she finished her run. We were preparing to break the national record in the four-times-one-mile relay coming up in Eugene, Oregon—Katie, Kelly McKillen, Kathy Branta, and me—but none of us were that close to Katie. Nobody went to see her when she was in the hospital, we didn't send her anything. She never really came back after that. She couldn't practice at our level, and she lost heart. Peter knew she could beat other people, but she couldn't beat her teammates. We never ran the relay, either. Could we have broken the record? Oh, yes."

Herbst looks to see if any of this sounds reasonable. Engaged to be married, she has already decided that if she has children, they will not be distance runners. "Practices were part of the problem," she continues, "because they were so competitive. You tried to please Peter all the time, so you had to beat your own teammates all the time, you couldn't be a friend. We drove each other nuts. Peter is such a wonderful, understanding man. I don't know how he dealt with all us girls."

Herbst thinks that Tegen was relieved when Suzy Favor came along, seemingly without debilitating obsessions. "Suzy was intense, but only about the race," she says. "She could lose at practice and not let it bother her."

The psychic break for Herbst came at the 1986 NCAA Indoor National Championship, after she won the 3,000 meters and felt so devoid of joy that she almost panicked. "I got off the track and I had this realization that this is all for nothing. There was nobody there for me—no family, no friends, nobody. The only people who had come were Peter and Katie Ishmael, and I'd have rather been by myself than with her. Nobody patted me on the back. It was scary. I didn't date, had no friends, no boyfriend. I never had a period, my hormones were all screwed up, dark hair would start growing above my lip. I'm wondering if I have any calcium, if I'll be able to have babies. The newspaper has a photo of me crossing the finish line, and I have an expression like, 'God forbid, this is all we do this for?' I wanted to quit right then, but I couldn't get out of the loop."

What she did was to see Rick Aberman. She sat and told him her story, why she didn't want to run anymore. She ultimately did sit out for a year, and during that time she got an unlisted phone number to keep people from trying to persuade her to run again. "I went to an awards dinner with Paula Bonner, who was then the women's AD, and she was so sweet," says Herbst. "She started crying and said, 'Why did this happen? Is there something we could have done better?' And the truth was, they were great. I loved the athletic department. People were there to help."

But she didn't trust people. "Everybody said I was crazy for quitting when I was doing so well, but I needed to find peace of mind. Did Rick help me? Not really, because I only went to him a couple of times. He was in his listening phase, but I knew he was a runner, so I thought he'd probably try to get me to stop running, just so I wouldn't do well. I was so paranoid. And the irony is, if he hadn't been a runner, he couldn't have related to me so well."

She falls silent for a moment. "I should have continued with him," she says. "I know I was close to the edge, and I could have gone over."

She takes a break to get lunch, riding the elevator down to the street and stopping at a sandwich shop around the corner. She orders a turkey sandwich, no cheese, no mayonnaise, no butter, no mustard, and a Diet Coke. She looks athletically lean at 125 pounds, and she still runs often, though never competitively. But still, she says, "I think I'll feel better about myself if I lose five pounds."

And what of the skewed eating habits of her and her group? Was that simply a manifestation of deep underlying emotional problems?

"I don't know," says Herbst, sipping from her soft drink. "Did we all have eating disorders? The thing is, there was a purpose to the way we ate. We were reducing our calorie intake to be intense runners. It was a great feeling to be standing on the starting line thinking, 'I'm thinner than her.' "

She finishes the sandwich half and looks out the window at the noontime pedestrians moving up and down the street. "When you're thin you feel very strong," she says. "Your body is incredibly efficient. You have a bowel movement very fast after eating anything. You have no body fat, so you're cold all the time. Especially in the winter. When I went to bed, I'd wear sweatpants and socks because I was so cold, even when other people thought the dorm was hot. And, of course, you have no periods. For nine years, all through high school and college, I had maybe one."

She eats most of the other sandwich half, and then it's time to get back to work. She is an attractive woman, gentle and shy and well dressed (she always wore makeup in races—eye shadow, eye liner, lipstick), and no one would guess from her demeanor that she was once an assassin on the track. Or that she was as confused as a person could be. The only people who could have known for sure were her teammates and her coach.

"So much is going on in your mind that you need somebody to take care of the logistics of being a runner," she says, waiting for the elevator in her building. "I needed Peter. He's a good person. He's a little man, who has this march to him, this glow in his eye."

She looks up. The elevator is almost here.

"I think Peter was the best coach in the nation."

*   *   *

RICK ABERMAN WENT WITH THE MEN'S CROSS-COUNTRY TEAM TO A LARGE MEET last weekend at the University of Minnesota. While in Minneapolis he went to the hospital to be with his brother David for the birth of David's third child, a daughter. The event impressed Rick, who more and more feels the desire to have his own link to the future, to create his own genetic legacy. "It was great," he says. "I'm not a father, but it was something. It just cuts through all the crap."

The meet itself was a testy affair. Aberman watched as much of it as he could, as the runners from about thirty teams raced over the still-green fairway at the school's golf course. The University of Wisconsin's head coach, Martin Smith, came up to Aberman as the race was ending and said, "Did you see the fight?" Aberman had not, but apparently one of the UW assistant coaches had. Two runners from different schools had been elbowing for position, when one of them suddenly pushed the other. The runner who had been pushed recovered and threw a punch at the other runner. They both finished the race, but it still wasn't clear what punishment would be meted out by the race officials or to whom.

"These guys were cruising, doing four-twenty miles and fighting," marvels Aberman. "You just wouldn't expect skinny guys to do that."

Back on campus, Aberman learns that there has been some trouble on the football team. Two players, former starting running back (recently demoted to fourth string) Robert Williams and injured wide receiver Lionell Crawford, were arrested for shoplifting at a department store. With them at the mall, but uninvolved in the crime, was Tony Lowery. All three of the players have been having tough times.

Lowery had injured his right thumb in the Badgers' loss to Ohio State, a game that dropped UW from the heady ranks of the undefeated to a tie for last place in the Big Ten. At 3–0 the Badgers had even garnered a couple of random votes in national polls as the best team in the country. But at 3–1, with wins over teams that were little more than crash-test dummies and a loss to a mediocre Buckeye team, the Badgers aren't fooling anybody. Lowery has been erratic at best, and his recent thumb injury, though not serious, gives Alvarez the perfect excuse to bench the quarterback. Lowery missed one session with Aberman, but he left a note under the psychologist's door, asking to schedule another office visit.

AL FISH BLITHELY STUDIES A COPY OF AN ARTICLE FROM *INCENTIVE* MAGAZINE, given him by one of the marketing consultants for the athletic department. The article is entitled, "How Lousy Teams Fill the Seats." The world is Al Fish's cow, and he has a dairy farmer's ability to milk it.

"The signs on those new athletic carts cost four or five thousand dollars apiece and the sponsors bought each one," he says proudly. "That's for three years. After that we extract more cash or take the ads off."

There is another bit of business on his desk. It is a thirty-page proposal done by a company called Stall-Tactics, a group that specializes in advertising in rest rooms. At the beginning and end of the company's logo are the symbols for men and women that identify the sex on public rest room doors. "The deal here is that advertisers will buy panels that go above the urinals and on the walls of the toilet stalls in the stadium and Fieldhouse," notes Fish, looking over the top of his glasses. "You figure the reader value for women is smaller, generally, but then they probably read more copy." Urinal copy, he explains, would have greater reader turnover but less intense scrutiny. None of it, of course, would have quite the effect that Don Morton produced a while back when he placed small figurines of Iowa football players in the locker room urinals for his players to pee on during game week. But no one has offered Fish such a campaign yet.

"We stand to get twenty thousand to thirty thousand dollars a year from this project," Fish continues. "Will we do it? Probably. But we haven't fully flushed it out yet. I put Mike Greene on the case because, as they say, shit runs downhill. Let me put it this way: We haven't zipped this one up yet."

Fish leans back in his chair and reflects on the new advertising basketball scoreboard that is being installed over center court in the Fieldhouse. "We don't actually own that," he says. "Dactronics owns it, and they simply pay us a royalty for making the space available. I believe *royalty* is the right word, legally speaking. Ohio State ran into its problems because it didn't set its scoreboard deal up right. We will tell the IRS that we don't own our scoreboard—which we don't—and therefore we are exempt from UBIT, the unrelated business income tax." Again, Fish looks over his glasses, innocently. "It's worth a try."

ON FRIDAY EVENING BEFORE THE HOME GAME AGAINST THE UNIVERSITY OF Iowa, members and coaches of the UW football team take buses to the Inn-Towner Motel and check in. On Thursday, Alvarez had said privately of freshman quarterback Jay Macias, "In two days he goes from being redshirted to, well, being a major factor. He's really unflappable. The press has been hounding me to tell them what I'm doing at quarterback, but I don't see any reason to help Iowa prepare. Nobody knows Jay is starting."

Indeed, after last week's game Alvarez had said, "Tony Lowery is our quarterback. He is going to be our quarterback." And on his Sunday TV show he told viewers, "We're not going to throw [Macias] in there." But Macias knows now he is starting, even if the press doesn't, and he sits in the lobby of the motel, looking the way Alvarez described him, unflappable.

"I'm hardly ever nervous," he says. "People telling me to relax—that's what makes me nervous." He laughs at that, adding that his dad had seen him in a brief film clip on CNN, from when he got in against Ohio State and threw two touchdown passes in the fourth quarter of the 36–16 loss, in front of ninety-four thousand Ohio State fans. The highlight made his dad very proud. Things have just been going very well for Macias, overall. The people in Wisconsin are so nice that it's almost disorienting to him.

"They go out of their way to help you," he says. "Strangers come up to me and just start talking. In L.A. your first thought is to protect yourself; here it's to shake hands." He slumps down comfortably on the couch, his legs clad in red pants, his hands stuck in the pockets of his red football-issue windbreaker. "I'm not homesick at all," he smiles. "I'm not going back until Christmas."

An assistant coach approaches.

"Let's go, Jay," he says. "Time to get on the bus."

Macias leaves with the rest of the squad to see Joe Pesci in a movie called *The Super*. It's so new that nobody knows yet that it is a bomb.

*   *   *

RICK ABERMAN HAS A FULL LOAD TODAY: AN ATHLETE WITH AN ALCOHOL problem; one with an eating disorder; a third who was a victim of date rape. When he is done with his consultations, he thinks about his sessions a few years ago with Stephanie Herbst.

"Poor Stephanie was under a lot of stress," he says. "She was so focused, but she also was defending against other things in her life. She was burning out. Her grandmother, her real mother's mother, was dying, and Stef was going home each weekend to see her. Her father wanted her to keep running, but she had won the national title and she had nothing left. And Peter still wanted her for championship races. She was terribly lonely. She idolized Peter."

Aberman thinks about some of his other clients. His main purpose, he often explains, is to let the athletes know that they are *not* going crazy when they think they *are*. He speaks to them at times about the paradox of the double bind: occasions when there are two choices that can be made, and this one's incorrect, and so is that one. But a choice must be made, and an athlete particularly needs someone to hold his hand at that moment, to reassure him and let him know that his dilemma is real and this duress is natural, proper, and understandable.

Aberman sees some of the double-bind conflict at work in the athletic department itself, as Richter, Fish, and the new bean counters try to make workers more efficient and business-oriented, and ultimately the whole department more impersonal and machinelike. Fish's goal, Aberman feels, is to make workers easily replaceable, much as they are in governmental bureaucracies and large corporations, where only the system is king. More and more athletic department employees are coming to Aberman and saying their response to the new whip-cracking is simply to throw up their hands and say, "I don't care." And yet, as Aberman says, "We're only here because we *do* care. But the system won't let us, which drives us nuts. The double bind. 'I don't care' is a creative solution to a nuts situation. And it's very liberating, but, as you might guess, it's not very productive."

He considers the plight of Tony Lowery, who has already run into the insecurity problem as a starting quarterback that Aberman thought he might. "I feel sorry for Tony," says the psychologist. "This stuff happened sooner than I thought it would."

28

MIKE GREENE IS A DUTIFUL FOOT SOLDIER. HE HAS FOLLOWED THROUGH ON Al Fish's orders and has spent part of a day making notes while wandering the recesses of UW's two large sports facilities. His report to his superior:

Enclosed is the information you requested on the Camp Randall Stadium and the UW Fieldhouse.

The breakdown of restrooms used by patrons in the Stadium:

—20 Men's Restrooms   —18 Women's Restrooms
—160 urinals   —144 total stalls
—20 troughs
—93 stalls

Fieldhouse:

—1 Men's Restroom   —1 Women's Restroom
—31 urinals   —29 stalls
—8 stalls

In 1990–91 the stadium held 14 total events and the Fieldhouse hosted 68 events.

If you need any other information please contact me.

Sincerely, Mike Greene

*   *   *

THERE IS A GREAT DEAL OF ACTIVITY OUTSIDE CAMP RANDALL STADIUM TODAY, as an honest-to-God huge crowd streams toward the arena for this clash between 3–1 Wisconsin and 3–1 Iowa. No matter that over twenty thousand Iowa fans have driven in from the cornfields to the west, this is reminiscent of the good old days in Madison.

Abortion protesters work the sidewalks in front of the stadiums, as do T-shirt vendors hawking a new work of art that reads AFTER FURTHER REVIEW—THE BEARS STILL SUCK. A Wisconsin & Calumet passenger train rumbles slowly up the tracks that run directly in front of Camp Randall, and happy fans from Milton and Edgerton and Stoughton clamber off, looking like boosters riding in from a half-century ago.

Up in the press box there is also unusual enthusiasm. Elroy Hirsch moves through the long room, greeting everyone, getting everybody fired up.

Steve Yoder watches with bored bemusement as Crazylegs slaps backs. "Watch Elroy now," he says quietly. "He's going to do a coin trick for those kids." Sure enough, Hirsch approaches two young boys and gets them to laugh as he makes first a dime disappear and then two quarters, finding the coins in the boys' ears.

Donna Shalala bounces through the room, glancing out at the near-capacity crowd of 75,053, the largest home crowd in five years. She turns to a journalist who is writing a book about the athletic department. "You should end it right here," she proclaims proudly. "We've done it. We've filled the stadium!"

But that is slim compensation for the terrible display soon made by the Badger football team, which stumbles and bumbles about before losing, 10–6, on a last-minute, fourth-down touchdown pass by Iowa quarterback Matt Rodgers. Young Jay Macias looks as bad and as overwhelmed as a quarterback could in a college game, completing just 5 of 16 pass attempts for a paltry 22 yards and no points. The only score for the Badgers comes on an interception return for a TD by cornerback Troy Vincent; the extra point is blocked. For those Badger fans looking for further humiliation, there is this fact: Iowa's game-winning pass reception was made by wide receiver Mike Saunders, a Wisconsin boy from nearby Milton. Another blue chipper gone astray.

Alvarez is livid in the postgame press conference, snapping, "I think you see now why I didn't want to throw a freshman [quarterback] out there. We're playing like a jayvee team!"

Of course, he wanted the freshman out there more than he wanted Lowery, his "starter" whose sprained thumb was not so damaged that he couldn't have played. After a game like this, when the offense totaled just 82 net yards and the potential winning touchdown run was called back on a needless holding penalty, a coach can be forgiven for being upset. But when a member of the press asks Alvarez about something that apparently went wrong on the *coin toss*, Alvarez snarls, "One of our captains made a mistake."

On the coin toss?

After everyone has left the interview room and Alvarez is alone except for the little old security guard who lingers, the coach shakes his head in disgust. "Fucking Lowery blew it!" he says. "They won the coin toss at the start and they deferred their choice and Lowery says, 'We'll defend this goal.' The ref asked him three times. I *told* him what to do! So we kick off twice! Lowery's fucking mind isn't in the game."

Alvarez has aged a decade in the last week and a half. His once undefeated team is now 3–2 and listing like a damaged barge. He looks depressed, crushed, sick.

"Macias, he fucking choked," he says in a low voice. "It's a little different than in practice, with guys out there jumping around." Alvarez's eyes resemble a bloodhound's. "This is the state of the program," he says. "I don't have a quarterback."

Outside the locker room, a dejected Jay Macias slouches against the wall. "That's the worst game I've ever played," he says. "I gotta regroup." Reporters ask him questions in a gentle fashion; he is, after all, just a kid. But after the journalists have left, Macias continues to question himself.

"I overthrew Lee DeRamus across the middle," he says somberly. "As fast as he is. Think of that. I *overthrew* him. It would have been a touchdown. Oh, man."

In the Fieldhouse, Pat Richter, Al Fish, and Mike Greene stare up silently at the brand-new massive scoreboard hanging over center court. It looks out of place in this old, dilapidated building, like a gigantic, gleaming computer in a tar-paper shack. Richter is stunned.

"We may come in some morning and find a fricking hole in the roof and this thing on the floor," he says.

Fish walks around the floor, looking at the scoreboard from its four sides, noting the various advertising panels that are still blank. "We've got four sponsors left to sell," he says. "I'm real pleased." He walks over to a former storage room under the bleachers and opens the door.

"Look at these amps!" he says triumphantly, indicating the stack of amplifiers that are hooked through thick electrical cables to some distant power source and then, through other cables, to the scoreboard itself. The gadgets look big enough to power a Grateful Dead concert, maybe a missile silo. Fish closes the door and looks again at the dark scoreboard. The contraption actually has precious little space dedicated to the function for which it ostensibly has been built—displaying the score of the game. Fish waves his hand in dismissal.

"People will figure the score out," he says. "We'll also announce it over the P.A.—'Excuse us! In case you're wondering, the score is 79–70!' "

Another mission accomplished.

"I STARTED IN 1970," SAYS DICK SCHROCK, THE RECLUSIVE FORMER HEAD accountant for the UW athletic department. "Elroy hired me. Back then there were no women's athletics at all. The women's sports started with a budget of around fifty thousand dollars, and it just went up and up. A lot of it was absorbed internally, and I'll bet, even with the new coaches and trainers, there were only forty total people in the whole athletic department. But all the expansion wasn't the problem. That was second. First was the decline of football."

Schrock hasn't spoken with anyone from the press since he left the department more than a year ago under questionable conditions. He has blue eyes and blond hair and looks a little like Ted Koppel, only more furtive, perhaps because he has been dealt with so shabbily by those people he thought he was assisting. His apartment, which he shares with his wife, is immaculate; so, too, in its peculiar way, was his accounting handiwork, the reams of paper with tiny, precise, handwritten words and numbers on it like hieroglyphs on a cave wall—logic to him, arcana to all others. He hasn't spoken to anyone, because he has just wanted the financial tumult in the department to subside and to be left alone. But he has heard that he has been made the scapegoat for a lot of the red ink that exists at Camp Randall, and that has made him mad enough to finally agree to talk about his old job.

The decline in football attendance, he says, was particularly harmful because people quit coming en masse to the non-conference games, and those are the games where the department makes its most money. "You make more for playing a team like Western Illinois if you have fifty thousand in attendance than if you have seventy-six thousand for Ohio State. That's because you have to split the ticket revenue with the Big Ten team, but you pay the little team just a flat fee—I think the minimum now is one hundred thousand dollars, but we did Ball State once for fifty thousand and Northern Illinois once for thirty thousand. Of course, you can't force-feed the people that stuff."

No, you can't. Nor can you force-feed them a budget running deeper and deeper into the red. But that's what irritates Schrock, a middle-aged man who seems uncomfortable talking about himself except through his affiliation with numbers and financial acumen, this notion that bankruptcy suddenly dropped on the department like a bomb from the sky. Even with the football decline, he says, "We've had money all along. The great accounting error of seven hundred thousand dollars—there is no error."

He is a little heated now. He wasn't going to get into casting stones at those he thinks wronged him, but he can't keep this in any longer. "Oh, what the hell," he says angrily. "In the year of the *infamous* accounting error, the McClain facility payment of around three hundred and fifty thousand dollars was coming due. Remember, there were several of us who were against the McClain facility from the start, because the department didn't have the money to build it. I wanted to do a bond issue, like we did for the upper deck at Camp Randall. But no, we go through a bank, M & I Hilldale Bank, and get a loan for around four million dollars. I did the projections on payments, and I knew we'd be short. But there was always money in the Foundation.

"So to make the payment, we took money out of the Foundation—it was going to come out of there anyway. We had the money in there, just not in the right account. So we took it out of the unrestricted account, and we were just going to wait a couple months to pay it back, so we didn't have to go to the boosters for more money. We could have just called it all a loss of seven hundred thousand dollars, but that didn't seem right, because the money *was* in the Foundation. This was talked about with Fish. I didn't do anything wrong."

Who really knows? In certain ways the coffers at any university are like shells covering peas; move the shells around, hide the peas, use sleight-of-hand and talk a fast game, and it's almost irrelevant whether any peas are there. What's important is the *perception* that the peas—or money—is there. Schrock is out of this stuff for good, anyway; he plans to open a Maid-Rite hamburger stand in Madison soon, a business venture that will be more suitable to his small-scale, small-town way of thinking. Maybe he should have gotten out of the athletic department a long time ago, he thinks; when sharpies such as Al Fish start taking charge, it's way too late for the little guys like him.

But he's going to get his shots in now.

"The thing that shocked me was that just a couple months ago the department went into the Foundation and borrowed over a million dollars to cover the shortfall from just this last year, to show a ninety-thousand-dollar profit. Why didn't they do that the year before? That's the great question. And the other question I have is, Why cut the sports? I mean, men's and women's *fencing*? And then you go out and hire Jim Bakken as director of community affairs? I've never heard of that position. How do you create that? How in the fuck do you pay him forty-five thousand dollars a year, with benefits up to sixty thousand? For that you could have saved those sports."

Schrock is plain furious now, with the hurt of the wronged employee spilling from him in a torrent.

"If we can play Western Illinois in football, why the hell can't Mary Murphy and her women's basketball team play UW-Platteville and Eau Claire? What the fuck are they paying Pat Richter one hundred and fifty thousand dollars for? You know something—Elroy Hirsch, I love him. He's not a stupid, dumb ex-jock. He's a personality. He had the people in the stands excited! Some journalist wrote that Elroy doesn't know a spreadsheet from a bedsheet. That's bullshit! Or maybe it's true. But neither do Richter or Fish."

Schrock looks over at his wife. The look on her face tells him plainly enough: take it easy. But he's taken it easy for far too long. Things should be known.

"Scoreboards!" he snorts with true venom. "We wanted to have new scoreboards in 1975. But they wouldn't let us. Up on the hill they said, 'That's degrading.'"

He smiles a humorless smile. "Don't times change?"

IF A FALL DAY COULD BE MORE BEAUTIFUL, IT WOULD NOT BE OF THIS EARTH. The sun beams down on the rolling hills of Nashotah, fifty miles east of Madison; the wind is gentle and the few white clouds only add contrast to the azure-blue sky above the flaming palette of autumnal fields and forests. Rick Aberman pulls into a long driveway off a farm road and nearly runs over a white-haired man on a small tractor, his machine sucking leaves into a bin on a small connected trailer.

The man is Carl Whitaker, the Emeritus Professor of Psychiatry at the University of Wisconsin Medical School and Aberman's one-time teacher and professional guardian, and full-time spiritual guide. Whitaker is seventy-nine now and allegedly retired, though he does more consulting than most active psychotherapists half his age. He and his favorite disciple have not seen each other in several years, and they shake hands now with the openness and good humor so reflective of Whitaker's teachings. Aberman learned everything he knows about counseling from watching Whitaker, accompanying him to countless sessions with patients, and discussing every aspect of the trade with the man who generally is credited with founding one of the major schools of family therapy. He's happy just to see his mentor, a rock in the storm, unchanged.

Whitaker immediately asks Aberman about his job in the UW athletic department. "How did you con them into letting you into their world? That's an art. How did you get on their turf?"

Aberman laughs. Whitaker believes in asking what's on his mind. In the forward to Whitaker's 1982 book, *From Psyche to System*, Salvador Minuchin writes of Whitaker's impressive range of "interventions. He uses humor, indirection, seduction, indignation, primary process, boredom, even falling asleep as equally powerful instruments of contact and challenge. . . . He brings up an association with his own life, an anecdote about his brother, a slightly different comment another family member made, or a joke—'What would I do if God retired?' Though seemingly random, his interventions all are directed to challenge the meaning that people give to events." Aberman appreciates having his meanings challenged.

He explains that he got the job because he is a "quasi-athlete, a runner," and that one of the first people he was brought in to assist was a female runner whose opponent in a national championship race tried to kill herself.

Whitaker nods knowingly. "Their need is great," he says. "It's a turf problem, really, getting in there. Like the father-mother pull. The mother is there first, and then the father—what did Margaret Mead call him, 'the social activist'?—comes in. That's tough."

The two men walk around Whitaker's cottage to the backyard that slopes gracefully into Pine Lake. They sit under an oak tree, on grass as green as poker felt, and look out at the water, talking about their profession. They look exactly like what they are: a wise, old teacher and his student. From the kitchen window Whitaker's wife, Muriel, waves cheerfully.

"Transference," says Whitaker. "The world runs by transference." He means the substitution of another person for the one who has created the initial but now repressed impulses and feelings in the client. And everybody's a client—even he himself. "You spend your life trying to get where your mother or father wanted you to get," he says. "I had a client who as a boy hated his rich but restrictive upbringing in Boston. So he runs off to San Francisco, gets a domineering boss and makes him into his father, and then takes a wife just like his mother. Presto, he's back in Boston! That's not growth, that's adaptation."

The old man looks up at the kitchen window. "Here I am, eighty in a couple months, and I'm still my wife's little boy." He laughs out loud. "And I think I'm her mother!"

"It's like with coaches," says Aberman. "They think they're fathers."

Whitaker nods. "There is a golden opportunity for you as a therapist to relive your own immaturity and to sleep with the patient," he states. "You become the foster parent and commit psychological incest—the patient sleeping with her father. Quite often that's the patient's contract: 'Will you be my new parent?' " He looks at Aberman.

"You get paid?" Whitaker asks.

Aberman nods.

"Good. That's the difference between a pro and a promiscuous imitation. Pay. It makes you more able to keep your patients from being indebted to you. The kid becomes more free—he can hate or love the therapist. It also can help him get over the delusion of the coach as parental figure."

Aberman twists this in his mind. It is an axiom of therapy: Clients must have a real investment in their treatment or else the work is somehow fraudulent. In truth, the UW athletes he sees do not have this monetary investment, not really. The school pays his salary. If an athlete breaks an appointment or walks out of a session in disgust, who suffers? Whom is Aberman really assisting in his work? Can his good intentions make things right? Therapists, he knows, can be as confused as anyone.

A sailboat glides silently far out on the lake. Aberman brings up the concept of the family and how so often people in groups tend to form themselves into pseudo-families. Whitaker watches as the boat tacks toward the north shore. He nods. There are, of course, three basic families, he reminds his pupil. "There is your biological family," he says. "That's the most powerful, your genetic family. Nothing's more powerful than that. Then there's your psychological family—your wife, whomever you fall in love with. And there's your social family. The team. All teams are social families."

Whitaker stands up and walks over to a wind chime, which he tethers, because the wind is picking up and even a lovely wind chime can make too much racket. The two men go up to the house and take seats on the screened porch. The wind rustles high up in the pine trees. A collie walks in, lies down, and falls asleep instantly. The peacefulness of the day is almost hallucinatory. Aberman tells his mentor that he's considered moving to Minneapolis and getting into some kind of small business counseling practice, using his father, still active in his own job placement company, as a sort of partner/co-consultant.

Whitaker ponders this. "That's a courageous thing you'd be doing," he says. "You have to appreciate each other's separateness. You know, separate but together, breaking away so you can get closer. It didn't happen with my mother and me. She was ninety-three and dying, and I was sixty-five, and she decided on her deathbed what I should do with my life. Like I was sixteen." He shakes his square-jawed head.

Muriel has made coffee, and Whitaker holds up his mug, which shows a man facing two doors. A devil has a pitchfork in the man's back, and underneath are the words, DAMNED IF YOU DO. DAMNED IF YOU DON'T.

"If you become a father to your father, that makes you your own grandfather, Rick," he says. "That's scary."

They both burst out laughing at that truism. All relationships are complicated ones, and sometimes people go nuts just trying to unravel them. Sometimes they should just get on with their lives.

"Green Bay!" says Whitaker, addressing the point. "The Packers and all the people up there need to bury the 'Big Chief.' Lombardi. They need to all go out to a grave, do a war dance, and get it over with. So they can move on. Play football in the nineties."

Whitaker comes back to Aberman's situation, to his dealing with athletes who are growing up at the same time they are performing physically at an elite level. "Your clients are make-believe children for you, Rick," he says.

"I know I have to be careful about that," Aberman replied. "I want real children. Not make-believe ones."

They walk out onto the front lawn that is more like a wooded field, leading up to the access road.

"John, my colleague, says, 'This is the only job I know where you can spend your whole life working on yourself,' " says Whitaker. " 'And get paid for it.' "

This is true. A therapist's real canvas is a self-portrait, always in progress. You get into patterns in your life, thinks Aberman, and once you know why you are in them, you are free.

"Transference rules the world," says Whitaker. They shake hands as a squirrel runs across the lawn, gathering food for the winter ahead.

29

"He said he asked me three times?" says Tony Lowery. "He didn't ask me *once!*"

He is speaking of the ill-fated coin toss in the Iowa game, and of the referee who supposedly asked him if he was sure he wanted to kick off. Lowery is back to see Rick Aberman, feeling none the better for wear. He played in last Saturday's debacle at Purdue, a 28–7 thrashing in which he completed 15 of 27 passes for just 99 yards and two interceptions, before getting hit square on his left knee by a defender and suffering a second-degree sprain of his medial collateral ligament. The Badgers are now tied with Northwestern for last place in the conference.

"Third-degree, and I'd need surgery," Lowery tells Aberman. But his physical ailments are not what is bothering him. It's the mind games being played on him by the coaching staff and the lack of support he feels he is getting from Alvarez that troubles him. He thinks Macias, who came in after Lowery was hurt, is getting yanked around, too.

"I feel sorry for the kid," Lowery says. "I could have told you this was going to happen to him. I *did* tell you.

"They told us the Monday after the Ohio State game that he was going to start against Iowa. Then they told the media that it was because of my injured thumb. But it pisses me off—he was going to start, no matter what."

But because Macias was so ineffective in that start, suddenly Lowery was back to being top man. But still, no respect. "Alvarez hasn't even talked to me in two weeks. Robert Williams is across the hall from me, and we talk every night. He used to be first-string; now he hasn't even played this season. They were mad at him because he went home to Columbus, Georgia, for a few weeks during the summer. But I don't need a lot of praise, just give me a little support. Last week during the practice for the Iowa game, for the first time I really, really felt used."

"It would be better if they were up front about everything?" asks Aberman.

"We're, you know, people," says Lowery. "Talk to us."

The quarterback adjusts his left leg to ease the throbbing in his knee.

"I'm only looking out for Tony Lowery now," he says. "I only need two more yards to be the University of Wisconsin's second-leading career passer, behind Randy Wright. And that's funny, too. I had 1,800 yards passing last year, and after the season I was only 1,600 yards behind Wright for first place. He was at 4,698 yards. Then I come back this year and Wright is at 5,269 yards. How did that happen? They added his bowl games? I figured that in—306 yards—and it's still 200 yards short. I missed my high school basketball scoring record by eight points because I sat out a game with a twisted ankle, and I vowed that would never happen again. So now, if I have to run into the game on my own, I'll get those two yards for second place. Macias and Jay Simala, the other quarterback, know—and if they have to fake an injury to get me in, they'll do it."

Lowery looks at Aberman, then looks away sadly.

"I feel bad even having to think like that," he says.

"It doesn't have to be this way," says Aberman.

Lowery shrugs. "I keep telling Jay, 'They may like you now, but they really don't. If you can't help them, watch out.'"

"There's some of what my mentor, Carl Whitaker, calls transference going on here. Seeing your coaches as parents. Parents don't usually stop giving support, but coaches may."

"I can't believe they're doing this to me," says Lowery with a frown. "They *asked* me to come back. I'm a team player. I've been used."

Silence fills the room as the player leans back on the couch and looks at the clock. It is four hours ahead of time.

"I'll be rooting for the two yards," says Aberman.

TONY LOWERY HAS RECEIVED A LETTER OF ENCOURAGEMENT FROM A FORMER star player at UW, Thad McFadden. A receiver and kick returner from 1980 to 1984, McFadden led the Big Ten in punt returns his sophomore year and played for a time in the now-defunct United States Football League. He has known Lowery for several years, and has become aware that the quarterback is having a hard time with football matters.

His letter arrived today, two days before the Indiana game.

Hey Tony—

What's happening? I know that you are going through difficult times right now with the team and hope that you guys can turn things around soon. After reading an article from the last game, I kept reflecting on your remarks about how you were hoping to participate in a bowl game this year and that it seems apparent that those goals cannot be accomplished. Well, they *can*—only if you and the team want them to. In almost any situation in your life, good or bad is affected by the attitude you bring to it. . . . Sometimes it takes adversity for an individual to find his true identity. I have faith in you. . . . You can't get tired, you have to hang in there and just keep on keeping on, no matter what.
P.S.:
I had some great news myself. The parole board is sending me to boot camp, and I will be released in just 6 months.

> Your caring friend,
> Thad McFadden
> Dodge Correctional Institution
> Box 661
> Waupun, WI

*   *   *

ON THE SATURDAY FIVE DAYS BEFORE HALLOWEEN, RAIN POURS DOWN IN sheets, covering the artificial turf at Camp Randall Stadium with a film of water that slowly streams off the crowned field onto the surrounding track. It's homecoming, and the Badgers are playing Indiana University, and 54,052 die-hard fans have shown up to watch what will supposedly be a turning point in UW's fortunes. While Barry Alvarez does his pregame radio show, his assistant, John Chadima, stands looking out at the glistening field. "Barry is suffering," he says. "He's taking things kind of hard."

And well he should. His team has gone from 3–0 to 3–3, and even though all the hype and early expectations have jacked up attendance, at some point this UW team is going to have to play like a team that is worthy of being watched.

Today just might be the day that Alvarez finds relief. The Badgers go up, 7–0, on the Hoosiers, then 14–0, then 17–0 just before half, with Jay Macias looking competent in his fill-in role for the injured Tony Lowery. At the intermission, the UW officials in the press box chatter excitedly in anticipation of a nice, confidence-boosting blowout.

"Boy, did we luck out," says Al Fish as he looks down on Jim Bakken, who is interviewing Chancellor Shalala near midfield for a TV cable hookup that was put in by the athletic department just for this game. The homecoming contest is being beamed to twenty-three University of Wisconsin alumni clubs across the nation, to show alums the grandeur of the UW grid program, and, of course, to soften them up for contributions. Seeing their team ahead by seventeen points should make the alums feel exceedingly generous as well as reassure them that they are giving to an ascendent enterprise. "We'll hit them up for cash after the game," Fish says. "I've been thinking of brass offertory plates. It works for the church."

Pat Richter is equally upbeat about the TV deal. "The technology for this is amazingly simple," he gushes. "Just get a satellite linkup, and each alumni club can pull it in."

Television is a remarkable tool for the promotion and marketing of big-time sport, one that many athletic departments learned about long before UW. In fact, when a representative from Channel 5–TV in Madison, a low-power broadcast station, came to the athletic department before the 1989–90 football season and asked if his company could televise Badger games, he met with departmental people who reminded him of Stone Age natives greeting a time traveler stepping from a rocket ship. Bob Dobrowolski, who was then a junior producer for Channel 5 and the point man in the station's sports-broadcast efforts, recalls that then–athletic director Ade Sponberg "knew nothing about television whatsoever."

Dobrowolski, now a weatherman and talk-show assistant at Fox TV in Chicago, says, "It boggled my mind. I walked in wearing jeans and a T-shirt to ask about the rights fees to do a major Big Ten sports broadcast, and they asked me how much I could pay, and I said, 'All I can afford is two hundred dollars.' And they said, 'Okay.' Ade knew nothing, *nothing* about rights fees. All of them were the nicest people, but I couldn't believe what was happening. We wanted several sports, so I'd say, 'I'll give you fifty bucks for this, a hundred bucks for that. Can you put this antenna on top of the Fieldhouse?' And they said, 'Sure.' No arguing. Nothing. I kept thinking, 'This can't be happening.' The station's sales manager would ask me, 'When is the bubble going to burst?' But it didn't. It was a total joke. It cost us nothing."

Richter is at least aware of the potential of TV revenue now, and part of his offer to Alvarez was the assurance that the coach would have his own television show, which would bring in a decent sum of money. And with Al Fish around, it seems certain that the new athletic department will be ready to pounce on TV money if any of UW's revenue-producing teams should ever merit extra attention from the tube.

The second half begins, and things look even brighter for UW— and for all the boosters watching on the twenty-three screens around the country. Macias completes a 13-yard pass to wide receiver Tom Browne on third-and-four at the Indiana 37, and Rich Thompson kicks a field goal to increase the lead to 20–0. On the sideline Alvarez seems to have a little more spring in his step than before. This should get that monkey off the coach's back, the rap about never having won a Big Ten game in his career. No team could lose with a twenty-point cushion midway through the third quarter.

Up in the press box Laurie Irwin looks down at Bucky Badger in the end zone doing lackluster pushups for every point that UW has scored. Irwin is probably the only Wisconsin backer concerned about failure just now. "That's a tiny Bucky," she says, frowning. "That's a woman in there. Liz Moeller. She's five feet eight, but I'll tell you, I'm not going to allow any smaller ones."

Moeller is, indeed, small for a Bucky. But UW women get to share all the privileges once reserved for men, and one of those is the right to be Bucky and to do pushups each time the football team scores. After the game Moeller would admit that she had never done twenty pushups before, certainly not with thirty-five pounds of gear on. But then, you don't expect a lot of points from the Badgers, she explained. Even so, she was upset that the crowd might have thought the Bucky she portrayed was a weakling. "It upset me so much!" she said, noting that the costume itself was the thing holding her back. "I'm not a wimp. My head was coming off!"

At the half, Moeller, a senior from Columbus, Indiana, majoring in elementary education, went under the stands and took off her Bucky headgear so she could breathe some fresh air. She's had her problems playing the character, she said, but that's just part of the game. "Today there was a guy insulting me on the sideline. I was shaking hands with a little girl, and he just kept banging on my head. I told security, and they threw him out."

Of course, there is always the problem with drunks trying to maul her, not even knowing she is a woman. But probably the worst events are the fights she's been in with other mascots. This year before the Ohio State game she went so far as to call up the Buckeye and ask him not to cause a disturbance at the game in Madison. "I asked him not to beat me up," she says, her blond hair darkened by sweat. "It's not considered appropriate to beat up a mascot at home."

A former high school swimmer and quarter-miler in track, Moeller is not looking for any sympathy, however. "I was worried that I was picked to be one of the Buckies because I'm a woman," she says defiantly. "If that were the case, I'd quit." Her fiancé, UW grad Brian Griesbach, looks on with amusement; he knows his girlfriend is tough enough to be Bucky regardless of her stature or sex. He watches as she pulls out a can of Walgreen's disinfectant from her duffel bag and sprays it inside Bucky's big fuzzy head. A lot of wacky people have worn this contraption.

"Just a little," Moeller says, putting the can back in the bag. "Too much and you'll asphyxiate yourself."

Back out on the field, things have suddenly started to go wrong for the Badgers. Dreadfully wrong. Hoosier running back Vaughn

Dunbar rips off a 45-yard sprint to the UW 3-yard line, setting up a touchdown run by quarterback Trent Green. 20–7. Green throws a 48-yard pass to wide receiver Eddie Baety, and Dunbar pounds in for another score, 20–14. In the fourth quarter UW's offense disappears entirely and its defense turns to mush. Dunbar picks up a first down on fourth-and-one at the UW 2-yard line, with ease. Green carries it in from the one. 21–20, Indiana.

Can the Badgers battle back? There are still seven minutes left in the game. Fish looks down in horror at the debacle in front of him. Dare he hope for redemption?

Forget it. Green scores again for the Hoosiers with just over two minutes to go; the final score is 28–21, Indiana. The humiliation is complete; all those alums at their big-screen linkups have seen the football team die a wretched, painful death. Seventeen consecutive Big Ten games without a win over three years. In the press box the student reporters look at each other with sneers.

"And you wonder why we're cynical?" says Rob Reischel of the *Daily Cardinal*.

JUST BEFORE MIDNIGHT ON HALLOWEEN, SKINNY TWENTY-YEAR-OLD KEITH Breneman from Rhinelander takes a punch to the head from a UW football player. He takes another and another, falling to the pavement behind Joe Hart's tavern on University Avenue, bleeding from his wounds, with part of an ear torn off, two black eyes, and broken facial bones. As Breneman lapses into a coma from severe brain damage, as his entire world fades to gray—so, too, does the story of what truly happened in the fight. Police chase down the fleeing linebacker, Aaron Norvell, who implicates teammate Gary Casper, the 6'2", 235-pound starting linebacker, and former quarterback Sean Wilson as being involved in the fight.

But who did what to whom? Two people at the scene told police that two of the football players held Breneman while the third hit him five or ten times in the face. One statement given to police by someone at the scene said that one of the players then kicked Breneman in the head. Other statements give conflicting testimony, saying that Breneman was the victim of a plain old street fight, that it was hard to tell what was happening, that maybe Breneman was the aggressor, that it was all the result of holiday partying. The only clear facts are that Breneman was legally intoxicated (at the hospital his blood alcohol level was measured at 0.21, with 0.10 being the legal level for intoxication in the state), that he weighs just 160 pounds, and that he is now in critical condition from the beating. Though Norvell and Casper are allowed to play in the UW-Illinois game a day and a half later, they are suspended by Alvarez for the November 9 game against Michigan State, pending the outcome of the police investigation.

Neither of the players will talk to the press about what went on that night, and this irritates Barry Baum as he watches practice in the McClain facility with other members of the media. He has just walked in from class, and his parka and stocking cap are covered with snow. He stamps his feet and brushes the flakes onto the artificial turf. Before practice, reporters are required to give Steve Malchow a list of the players they want to interview for that day. Baum wrote down that he wanted to talk to Norvell and Casper. Malchow has informed him that those players cannot talk to him.

"Their attorneys won't let them talk," says Baum angrily now. "Why? They haven't been charged with anything. I just want to talk to them about the game they're suspended from."

Baum has a point. The players have not been charged with anything—Alvarez suspended them from the upcoming game for breaking a team rule, partying too close to game time. Still, the whole affair reeks of larger issues, one of which—freedom of speech—was captured in today's issue of the *Badger-Herald*, wherein sportswriter Jay Gold stated in an article that Norvell and Casper "stand accused" of the beating. That, at best, is an inaccuracy; at worst it is slanderous, for the pair stand accused of nothing, yet. Alvarez became livid when he read the story.

In general, Alvarez looks like a man in need of a big pep talk these days. Like many coaches who rise to the top, he has always been associated with winning programs, until now. Back as the head coach at Lexington (Neb.) High School in 1974 and 1975 he won sixteen of twenty games and was named the Nebraska prep Coach of the Year. In three years as the head coach at Mason City High School in Iowa, Alvarez chalked up a 21-9 record and a class 4-A state title. After that he was an assistant on successful University of Iowa and Notre Dame teams, including being the defensive coordinator on the undefeated Irish team that won the national championship in 1989.

As a three-year letterman at linebacker for the University of Ne-braska from 1966 to 1968, Alvarez made the All–Big Eight team and played in the Orange and Sugar Bowls, as well as the Senior and Blue-Gray all-star games. But none of those achievements seem to carry much freight these days.

"My daughter got her first *D* of her life in calculus," he says. "And my wife's on me because I'm not sensitive to that. All the people with problems come back on me. I try to eat dinner at home three nights a week, just to see my kids.

"After games on Saturday I stay up all night, I can't sleep, and then I pass out on Sunday. I'll tell you what . . . I've always won. I keep telling myself we're doing it the right way, that there will be a day. I'm just obsessed with getting there. I know Dick Vermeil and guys like that talk about burnout, and I can see the day is going to come when I just can't take it anymore."

Right now Alvarez would make Eeyore from *Winnie-the-Pooh* look happy-go-lucky. His once-undefeated team is now 3–5; Alva-rez's career record at Wisconsin is 4–15; he has never won a confer-ence game; his offense ranks tenth in the Big Ten in both rushing and total offense; and his prospects for a sudden reversal of fortune look dim. But he has heard himself talking, and the fighter in him clearly is raising hell within. Okay, he admits, things could be worse. He sets his jaw.

"I'm a tough old coal miner from Pennsylvania," he says, recall-ing his childhood days in Burgettstown, Pa. "I remember watching the men go off to the coal mine in the morning with their lunch boxes hanging down and come back at night so dark you couldn't recognize them. Hey, I'm not in a mine and I'm not in a factory. My dad can't figure out what I do. He's seventy-two and he thinks I'm still *playing*. My dad was a greenskeeper at the local golf course, worked seven days a week. I make more in one speech than he made in three months. Ah, hell." He furrows his brow and sighs.

"I just want to win again."

30

KATIE ISHMAEL IS BACK, AND ALMOST NOBODY KNOWS IT. WHICH IS FINE with her.

The former All-America track and cross-country star at UW is now twenty-seven, and she looks different than she did during her competitive days, and she hopes to God she thinks differently, too. Back then she was an emaciated, frighteningly focused runner who seldom spoke to anyone or had any meaningful contact with the everyday world except through her running. While at UW, Ishmael ran ninety miles a week at a ferocious pace. "You do everything you can to gain a fraction of a second on your competition," she says. "You get caught up in it, training your guts out. There's a fine line between being at your peak and . . . bottoming out. I went over the edge."

She has been gone for three years—completely gone—to the extent that almost no one knew where she was, which was how she wanted it. After graduation she packed up her few possessions and moved to Vail, Colorado, where she knew not a soul. She moved there to ski, to work in a retail shop, to deal with people, and to attempt to become a functioning human being in the process.

When Ishmael was a junior in high school—she is from Madison, and the youngest of six children—she stood 5′2″ and starved herself down to 86 pounds. Her mother committed her to the eating disorder clinic at the UW Hospital, where Katie now works. "I was running way more than I should have been," she states. "My jeans didn't touch me any place. I had to stay in for three weeks."

She looks out at the other people scattered through the cafeteria tonight. Each of them no doubt has his or her own story of a mistake-ridden past. Ishmael, like Herbst, blames no one else for her athletic travails. "They brought in my family and psychoanalyzed everything, and it had nothing to do with anything at all. It was me. I'm intense. I just . . . crossed that line. Dr. Landry asked me recently, 'What do you think we can do with these people?' He meant girls with eating disorders. And I told him I don't think you can do much of anything. You've got to shock them, that's your only hope."

She thinks about the runners on this year's team and is reminded of her own experiences. "I see Jenny Kraeger on TV," she says. "I see some of myself there. She's hobbling along. She's going to go from one injury to another. It's sad."

Doesn't Peter Tegen come in for some responsibility here, Ishmael is asked. Shouldn't a grown man, an instructor, help his pupils make proper decisions? "Peter," she says, fondly. "I wish he would have said something to me. If he had said, 'You can't run,' I . . ." She doesn't finish, only stares off. "I put a lot of stock in what he said. Maybe I would have run on my own. I valued what he said, but I didn't want to burden Peter. I knew how many other things he had on his mind. Peter is one of the best coaches there is. I wouldn't want anybody else. You bring this stuff on yourself."

Vail was like an elixir for Ishmael, who now weighs a normal amount and no longer runs long distance. "When I went there I had no job skills, no social skills, I was afraid of my own shadow," she says. "In Vail, I learned how to become a person. Three years ago I wouldn't have been able to look you in the eye."

She laughs. "You know, I saw Rick Aberman the other day. I was going one way on Monroe Street and he was running the other way. I said, 'Hi!' And he looked at me and had no idea who I was."

For the Michigan State game, Al Fish wears a pair of new sneakers that have an image of Bucky Badger on the back. These are a pro-totype of a shoe that Famous Footwear might make in a deal with the athletic department, selling the shoes to the public for about forty-five dollars, with 6½ percent going back to the department as a rights fee. "You can use them while you pee in the urinal and look at the ads," says Fish.

In the press box area reserved for the student writers, Barry Baum ignores the game for a while and reads a few irate letters sent to the *Daily Cardinal* about his work. One of them refers to his latest column as "degrading drivel" that is "racist/sexist/classist."

"I called the lady who wrote it," Baum says. "Basically, she didn't think I should have used Idi Amin as an example of a poor sport."

The game is more of the usual for Wisconsin, with Michigan State moving to a 20–7 lead in the fourth quarter in front of a bored crowd of 41,074. The only excitement occurs when Tony Lowery enters the game in late relief of Jay Macias, in pursuit of his two passing yards. Even then, almost no one in the press box is aware of the milestone that Lowery can achieve—second-leading passer in Badger history—except for the student writers. "Lowery, for the record," says Baum, as the quarterback drops back to pass. Lowery is smeared for a sack. He drops back again. Another sack. On third-and-26, Alvarez calls a draw play that goes nowhere. Punt.

"Player request?" asks a publicity assistant, moving through the press box, taking names from the writers.

"Al Toon," says Baum when the assistant reaches him. Former Badger star Al Toon has played for the New York Jets for the last eight years.

With just over two minutes left in the game, Lowery re-enters the game and completes a short pass to move into second place on the all-time list. There is no sound from the stands or the press box. And there will be nothing written about the achievement in any of tomorrow's papers.

ON WEDNESDAY LOWERY COMES BY TO SEE RICK ABERMAN AGAIN. HE TALKS about his record and how he finally told fullback Mark Montgomery, "I'm getting the record now, and I'm just passing it to you over the middle." No look-offs, no fakes, no nothing. Just business.

"I wouldn't want anybody to go through what I went through here for four years," he tells Aberman. "But now I'm out for fun. I'm clowning around in practice. I'm laughing. Throwing left-handed passes. What are they gonna do to me? Bench me? They don't have anybody else. Barry hasn't talked to me since the Purdue game, and then on Sunday he said to all of us, 'We love you all like our own kids.'"

Lowery is still as slender as ever, his weight lifting and protein shakes having had little effect on his basic body shape. "I'm fine, really," he says after a time. "Barry can definitely coach, but I wonder why he does some things. I think about Robert Williams. He hasn't *touched* the field this year, not even on special teams. He hasn't even traveled since the shoplifting."

Lowery exhales softly. "I remember back last spring—I'll never forget it—I handed the ball to Robert, and he got hit in the backfield and then he spun and ran right instead of left where the play was designed, and he broke the play all the way. Brad Childress, the running backs coach, said, 'Robert Williams, we don't want none of that shit this year. Run where you're supposed to!' Looking back now, I see how it started. But, I mean, we're last in the Big Ten in rushing. And with his talent . . . ?"

LOWERY WALKS BACK TO HIS SMALL ONE-ROOM APARTMENT ACROSS FROM THE Nitty Gritty Restaurant on the corner of Gilman and Johnson Streets. The room is tidy, with a small microwave and refrigerator at one end. Attached to the refrigerator door by a Domino's Pizza magnet is a paragraph from yesterday's *Milwaukee Journal* noting that Lowery moved ahead of Neil Graf into second place in the UW all-time passing yardage category. "It wasn't in any other paper," Lowery says.

On his desk are some sheets of paper containing his current statistics as well as his goals for this final season, goals that are mostly far out of reach now. He also has a page titled "Black Quarterback Stats," in which he has compared himself to the starting helmsmen at Purdue, Northwestern, and Minnesota. Under that is a heading entitled "Other," with the statistics of the white quarterbacks in the Big Ten.

On a shelf next to a Halloween pumpkin are seven practice footballs Lowery has taken from the practice field. "They don't know I have them," he says. "But I'm going to paint them myself."

He has determined that in his career he has done seven things for the team that are worthy of being honored with commemorative balls, game balls, if you will. He will even have a little ceremony for himself after he paints them, he says, even if it's just in his mind and he is the only one in attendance. Nobody else needs to know or celebrate with him; it's likely, he feels, that nobody else would want to.

AT HOCKEY PRACTICE, TEAM CAPTAIN AND LEADING SCORER DOUG MACDONALD stands glumly in street clothes, watching the other players skate through their drills. Macdonald had surgery on his left shoulder a few days ago after it was badly separated when he was cheap-shotted into the board by a University of Minnesota-Duluth player. The UM-D player got a five-minute major penalty; Macdonald got an injury that will haunt him for a lifetime. His left arm is in a sling, and the senior will be out of action for at least two or three months, and even then it's not certain how much mobility he will regain in the joint. Macdonald has never been injured severely before, and he is going through the pangs of reckoning that come with this new territory.

"There's so much time to think," he says unhappily. "I used to think I was invincible."

He watches as a new skater slaps a shot at the goal. The player is a twenty-three-year-old Latvian named Ulvis Katlaps, whom Jeff Sauer hopes to have declared eligible to play someday soon for the Badgers. Katlaps, who used to play for the then–Soviet Union professional team Dynamo Riga and was formerly in the Soviet army, came to this country a few months ago to live with his cousin in Milwaukee and, with luck, to be admitted to the University of Wisconsin on a hockey scholarship. Sauer is disgusted with the foot-dragging being done by the NCAA regarding Katlaps's eligibility. Hell, the guy just wants to play, Sauer tells everyone. Sure, he could help the Badgers, but that's not the point. Isn't this America, where you follow your dreams? Where you're free to become all that you can be?

"In all this time we've made it past two offices at the NCAA," says Sauer sarcastically. "Two offices. Imagine that?"

For Macdonald, watching Katlaps is especially painful. The Latvian is 6′2″, 205 pounds, and a fine skater, and his presence only makes the point sharper that an athlete is just a replaceable part in a big machine. Sauer has done everything he can to cram Katlaps through the system, because the big foreigner with the ragged neck scar (from being stepped on and nearly killed by an opponent in Latvia) can help UW win games, bring in money, and keep Sauer's job secure. One day this fall Sauer sat for a good part of an afternoon, trying to make sense of a document he had received via fax from Latvia, which supposedly showed that Katlaps had taken the high school courses and received the grades needed to qualify for NCAA play. The document was written in a foreign alphabet and could have been anything from a birth certificate to a restaurant menu, for all Sauer could tell. Such is the recruiting process.

"My dream is still to play pro hockey," says Macdonald, as the team circles around the coach near center ice. Nobody looks over at Macdonald, their captain. Nobody notices him at all. "It's scary to think about leaving hockey. So scary. When it happens to guys, what do they do?"

DEER HUNTING SEASON HAS BEGUN ONCE AGAIN, AND AL FISH STOPS BY TO CHAT with Rick Aberman and tell him that he himself may actually be going to a real, functioning deer camp one of these weekends.

"I went to one before," says Fish. "I had a deer in my sights, and I didn't shoot. It wasn't buck fever or morality or anything."

What was it, asks Aberman.

Fish shrugs. "I just forgot to shoot."

Aberman thinks about this a moment. "Want to be part of our pool?" he asks. "You make a prediction on how many people will be fatally shot, die of heart attacks, fall out of trees, be mistaken for bucks, shoot themselves, that sort of thing. Just during the season."

Fish considers this briefly.

"No," he says after a time. "I just want to be one of the six hundred thousand hunters."

BARRY BAUM HAS BEEN ABLE TO HUSTLE A GIG TO HAWAII TO COVER THE upcoming Rainbow Classic basketball tournament in which the UW men's team will be playing. Naturally, the *Daily Cardinal* will be paying him nothing, but by lining up stringer jobs with the *Wall Street Journal*, the *Delaware County Times*, the *Baltimore Evening Sun,* and several other papers that have marginal interest in one or the other of the eight teams in the tourney, Baum has been able to buy a plane ticket and reserve a cheap motel room in Honolulu.

"I think if I write for all those papers I can break even," he says triumphantly. "Wait till Yoder sees me on the plane. I'm going to ask for the seat next to him. What a coup!"

Baum has recently focused his critical powers on the faltering men's hoops team, with some of his special juice being reserved not only for the despised Yoder, but also for slumping senior guard and team captain, Billy Douglass. "I don't know what it is about Douglass that is the problem," Baum says thoughtfully. "It's more or less his play—it's just so bad. There's, like, nothing there. It's hard to explain."

Last season, when Douglass was still playing mostly at point guard rather than shooting guard, Baum referred to him in one column as the "pointless guard." Now Baum and a couple of the other writers want to put a small section in the *Daily Cardinal* every day dealing with Douglass. "We want to call it 'The Billy Club,' " he says. "But Mike Bresnehan is very nervous."

Naturally upbeat, Baum is thrilled with the chance to write from Hawaii for some of the nation's biggest newspapers. The only thing that would make his life richer, he admits, would be to hook up with a grass-skirted wahini while there. Madison has not rewarded him with an abundance of romantic interests. "The girl situation is at an all-time low," he says, momentarily downcast. "Even with my picture on my column. I don't get it. I thought the *Cardinal* was bigger than that."

JENNY KRAEGER, DRESSED IN A SWEATSUIT AND LIMPING SLIGHTLY, SEES RICK Aberman outside his office. She is preparing to leave with the team for the NCAA cross-country championship in Tucson, along with six other runners, Peter Tegen, and Mary Grinaker.

"We're expecting to shock a lot of people," Kraeger tells Aberman happily. "We were ranked tenth in the nation, but people better look out."

Aberman asks her how she is feeling.

She looks at the floor. "Honestly?" she says. "Like shit. The overall wear and tear is taking its toll. I don't know what it is. It's not the stress fracture, it's the tendons and ligaments and all that."

Aberman asks if she has been getting enough nutrition.

"I eat all the time," she replies.

THE FOOTBALL TEAM BEAT MINNESOTA, 19–16, LAST SATURDAY FOR THE FIRST Big Ten win of Barry Alvarez's career, as well as his first road victory. Tony Lowery started the game and completed 10 of 15 passes for 95 yards and no interceptions. He passed 14 yards for one touchdown and ran five yards for the other, thus gift-wrapping a present that his head coach desperately craved.

Now, on the Thursday before the final game of the season against Northwestern at Camp Randall, Alvarez reflects on what might have been. Of playing Jay Macias he says, "It was, damn, just too much to ask of an eighteen-year-old. It was like throwing a kid to the wolves." And of Tony Lowery, the only quarterback who ever has won a game for an Alvarez-coached college team, he says, "He's a funny kid. He's got the tools, a rifle for an arm, and he's quick enough. And I always thought he had charisma. But being a leader, that comes from confidence.

"Tony's tough to get close to," continues the coach. "We tried, offensive coordinator Russ Jacques and I. But I don't know if Tony trusts people. He'll give you the image of being cool and in control, but basically, he didn't perform for us. It was there for all to see. He didn't improve. He regressed from last year."

Alvarez rubs his thinning hair. "We gotta recruit better. If we'd had a middle-of-the-road quarterback, we'd have won seven games this year."

The Badgers are 4–6 now, and they have a chance to finish at 5–6, a poor record, true, but still the best any UW team has achieved in six years. And Tony Lowery has been at the helm for every victory, every measly one. The announcer on a recent local radio sports broadcast referred to Lowery as the UW football team's "whipping boy," but Alvarez at least admits that "Lowery has earned this start" against Northwestern. But then, as Lowery himself has noted, who else could have earned it? Who else could Alvarez put in there? It's not hard to pull a can of soup off a shelf when there's only one can in the cupboard.

* * *

TOMORROW WILL BE THE FINAL GAME OF THE SEASON, THE FINAL GAME OF Robert Williams's rocky college football career. A 5'9", 185-pound senior from Columbus, Georgia, Williams has had a sports history at UW that has followed the trajectory of a small artillery rocket, starting off at ground level, rising loftily into the sky, then sailing abruptly back to earth and exploding.

He did not play as a freshman, but his sophomore year he started six games at tailback, rushing for 354 yards on 73 carries, including a career-high 129 yards on 21 attempts versus Minnesota. His junior season he started seven games and led the Badgers in rushing with 541 yards on 139 carries. The highlights of his season were a 10-carry, 114-yard game against Ball State and an 18-carry, 111-yard effort against Iowa. Then in last spring's Cardinal & White intrasquad game he led both teams in rushing and scoring with 77 yards and three touchdowns. In the 1991 media guide it states that Williams will be "tied for the top spot at tailback with Theo Carney entering fall."

But something happened between then and now, and Robert Williams wishes he knew what it was. He has not played a down of football this season.

He sits on his bed in his room across from Tony Lowery's room and looks out the window. Where did he go wrong? He wears his Rolling Red Thunder spring game T-shirt and a Penn State baseball cap; a hoop earring dangles from his left ear.

"I'm mystified," he says, still gazing out at the November sky. "I talked to Coach Childress after the Western Illinois game, and he said it basically came down to a business decision that I wasn't playing. He didn't say what business."

Williams does not have the aura of a star football player to him; he is short and squat and not overly dangerous-looking. But then, good running backs come in all shapes and sizes, and most of their success comes from attributes that can't be appreciated until the players cut upfield. "Okay, I can see not starting," he says. "But not even playing? To go from starter to scout team? There are three backs better than me? At Wisconsin?"

He has been told several times during the season by various coaches to be patient. But now the curtain is coming down, and there's nothing to be patient for. "I was told yesterday by Childress that as time allows, as 'the situation presents itself,' I might get in," he says sadly. "My dad is coming in today from Columbus. He's in the Sheriff's Department there. I didn't want him to come. He came to the first game, and I saw so much pain and frustration in his eyes, I saw how much he hurt for his son . . . so I called him last night to tell him not to come, but he's coming anyway. Basically, I don't want to play tomorrow."

Williams often wanders over to Lowery's room to talk about football things, but Lowery is not much help to him anymore now that Lowery is also getting jerked around.

"It doesn't have to be like this, does it?" Williams asks. "I just think, 'Why?' Barry would say, 'Hey, it's just business.' But even in business it doesn't have to be like this. Does it?"

Williams is not the kind of figure to elicit much sympathy from the public; after all, he's a convicted shoplifter, charged with three counts of misdemeanor retail theft in the West Towne mall. He and teammate Lionell Crawford got caught by store detectives when they met up in another store with Tony Lowery, who had driven the players to the mall. Lowery knew nothing of the thefts; all the merchandise in his bag had been paid for and when he showed the guards his receipts they exonerated him from any wrongdoing. "Tony wouldn't have let me do it," says Williams softly.

Williams speaks in an even, demoralized voice as he rehashes the incident. "I'll take full responsibility for what I did," he says painfully. "It was stupid. I was just messing around, but that's no excuse. I just had so much frustration built up inside of me that I think I needed somehow to draw attention to myself. I mean, I used to get interviewed by the press almost every day in other seasons. This year, nothing."

He has been trying to understand his behavior that night, struggling with the implication that he is just a weak individual who can be easily manipulated by those in power over him. As he points out, he has never been a disruptive force at UW. "I was the guy who led Bible studies." But this was different.

"I have never in my life done that. I had money in my pocket and I was ready to pay for the stuff, three neckties, but then there was just this impulse: 'What have I got to lose?' I was getting a new tie because I was going on my first travel game of the season, to Ohio State. The guy I was with, Lionell, he was depressed, too."

Williams is no longer looking for sympathy, just understanding.

"I see it as . . . a cry for help," he says, gazing out his open door as another student walks past. It is Tony Lowery. The quarterback waves and goes into his own room. "If it hadn't been shoplifting, I think it would have been violence. Just go out looking for someone to beat up."

He knows how pathetic that sounds, but he wants people to know it's the truth. "I just want the team to know why I did it," he says. "People think I'm a kleptomaniac. Lionell and I even asked if we could apologize to the team, but Alvarez said no."

There's nothing left to say, really. Williams remains seated on his bed, waiting for his father to arrive, the one man he does not want to see.

31

RICK ABERMAN WATCHES THE LOCAL TV NEWS TONIGHT AT SIX AND SEES A brief video report on the hospital patient Keith Breneman. Breneman is a shell of the person he was before that Halloween night, still suffering from the massive brain trauma he received at the hands of one or more UW football players in the parking lot behind Joe Hart's bar.

As the camera follows Breneman's attempts to deal with partial paralysis on his right side and both short- and long-term memory deficiencies by answering simple questions and attempting to put a nut on a screw, Aberman looks on in shock. He decides to drive over to Meriter Hospital to see if perhaps he can talk to Breneman or to his sister, Mary Ann Seuss, who has been helping to care for her brother. Something about this situation just isn't right, Aberman feels. Maybe he can help. Or maybe he can learn something that will help him.

In an article in the *Wisconsin State Journal* a few days ago, the hard-working Vic Feuerherd had reported on his own visit to the hospital and what he had seen of Breneman's condition. He described Breneman as having blackened eyes, stitches on his face and above his right ear, and being unable to walk without assistance, as well as being confused and unable to speak more than a few words at a time. He quoted Seuss as saying of the attackers, "It was like they meant to kill him. . . . Our biggest concern is not who injured whom, but the bottom line is how could someone—three people, two people, one person—do that to another human being and live with it."

In a sidebar entitled UW OFFICIAL WARNS AGAINST PREJUDGING, Feuerherd also quoted Mary Rouse, the University of Wisconsin dean of students, who urged the public not to judge the football players prematurely, but to wait until all facts come in. "I am deeply concerned about the trial by public opinion that seems to be taking place," she said. "Because UW-Madison football players were involved, the level of public interest has been intense." She then implored the public to "take a deep breath and let the legal process run its course."

Rouse, who has worked hard at UW to educate the student body about the dangers of alcohol abuse and immoral behavior, knows better than most about the damaging, rippling effect anger, violence, and prejudgment can have on people. The child of abusive parents who both committed suicide, Rouse watched as her only sibling, her older sister Catherine, forty-six, descended into insanity last January, gunning down her former lesbian lover and then barricading herself into her house on Van Hise Avenue, just a block and a half west of Camp Randall Stadium. As police closed in, firing tear gas into the house and igniting smoke bombs to cover their assault, Catherine Rouse killed herself with a bullet to the head.

Aberman parks his car in the hospital lot and asks at the front desk for directions to the third-floor rehabilitation center. He walks down the squeaky-clean hallway to the nurses' station and asks a nurse if it would be possible to visit with Keith Breneman.

The nurse walks down the empty hallway to a partly opened door, where she confers with a woman who is standing in front of the opening. Aberman recognizes that woman from the telecast as Breneman's sister. She looks at Aberman, then says something to the nurse, who pads silently back up the glistening hall to the nurses' station and faces Aberman.

"He is not seeing anyone," the nurse says.

Aberman looks back down at the sister, who goes inside the room and closes the door. It's been twenty-two days since Breneman was beaten like a punching bag in a gym. Aberman wonders if the boy will ever know what hit him.

*   *   *

As SNOW SWIRLS DOWN, MARKING THE CLOSING OF ANOTHER LOOP IN THE great seasonal chain, Robert Williams gets the call from Coach Barry Alvarez. There are four minutes left in this final game, in Williams's career, and it's time to play.

Williams jogs onto the field in front of stands that are emptying fast of spectators. 38,620 people supposedly came to this game—though 6,000 tickets were handed out free to Madison school kids during the week, and at least 5,000 other ticket-holding fans never showed up—but only one of the people in attendance means anything to Williams.

The Badgers line up with Williams at the tailback position. He goes in motion, but the ball is handed to another back for no gain. On the second play Tony Lowery fakes to one back and then gives Williams the ball and the frustrated young man bulls ahead for five yards. In the press box, the only people making note of this minor, yet emotionally complex, event are again the student writers.

"Is that a necktie he's wearing?" Barry Baum asks the group.

Williams gets the ball again on the next play, third and five, and crashes ahead for four yards. That makes it fourth and one, and Alvarez elects to punt. The ball sails away, and with it goes Williams's hopes, dreams, and torment. Wisconsin will not get the ball back. He's finished here. It's all over for Robert Williams, college football player.

The Badgers are ahead of Northwestern 32–14, and that is how the game will end. Before the gun sounds, though, Williams breaks away from his teammates on the bench and walks down near the west goal line. There he meets up with a man in a brown overcoat who has worked his way down out of the stands, past the fence, and onto the sidelines. They look at each other briefly, and then they hug each other hard.

Robert Williams and his dad.

When time expires, the players and students remaining raise a cry of victory. The seniors on the team stay on the field as the band plays to them. Those players who have already run into the locker room return for the celebration. It's cold and miserable outside, but nobody cares—this was a win, the second in a row, giving the Badgers a 5–6 record, something they haven't achieved since Dave McClain was alive—and is it not party time?

The entire team is now back on the field, and the players dance with cheerleaders, with Bucky Badger, with the trainers, with each other, as music director Mike Leckrone puts the band through its silliness. Players do the "Chicken Dance"; they surf to "Tequila"; they boogie to "Louie Louie"; they do the things that seem to have been handed down from year to year, student to student, team to team—like artifacts from one civilization to the next. Lowery walks amidst the revelers, smiling and occasionally letting fly with a directionless whoop. He threw a nice touchdown pass today, scrambled smartly to avoid the rush, and played pretty well overall. His burden, too, has been laid down.

Yesterday he thought about his relationship with Alvarez, and the relationship he'd had way back with Don Morton.

"Alvarez ended his twenty-three days' of 'no talking to Tony' last Wednesday before the Minnesota game," Lowery recalled. "He said, 'Good pass,' I think. Then, when we were on the field stretching in Minnesota he came up to me and said, 'Ready to go?' "

The Minnesota win was a big one, and at the end the Wisconsin quarterback had found himself jumping with ecstasy, leaping into the arms of the nearest person to him. It happened to be Barry Alvarez. "I didn't know it was him," Lowery said. He thought of Alvarez's treatment of him this year, "I don't think it's personal. I think it's business."

That's the word that came to him after he quit the football team following his sophomore season—*business*. "Don Morton is one of the nicest men I've ever met, but coaching, he couldn't do it. The veer. I had dreams of playing pro ball, but I knew it wasn't going to happen in that offense. We called everything at the line—things like 'Red 18 Option,' or 'White 19 Option.' Red was right and white was left. Now, if I'm a defensive end, I think I'll figure that out after a while. Red was *always* right; white was *always* left. So I hoped Morton would get fired after that third year. And he did. I mean, nothing personal. Just business."

The snow has stopped, but there is an icy glaze remaining on the field from the flakes that have fallen and melted on the turf, then frozen again as the temperature has plummeted. Jason Maniecki has the look of a young boy at a birthday party. He dances the polka with great gusto, then sways back and forth with his brethren as the team joins the crowd in singing "Varsity." The future beckons to him. He hollers with delight as the UW band finally plays the school's true anthem, the Budweiser song.

In the UW men's non-conference basketball game against Southeast Missouri State, a strange thing happens: Every time guard Billy Douglass enters the game, a large part of the crowd boos him lustily. When he comes out of game, the same fans cheer. Mostly, those fans are students—but they are several thousand strong, and their sarcasm trickles down to affect all in attendance, until it seems the entire Fieldhouse crowd is eager to heap derision on the beleaguered player. When Douglass commits a turnover and then is removed by Steve Yoder, the audience rises and gives the senior player a raucous standing ovation.

One of the most shocked people in attendance is Barry Baum. He can't believe what he is seeing and hearing, feeling an odd mixture of pride, significance, and shame over his role in this affair. He and fellow scribe Rob Reischel have ridiculed Douglass to such an extent in the *Daily Cardinal* that their cynicism has spread to all Badger basketball fans. Baum asks *Milwaukee Sentinel* writer Michael Hunt if he has ever seen anything like this at a UW home game. "No," says Hunt. In his basketball column tomorrow, Vic Feuerherd will describe the tumult as "the longest and loudest chorus of boos ever delivered to an individual UW player."

After the game, which UW wins in overtime, 82–71, Yoder complains bitterly about the unfair treatment of Douglass by the crowd and the student writers, describing the behavior as a "sickness." He then says, "Some of our school newspaper writers beat that poor kid up all the time. But then, I don't have any idea what they're all about sometimes, either."

Baum stands to the side, listening. He feels a tap on his shoulder. It's forward Carlton McGee. The two move off and McGee tries to explain to Baum how hard it is for the team to try to play with enthusiasm and unity when it feels undermined by its own peer group. "We're family this year," the 6'7", 205-pound McGee says. "Not like last year." He tries to explain more about the hurt of seeing a teammate ridiculed, and suddenly he is crying.

Baum looks up at the player in disbelief. Here is a skilled athlete, twenty years old, from Milwaukee—a guy who can dunk from just inside the free-throw line, a former two-time Wisconsin state high-jump champion, a black man who might not have that much in common with Douglass, a white from affluent Lake Forest, Illinois. But he cares. And he can't stop crying. He can't even finish what he is saying. He just looks at Baum and walks away.

Late at night Baum is still sitting in front of his word processor at the *Daily Cardinal*, looking at the keyboard as if the symbols are printed in Chinese. He's way beyond deadline on his story, but no matter. He's been rocked to his soul. Again.

"I felt bad when the students booed Douglass," he says. "But it didn't hit me until McGee broke down. You see what words can do to someone. That's the first time in my life. It's different even from Steve Lowe's death. I don't even remember the game. And it was an overtime, and Tracey Webster played great. But the game doesn't mean anything anymore."

Things were a lot simpler for him before tonight. The Steve Lowe incident affected him, but he was not a participant in that sadness, only an observer. This is different. "I feel like I grew up," he says. "It's corny, but I feel that. What I can do to people . . ."

He is overwhelmed by the flood of uncertainty pouring over him. The news is an easy thing to discern. But how do you write the news without hurting people? How do you say anything about anybody? How do you judge? How do you have fun? How do you rip? How do you control yourself once you have people's attention?

"Is it the money?" he asks. "Is that what makes people boo? People pay to see these guys play, but does that give them the right to be mean? It's not like they're paying eighty dollars to see a Knicks game. These players do have scholarships, and the rest of us have to pay for our education, but I don't know if that means all that much."

Thad McFadden, twenty-eight and out of college football since 1984, walks into a bare-walled conference room sixty miles from Camp Randall, wearing a short-sleeved shirt, Lincoln-green pants, and simple work boots. Outside it's four degrees above zero, with a windchill of twenty below, but this room is toasty. The state clearly does not scrimp on its heating bills.

McFadden is here at the Dodge Correctional Institution in tiny Waupun, Wisconsin, because he pretty much took all the concepts he learned in school and athletics about hard work and discipline and fair play and stomped on them like little porcelain teacups. He played for the USFL Birmingham Stallions for a while, made some decent money, discovered cocaine, and the rest is, well, right here in his prison record: six years for five counts of burglary, nine months (to be served concurrently) for retail theft, five years of probation for two counts of bail jumping, issuing a worthless check and forgery. "I'm glad it's stopped," says McFadden. "You know, that don't-give-up attitude, the attitude of the athlete? I have it."

It is why he felt compelled to write to his friend Tony Lowery to tell him to keep his head up and fight through the hard times at UW. McFadden put his own head down and took whatever he wanted for a while there, and look where it got him.

"Yessir, my drug use had really gotten out of control," he says. "That's really why I'm in here. I didn't do any physical harm to anyone. Just myself."

McFadden's father was a Baptist minister back in Flint, Michigan, and the family of six was fairly close-knit, until one day the Reverend McFadden walked out and didn't come back. Thad was going into tenth grade, and the ensuing divorce hurt him a lot, but he doesn't blame it for his problem. He doesn't blame anyone. He can't. Athletes are supposed to rise above the normal strife.

"Athletes are used to being praised and getting that VIP treatment," he said. "But when it's gone, it's tough. They say life goes on, and it does, but sometimes your identity is gone." When he injured his foot in a tryout with the Minnesota Vikings and then began the quick fade from professional sport, McFadden lost sight of himself, and his drug use kicked into high gear. Soon he was just a con man, using any means he could to get money to party onward.

"It all started when I was a rookie with Birmingham, and I went to a party for Stallion players and all this free coke was laid out, right there in the bathroom," he says. "I tried a line, and the thing was, I didn't really like it. Then I went to another party and I tried it again. And the thing I remember, as though he's talking to me right now, is this guy saying, 'That stuff right there destroys dreams.' I can hear it perfectly."

A guard looks at the door of the room. There's no place that

McFadden could run to, because this wing of the prison is well within the compound, deep inside the fences and lights and concertina wire and guard towers, so that any freedom here is really not freedom at all. But guards must check, because you never know. McFadden is twenty-five pounds above his college playing weight of 190, his head is shaved, and he wears a mustache, all of which combine with his prison clothes to make him look more like a middle-aged janitor than the speedster who caught a touchdown pass in the 1984 Hall of Fame Bowl. At any rate, McFadden is not breaking out of this joint; he's going to do his time (he's been in various jails for over half a year and may get early parole after going to boot camp next spring), and he's going to get back with his wife and two kids and make something of himself—he says.

"I talk to my mother now and I say there are two things in my life I've been successful at. She says, 'What is that?' And I say, 'I was a good athlete, and I was real good at drugs.' When I look back on it all, though, it is amazing. The cocaine, the girls, the parties. One day this teammate came in and cooked up some freebase, and I took a hit and almost passed out. He said, 'Thad, you all right?' And I kept smoking. How crazy is that?

"The crime started basically to support my habit after I'd run through everything I'd saved from my pro days. I went through sometimes a thousand, fifteen hundred a week. Like water. You know, I'd made all-league as a return specialist, and I thought that was just the beginning. 'Hey, you're really good!' I thought I was going to be around as long as Walter Payton. It's very dangerous territory."

McFadden nods to a passing guard. The office room across the hall was remodeled a while back by one Ed Gein, the Plainfield, Wisconsin, farmer turned human taxidermist, who was the model for Alfred Hitchcock's greatest movie character, Norman Bates. But that's another story.

"So a friend and I started burglarizing houses. We'd ring the bell, and if no one answered, we'd go in. I remember looking at my buddy and thinking, 'Here's this guy who used to come to Camp Randall to see me play. Man, what does he think of me now?' As it turns out, he would even get upset about it sometimes. He'd say, 'I remember watching you run back punts. I remember when you wouldn't even touch drugs. What happened to you?'"

McFadden sighs. "Even two of the cops who arrested me knew me from football. They were saying, 'What are you doing out here?' The thief I was with never got caught—people don't even know someone was with me. But it doesn't make any difference. I did the crime."

Indeed, he did, and when the police closed in, McFadden ran to an office building on Mineral Point Road to hide. He looked out a second-floor window and was stunned as he watched the news teams from different TV and radio stations arrive. It was almost like after a big game. "It was amazing. All these cameras and stuff, and I was thinking, 'How did they get here so fast?' "

He went into an office and called his wife, telling her he was in big trouble and that it was all over. Fortunately, it truly was all over.

Now, though, McFadden is preparing for the day he is released. He wants to move back to Madison, because, as he says, "It's a place where you want to raise your family." He also will try to reenroll at UW, since one of Dane County Circuit Judge Gerald Nichol's sentencing recommendations was that McFadden finish the fifteen credit hours he needs to graduate.

Back on campus, older but wiser, maybe this time he can get it right.

32

TODAY MARKS THE LAST CLASS OF THE SEMESTER IN WOMEN'S STUDIES 193, "Women and Their Bodies: In Health and Disease." The twenty-one students at the discussion group in Birge Hall pay attention as teacher Katherine Rhoades goes over some of the things that will be covered on the final exam—the benefits of an epidural block during childbirth, the sexual response cycle in females, the definition and properties of progesterone and estrogen, the purpose of balloon catheterization, among other things. Rhoades adds some practical advice as well. "Don't ever reuse a condom," she says. "Sloane writes that you can. Take my word for it—*don't*."

Nineteen young women listen attentively. They represent a cross-section of the many types of females on campus. One wears a lumberjack shirt. One wears a long skirt. Another woman has very short hair and a nose ring. Another wears a pink Ralph Lauren polo shirt and a pink bow in her hair. There are only two males in the class—a guy with longish hair and a distracted look, and Barry Baum.

This may have been Baum's favorite class of his four-and-a-half-year career here at UW. His love life is still a nearly invisible smudge on the horizon, but at least in this class he has ferreted his way into the temple of the sacred goddess queen herself, Woman, and he thinks he now knows better how to prepare his attack on her impregnable fortress. He has also spotted some candidates, some potential date material, right here in the inner sanctum.

The teacher asks the students to go one by one around the room and describe what they feel the benefits of this class have been for them.

"I know so much more about the shadowy things going on in my own body," says the first woman. "I use the knowledge every day. Or every month." Chuckles fill the room.

"It's made it so nice to discuss things with my mother," says another. "We've gotten closer."

Another tells about the frustration she feels as a woman over the poor condition of health care in this country, made all the clearer to her by the class lectures. Another says that her mother had a mastectomy last month and that this class has been very helpful in enabling the student to deal with that fact and give comfort to her mom.

"And you, Barry?" says the teacher.

Baum takes a deep breath. "I always knew women were complicated," he says. "But not this complicated. Plus, I can now carry on an in-depth conversation about Fallopian tubes."

Most of the class members laugh.

The next woman says, "I didn't want to have children before this class, but now I do." Then she turns to look venomously at Baum. "*Daughters* only."

As the class disperses, Baum approaches an attractive young woman in jeans and sweater and starts up a conversation with her. "Can I call you?" he asks tentatively, not making it clear if he means to ask her about women's studies or out for a date.

"Yes, Barry, anytime," the student says with a smile.

"You've really helped me, you know that," Baum says earnestly. "You explained menstruation so well. Menstruation was the only thing I did well on the last test."

"Oh, Barry," the girl laughs. She gathers her things and starts to leave. Then she turns to him. "I did explain everything, didn't I," she says.

She looks at him and smiles. He beams. What a wonderful class.

"I AM GERMAN," PETER TEGEN SAYS. AND ONE SENSES WHAT THAT MEANS AND implies. He is precise, aggressive, passionate, intelligent, and independent. He can be brooding and arrogant at times, but he also can be sentimental and vulnerable. And he does not want anybody messing with him or his program. "I have never seen the dependence on counseling you have in this country," he says with disgust. "I like the commonsense approach to problems. Too much counseling can easily become a problem itself."

It has been suggested to him that some of his runners have had emotional problems and/or eating disorders that perhaps merited psychological therapy, if not direct intervention from someone in a position of authority. The names of Heather Rawling, Jenny Kraeger, Stephanie Herbst, Katie Ishmael, and others have been brought up. Tegen answers with a question.

"When is enough enough?" he asks. "It's a very sensitive thing. Especially with women it gets misunderstood. You want the weight-to-strength relationship to be very, very narrow—not too much and not too little. Heather went too far. Obviously, from looking at that picture [in the track media guide] you can see that she has crossed that fine line. She brought herself to the bodyfat limit, and then she kept going. She kept pounding the road and not eating enough."

But, Tegen quickly adds, "I'm not in favor of all this counseling. I'd rather catch these things in a commonsense sort of way, without painting labels on the athletes. Something like *anorexic* is a tremendously negative label."

Tegen is working at the UW track now, sprinting back and forth between different athletes, assisting them with their tremendously varied events. He dashes off now to help a high jumper, simulating the takeoff for her, raising his arms into the air with spirited gusto. A moment later he trots over to the shot put ring to describe the cradling of the steel ball under the chin to a female thrower. He walks back and continues his thoughts, expressing them in passionate bursts of language thick with the accent of his native land.

"I tell people that after they run a marathon, they must consider themselves injured. Their bodies need repair. Sometimes you tell them to stop, and they don't. When you confront someone who isn't eating enough, sometimes they say, 'I'm counting calories.' If an athlete runs a double at a meet—a five thousand and a ten thousand, as Jenny did at the Big Ten—then injuries may start popping up. And they take too long to heal, because there isn't enough substance and nutrients there to repair tissue. They forget how much they need."

But couldn't a coach make his point by not letting the women run—by benching them, in effect, until they get healthier?

"There is a limit to what a coach can do," says Tegen. He hurries off to the high jump area once more. A spirited man, Tegen occasionally will do pirouettes out of sheer exuberance as he coaches his athletes. Though he has his critics among other coaches and among some administrators in the UW athletic department, Tegen has nothing but disciples among his runners past and present. It might be safe to say that most of his long-distance runners, in a manner of speaking, love him.

"It is easier to become obsessed with long-distance running than, say, high jumping," he continues. "You become like a computer, with a pattern running over and over, a program rerunning in your head." He grows more and more animated as he talks about coaching this most internal and individualistic of sports. His eyes blaze. He talks of "breaking the mold," of "teasing the maximum level," of "relaxing the nervous system," of "replenishing chemicals," of "surge training." His hands move in broad, graceful arcs of illustration.

"I consider being a coach being an artist," he says. "I am an artist. I try to know as much as I can about the paint, the brushes, the canvas—whatever I can to complete this masterpiece. I believe at a point it goes beyond science."

In his hand he has a sports magazine, written in German, open to an article that shows Cory Everson demonstrating step exercises. He looks at it briefly.

"She was interesting," he says of his former star pentathlete. "She went through some phases, an anorexic phase. But she is an obsessed kind of person. I remember her mom was obsessed with clocks. In her house, in every room, there were twenty clocks. They were very nice people, though." He looks again at the photos of his old athlete, sees her in her high-tech workout gear with her buffed, ripped physique.

His mind moves to his most recent star pupil, Suzy Favor Hamilton, married since last summer. "Suzy," he says happily. "The All-American girl. She never got to the point of obsession; there was always room for the rest of her life. She was the most talented athlete I've ever had. There is a biomechanical fit that lets her glide in a beautiful way. The length of her levers is just perfect. *Effortlessness.* Is that a word? That's what she has—effortlessness."

Tegen looks at the magazine again, then out at the track. "And she has a fierce will to win," he smiled, "that is not sweet at all."

He himself feels his own will to win being undermined by the upheaval in the athletic department. He is king of all that he sees, but he sees less and less these days. His elite female athletes and his artistry seem to have nothing to do with whatever goes on in Richter's and Fish's offices.

"In the last year we coaches are being intimidated," he says. "It's like they're saying, 'If you don't like it here, leave. Shut up or ship out.' What you've done in the past twenty years doesn't matter, all of a sudden. They have us on one-year contracts? It's ridiculous!"

The little man kicks at the ground. "It's like they want to be able to replace us with anybody," he says.

BARRY BAUM GETS A MESSAGE ON HIS PHONE MACHINE FROM A GIRL TODAY. BUT it's not the lovelorn call he's been waiting for all these years. He flips on the tape and listens as the young woman's voice says, "Hi Barry, this is a friend of yours. I'm just calling to let you know that I really enjoyed your article in the paper. However, I feel that you're very much a Jew, the biggest asshole on this campus! And I really would prefer that you really kept your nose out of everyone else's goddamn business, you Jew!"

He ponders the message. "She's right," he says. "My rabbi says I'm a Jew, too."

Then he replays the tape, stopping after the first sentence, the introduction, as it were.

A sensual glow crosses his face. "You know," he says, listening once more, "she sounds kind of sexy, doesn't she?"

DEAN OF STUDENTS MARY ROUSE HAS BEEN TESTED DEARLY BY THE HALLOW-een night beating of Keith Breneman. It appears now that charges will not be filed by police against anyone involved in the fracas, because no witness can state clearly what happened. Nobody's testimony would stand up under the scrutiny of a trial cross-examination, and the victim himself, Breneman, is still disabled and remembers nothing of the attack. Complicating matters are two verifiable facts: almost everyone involved—fighters and witnesses alike—had been drinking, and most of them, including the UW football players, were wearing masks. It was Halloween, after all. Though at least one witness has stated that two men held Breneman and beat him mercilessly, others deny this.

Still, Madison residents have been calling for Rouse to do something, to take a swat at athletes they feel are being treated with kid gloves. But she will do nothing, because she feels it would not be fair.

"I've never had so many calls from people saying I should suspend these players, but that would be grossly unfair," she says. "The student disciplinary code is limited to UW property or school-authorized events. The fight occurred off-campus, it wasn't a student who was beaten, and it wasn't at a UW activity. When all the police reports are finished, I'll look at them. But the right for full due process is one of the rights that students fought for in the sixties, one that must be applied equally. And athletes are students first, athletes second.

"We all make a grave error in treating student-athletes differently from the general student populace. We need to integrate them as much as we can. Maybe I'm out of it, but I don't place winning up there at the highest level of attainment. We overemphasize winning, and treat athletes differently. It's a terribly difficult thing, trying to change culture and make winning not important. I have three kids—one fifteen-year-old still at home—and I see the magnetism sports and winning have for him."

She knows when she is up against a force over which she has no control, but she doesn't care about that. "I want athletes treated like students. We did not take good care of our black athletes in the eighties. Their graduation rate was terrible; but then we did not take good care of our students, generally. We need safe, nonjudgmental spaces for athletes, for everyone. I'm not going to give up."

AL FISH SITS AT HIS DESK, READING THE HEADLINE IN TODAY'S *BADGER-HERALD*: STUDENT CHARGED WITH ATTEMPTED POISONING. Fish whistles and shakes his head.

"There were days when I felt like transferring," he says. "But I never wanted to *kill* my roommate."

Fish feels pretty good these days, overall. Many of the target objectives rising from the turmoil of the old bankrupt athletic department have been reached or approached in this past year. The five sports are gone. Crew is capped. Budgets are more or less under control. Football came in eleven thousand dollars short of what it had hoped to raise from its seven home games, but still it pulled in nearly $3 million, up a lot from the lean years. Home attendance averaged 49,665 per game, which was slightly under the 50,000 per game Fish and Richter had hoped for.

"It's kind of a miracle we came out so close," says Fish. "But it's kind of sad, too. When I figured fifty thousand, I thought I was low-balling."

The athletic department still has a deficit of more than a million dollars, but the department showed an operating profit of close to one hundred thousand dollars for the fiscal year 1990–91. Don't ask how; it was all done through belt tightening and the miracle of accounting.

Fish has some time on his hands, so he strolls over to the Field-house, where Mary Murphy is putting her basketball team through its paces. The women shoot free throws, and if they miss they are forced to run grueling ladder drills as punishment.

"Marine training," says Fish approvingly. "I bet Mary was feisty as a player. All those brothers."

He watches Peggy Shreve at point guard with the first team and sees that the squad still misses the cohesion it once had under Amy Bauer. Why not bring the young woman back? "She would have to ask us to come back," he says. "And apparently she's not going to." And what of the lawsuit Bauer is still threatening to bring? "We'd crush them if they brought it. They have no case," says Fish ruefully. "It's a shame when a lawyer uses a kid."

There has been a bit of a problem with strength coach Scott Raridon, Fish admits, and it may not be so easily resolved. Apparently Raridon has been doctoring the time card of weight room employee Traci Ferren, his girlfriend, fleecing the university out of several thousand dollars. UW police have said they will be turning their reports on the matter over to the county district attorney soon, along with a request for charges to be brought against Raridon and Ferren, a former shot-putter on the women's track team from 1987 to 1989.

Fish says that the other day he and Barry Alvarez sat down with Raridon and had a heart-to-heart talk. "I said I'd been hearing things that aren't good," says Fish. "This was just about other things, not even this time-card incident—about bringing women into the weight room after hours, a pistol he brought into his office, the fact the black players don't get along with him."

Fish gets up to go back to work. "It's a perfect example of hubris," he says of Raridon's arrogance. "He had a boss who he thought would protect him from everything."

Why?

Fish ponders this as Amber Landrigan, a six-foot-four-inch freshman, rejects a shot.

"I don't know."

33

THE USUAL GUESTS START ARRIVING AT SEVEN, TAKING THEIR PLACES AROUND the dining room table that is actually in a corner of Rick Aberman's living room, since his little apartment doesn't have a dining room, per se. What it has is a tiny area like this, where a table barely fits. It is Sunday night and very soon it will be New Year's Day, 1992, and the time has come for the psychologist's annual year-end poker party.

The attendees are Aberman's buddies—a lecturer in the business school, a public defender; a local merchant, running partners. Just guys. The same ones who come for the poker games on all the other weekends once a month through the year, ready to blabber, kibitz, harangue, eat junk food, bet nickels on inside straights, and basically act like kids again.

Within seconds of the card deck's being opened, somebody belches long and loud. Pizza has been passed around, and crumbs and grease are everywhere. Aberman's baseball cards are scattered about, and somebody holds out the plastic-covered Billy Ripken card that has an obscenity, "Fuck Face," printed on Ripken's bat handle. One of Ripken's teammates wrote it on the handle, thought it was hysterical. "I bought that for Rick," says old pal Bob Schwartz, proudly.

"What did you do, go into the store and ask for the 'Fuck Face' card?" asks a player.

Karen Parker comes out of the back room, and she and Aberman exchange kisses. Aberman even has a sports card for her, printed when she was featured on the UW women's soccer schedule in 1985. Most of the men say hello to Karen, then ignore her. An argument ensues about Donna Shalala, and one player calls her a "midget radical weasel."

"I heard that she wishes she had nothing to do with athletics," says a UW writing teacher. "She's just a politician, and by definition politicians are corrupt and dishonest."

"That's not true!" shouts another man, but his comments are lost in the uproar from an argument over the ante.

Parker looks on in disgust.

"You sticking around, woman?" asks Schwartz.

She calls him a pig and leaves to visit Steve Myrland and his girlfriend. The game continues on for several hours, past midnight, until the revelers count their change, wipe their hands on paper towels, zip their coats, and shake hands before heading into the night.

Karen returns and marvels at the sight before her. The residue from the poker game has been largely cleaned up; she is marveling at the basic, everyday decor that cannot quite be called filth, just disorder.

"Rick, look at this," she says. "You told me it was just for a while. You were moving, remember? That was six years ago."

Aberman apologizes. He'll be moving one of these days, he promises. When and where, he has no idea. He picks up today's Madison paper and begins reading the sports section. He spots a byline by Barry Baum, covering the men's basketball team in Hawaii.

"Our man in Honolulu!" says Aberman with New Year's Eve cheer. "The tropical journalist."

TODAY'S RUN IS A GOOD ONE. ABERMAN FEELS UNENCUMBERED BY HIS BODY FOR long stretches of time, as though he is the most efficient of machines, one that needs no fuel, no maintenance, no supervision. In places the snow crackles under his feet, and that brings his mind and body momentarily back into union. But soon he is drifting again.

So many things to think about. And yet nothing, really. The athletes will adapt. They always do.

Yesterday Al Fish called him—actually, Mona, his secretary,

did—and she said Fish wanted to talk to him at three-thirty, so would he please come by. Sure, why not? Then Al had to go pick up his kid at school or something, so the meeting got pushed back to four-thirty. Aberman stopped in to see Martin Smith before heading over to Camp Randall. Martin's runners are such thoroughbreds; they have just won their seventh straight Big Ten title and finished third in the NCAA championships, and Martin was named conference coach of the year. Martin told Rick about taking brooms and shovels and having all his guys help clear a path through the Arboretum so they can run through the snow. What a low-maintenance sport, said Aberman. What are you seeing Fish about? asked Smith. Aberman said he had no idea, he just hoped it wouldn't be boring.

Aberman got to Fish's office and saw that trainer Denny Helwig was already there. They shot the breeze, and then Fish sat down, and for a while all three of them yucked it up, made small talk.

And then Al gets sort of serious-looking and he turns to me and says, "This is difficult for me to do," and I'm thinking that maybe I'm going to start smiling again, because this is so canned and impersonal, and he's done it to so many other people. I feel like sprinting out that second and telling Martin to come up, because he'll enjoy this, but of course, there isn't time, because Al is continuing right along with his talk and I've gotta be here. I feel sort of disembodied, but not bad, because this is interesting. He says, "We decided not to include your position in next year's budget. We decided to just rely on campus resources and put your money toward other services." It's so silly, and I may even be grinning a little. I mention to Al that the people making the decision probably don't even know what I do around here, and then it strikes me, "Jeez, moron. Al makes the decisions around here." So a lot of things are going through my mind, but all I can think to say is how I've always wanted to make a resignation speech. And we all have a nice laugh at that. And then I look over at Denny and wonder why he's even here, and it dawns on me that he's here, obviously, as a witness. Al knows about these things. So I leave, and I start thinking about my future and how even my tiny salary was something to live on, a habit that I'd grown accustomed to, and then I think about all the kids, wondering how they'll be, if they'll find what they need somewhere else in the university. And I think of all the times on my runs where I've planned what I'd say if I was fired. "That's all right, I was going to give my money back for season tickets, anyway." "No problem, I think I've healed everyone." "Twenty thousand dollars? My God, you could buy a third of a strength coach with that!" "Can I at least take my clock?" "Funny how the sick people never come in for help."

The white ground sails beneath the runner's feet, some of it rising briefly into the air as powder after each step. In the end, Aberman said nothing before he left the office, but what he thought through all the jumbled thoughts in his mind was this: *Hello, world.*

Postscript

On January 1, 1994, an unbelievable thing happened to the University of Wisconsin: its football team won the Rose Bowl.

No one could have predicted this. It had never happened before. When the Badgers danced off the field in Pasadena, 21–16 victors over UCLA, ranked fifth in the nation, first in the Big Ten, owners of UW's first winning season in a decade (10–1–1), there was one prevailing sentiment among delirious boosters, students, and alumni of the school—those who recalled the recent stormy athletic department past, at least—and it was: My God, did we actually do it?

The answer was twofold. A resounding, chest-thumping *yes!* And a much quieter *well, maybe.*

Certainly the turnaround of the football team—1–10 just three seasons earlier—was little short of miraculous. Barry Alvarez had recruited well since his rookie season, had coached well, and had made believers of all the people he needed to make into believers. The squad was rough and fast and strong and skilled, attributes not often associated with UW grid teams. It had at the helm a sophomore quarterback named Darrell Bevell, whom Alvarez had found in one of those moments of serendipity that are needed by any program hoping to rise out of the gutter. Bevell, from Scottsdale, Arizona, had gone to school for one year at Northern Arizona before leaving to serve on a two-year Mormon mission in Cleveland. UW offensive coordinator Brad Childress had been an assistant at Northern Arizona during Bevell's stay at that school, and he found the young man after the mission and persuaded him to continue his travel adventure by becoming a Badger. In the fourth quarter of the Rose Bowl, the mature leader—Bevell is married and will turn twenty-six as a senior—scrambled 21 yards for what turned out to be the winning touchdown. It was the longest football run of his life. "I can't believe somebody didn't catch me," he said in the locker room afterward.

It all was hard to believe, and yet . . . and yet this was precisely what Donna Shalala had in mind when she hit the deck running her first day in Madison. She left the university in 1993 to become the U.S. Secretary of Health and Human Services, but she left with dynamic people in place in the athletic department—Richter, the sports icon; Fish, the rainmaker; Alvarez, the turf messiah. She said it could be done—winning, making money, getting excellent—and she did it. What, she would ask everyone, did you expect?

For the 1993 season Wisconsin had an average attendance of 75,507 for its five home football games, an increase of more than 14,000 people per game from the previous season (and more than 34,000 over the low ebb of 1989), the largest increase in the nation. The attendance set a record for UW and pushed the athletic department's money needle well into the black. In September 1993, the department announced that it was out of debt. "As of June 30, 1994, we expect to have a half-million-dollar reserve," states Fish. Sums up Richter, "It was football that took us down, and football that brought us back."

So why the *well, maybe?* It is because none of the good things came without a price. Even as the football team was beating Michigan, 13–10, on October 30—the Badgers' first win against the hated Wolverines in a dozen years—disaster was brewing. Ecstatic students trying to storm the field at the end of the game formed an avalanche of humanity that rolled down the stands and over two fences and everything else in its path. Rejoicing players were abruptly confronted by mayhem, as bodies piled upon bodies near the edge of the field. It was Parents Day, and some mothers and fathers got to see their own offspring trampled in the stampede. Shalala, wearing a red Bucky sweater, had returned from Washington, D.C., for the game, and she likewise witnessed the chaos. Players Brent Moss, Joe Panos, Mike Brin, and others pulled suffocating people from the mounds near the fences; Panos could be seen later on national TV, weeping in sadness over the event. While no one was killed, seventy-three people were injured, six of them critically. To outsiders, Mad-Town looked more like Sarajevo than Florence.

Then, too, the athletic department's money problems did not simply vanish with the filling kitty. A finance-based pragmatism now colors everything the athletic department does. "We look at this as a business," says Richter today. "If we're not successful, we don't exist."

But with the increased revenue of success has come the pressure to spend money on those things the department needs, or believes it does. Though the five sports that were cut in 1991 are still gone, the department must add new women's sports to bring the school's male-female participation ratio closer to the federally mandated 50-50 split than its current 65-35 male/female ratio. The department has announced the addition of women's softball, beginning in 1995, with twenty-five players and two coaches included, and has hinted that it will add a second women's team in another sport beginning in 1996, most likely lacrosse or lightweight crew, adding another twenty-five women and two coaches to the roster. "We wouldn't do this if we didn't have to," says Richter. Of course, gender equity also could be achieved by jettisoning more men's sports, but Richter has put away his axe for good. He knows that successful businesses grow, not shrink.

The financially capped sports of men's and women's crew remain capped, at $180,000 annually for men and $150,000 for women. Starting this fall, women's crew will receive annual increases of $10,000 until its budget is the same as the men's. After that, who knows? All the sports need new equipment. Buildings need refurbishing. Coaches want more pay. Things have to *look* big-time. The department, once the laughingstock of its intercollegiate brethren, is now the fourth-highest-rated university sports organization in the country, according to the Sears Director's Cup rankings, which tabulate a school's success in all sports. Once an athletic department wins games, it always wants things, such as buildings and fields and locker rooms and uniforms, that surpass what's there now. Athletic departments have an implicit mandate to grow larger and more complex. It is a mandate that the UW athletic department is now following.

The football team played its final 1993 conference game against Michigan State on December 4 in, of all places, Tokyo. Originally scheduled to be played on October 2 in Madison, the game was moved before the season by Fish, Richter, and Alvarez to the later date and foreign location so that the players could experience something resembling a "bowl game." Not incidentally, the department pulled in $400,000 from the Japanese sponsors. While it seemed a good deal at the time, the move wound up costing UW at least $100,000 compared to what the resurgent team could have made playing in a sold-out Camp Randall Stadium.

That success came so swiftly and so unexpectedly to the UW athletic department has only added to the confusion. Has the athletic department, and sports in general, gotten too big and influential at UW? What about the academic mission of the school; has it been undermined by this newfound lust for victory afield? Do all those red-clad boosters waving Rose Bowl pennants have their priorities in order? It is noteworthy that while Alvarez signed a fifteen-year contract with the school this May, a deal promising him more than $400,000 per year, with $350,000 in bonuses kicking in every five years, teachers at the university were more than a little concerned with their own low pay. According to a 1993 survey, UW professors' salaries were at the bottom of the pay scale among the nation's top twenty universities. Even the new UW chancellor, David Ward, makes about a quarter-million dollars less per year than the football coach.

The athletic department's expenses just keep piling up. The hockey team has continued winning and is profitable, but now the athletic department is making $2.7 million worth of building improvements to the Coliseum as well as expanding the existing ice sheet to Olympic size. Basketball coach Steve Yoder was fired in March 1992, and former New York Knicks coach Stu Jackson was hired to take his place—at a sizable pay increase, to around $275,000, plus whatever else Jackson could line up on his own. His month-long 1993 summer basketball camp, held on campus, netted him over $72,000, for instance. Of course, Jackson was exactly what the department had been seeking—a savvy, sophisticated former pro coach who could maybe reel in some fellow African-Americans from the high school ranks to help turn the program around. Jackson quickly did just that, signing seven-foot phenom Rashard Griffith out of Martin Luther King, Jr., High School in Chicago in 1993. Griffith promptly led the Badgers to an 18–11 record and UW's first NCAA tournament bid in forty-seven years.

Still, this success gave rise to problems that didn't exist when the old team was fumbling through a typical season. The nineteen-year-old Griffith complained about Jackson's coaching, even threatening to transfer to another school or enter the NBA draft if things weren't done to "make me happy." Jackson himself was wooed in April by Iowa State for the head coaching job there at a reported $600,000 a year for five years. Jackson vowed to stay in Madison, and the department threw him some more money to keep him happy.

With the Fieldhouse sold out for the first time in UW history, it was time to bang the drum for a new, modern basketball building. Fish drops the concept drawings on his desk now and says, "We're making money, and the customers are advocating it." *Customers.* What the customers want, apparently, is a multiuse convocation center, which is rendered on the white page as a large gray trapezoid located between Regent Street and West Dayton Street, a couple of blocks east of Camp Randall.

"Fifty million, approximately," says Fish. "Approval can't come until July of '95, then eighteen months construction." It will happen, he implies. It can't be stopped.

Though the Badger football program has been a smash on the field, it has made academic concessions to the demands of the sport. Though UW administrators say they would like to have athletes on campus be no different from the students around them, clearly that is not the case on the football team. The average SAT score of entering UW students is 1090, while for those members of the football team who took the test and entered school from 1990 to 1992, Alvarez's first three years as head coach, the average is 825. Those SAT scores place Wisconsin ninth in the Big Ten among football programs.

There are more black players on the football and basketball teams than before, but that trend has not been followed by the school's general admissions. There are fewer black students at UW now than there were in the midseventies, just 794 out of a total enrollment of nearly 41,000 in 1993–94. A recent survey by a UW-LaCrosse psychology professor indicates that the Madison campus has by far the worst racial climate of the thirteen schools in the UW system. The black athletes at UW-Madison might be forgiven for feeling they have been brought in solely for their ability to contribute to the athletic department's bottom line.

Times change. In 1993, Wisconsin—the state—suffered the indignity of being overtaken by California as the leading milk producer in the nation. This was a crown Wisconsin had worn proudly for eighty years, and one it was loath to relinquish. Milk production "is just one small category" of the diary business, Governor Tommy Thompson sniffed defensively at a press conference in Madison.

Wisconsin is still the undisputed king of cheese-making, for example, and it has three hundred thousand more cows than California. The country's cheese prices are set at the National Cheese Exchange in Green Bay. Still . . .

Richter, too, sees changes in his field that are dispiriting. "The same problems aren't here from a couple years ago," he says, "but it will be a constant battle for us to stay solvent, because of the demands of gender equity, the escalating costs of all sports, and the uncertainty of TV revenue. We're always trying to find new revenue sources."

Revenue sources? Hello, Mr. Fish.

On the administrative officer's wall, where there once was a poster of a UW football player urging fans to come to a big game, there now is a framed photograph of the rock band U2, performing live in Camp Randall Stadium.

"The Edge. Bono," says Fish, pointing fondly at two figure writhing on stage beneath several automobiles suspended by cables from overhead beams. "The Zoo Tour."

The Zoo Tour's stop at Camp Randall in September 1992 netted the athletic department almost $150,000. Fish set it up that way. And three months before that windfall, he brought in Genesis, skimming another 150 grand for the department.

"I turned down McCartney," he adds with a shrug. "Not enough." Fish remains at UW, earning $72,000 a year in a relatively anonymous and thankless job, because he feels his duty isn't completed yet, and because he gets a kick out of messing with people's minds and playing with this giant money machine that is better than any carnival ride in the world. Athletic department official as rock promoter? Why not?

"Pink Floyd is coming this summer," he continues. "Sold out in a day and a half."

Three weeks after this conversation Fish will announce that the athletic department has signed the Rolling Stones to play in late August as part of the band's "Voodoo Lounge" world tour. The take should be about $125,000. Fish tells a reporter that he doesn't foresee any crowd control problems for the concert, despite the Stones' history of raucous behavior, because the band "is older than me, and any group older than me has got to attract a sedate crowd."

Any other schemes being worked just now?

Fish thinks. Sure. There's the UW Athletic Hall of Fame Terrace, the semicircular patio being inlaid with bricks in front of the Shell, next to the Camp Randall parking lot. A Badger fan can buy a brick for one hundred dollars, have his name carved into it, and then have it placed among the other bricks in the area. The terrace is outside and covered with snow a good part of the winter, and it's no place to hang out even in the summer, and the names carved into the early bricks are already fading away after less than a year of being exposed to the elements—but, heck, as the pamphlet says, "Bricks make great gifts—birthday, anniversary, graduation, etc.—especially for the Badger supporter who has everything."

The deal is almost all profit, the bricks being cheap as dirt, and Fish says that nearly two thousand of the objects have been sold so far. "Jim Bakken was behind this," he acknowledges.

Anything else?

Fish points to a pamphlet on the table. Its cover says BADGER MAX in black letters beneath a red-tinted photo of a track runner sprinting across a blurred background. To the left of the runner is a small logo stating OFFICIAL "W" SPORTS DRINK. At the top of the photo is the statement DEVELOPED AND USED BY U.W. ATHLETES. A yellow lightning bolt is superimposed across the word MAX.

"We're taking on Gatorade," says Fish with a little smile. "Product development. We're starting soon at seven hundred locations in Dane and Rock Counties. Grocery stores, convenience stores. We make two to three dollars a case, and our goal is to move one hundred thousand cases this year. Then we get bigger."

He suggests a walk to the football weight room in the McClain facility, to see Badger Max at work. En route he says, "We co-opted two hundred fifty thousand dollars' worth of advertising for our introduction of the stuff, on TV, radio, and billboards." He wrinkles his brow slightly, reflecting. "Yes, co-opted is the word."

And what did UW give to the promoters in return for their kindness?

"Tickets," he replies. "We're hot."

In a room at one end of the vast weight-training area, football players clad in gym clothes and lifting belts mill about, sweating and muscle-pumped, filling cups with brightly hued liquid from the four large vats. They guzzle the fluid, then go back to the benches and racks in the weight area. The drink is Badger Max in its four incarnations, as germinated right here in the football headquarters: red, green, orange, purple. No doubt there are fancy flavor names to entice the public?

"Nope," says Fish. "We want it simple. 'Cherry,' 'Lime,' 'Orange,' 'Grape.' Easy to order. Easy to buy."

He starts asking players which flavor they prefer. Some very large athletes think long and hard before answering. Cherry seems to win out.

Next to the Badger Max vats is another container with thick pink goop in it. Occasionally players fill a cup with the stuff and slowly drink it down. It is a high-protein muscle-building concoction that somebody in the football program developed. Fish is asked if having such a product here isn't a blatant violation of NCAA rules, since it is a food not available to the student body generally, and certainly not for free.

"Yes," he answers smoothly. "If it were solid food." He taps the keg. "This, you'll notice, is liquid."

On the walk back to his office Fish peeks into the old, stinking, overheated wrestling room off the second-floor hallway in Camp Randall. The old room has vanished; this new place is immaculate, white-walled, gray-carpeted, odorless, well-lit, with half a dozen people quietly sitting at desks partitioned one from the other by movable walls, tapping on computers.

"Tracking money," says Fish.

A few years ago the department didn't even have computers, let alone enough money to track. Whom did Fish scam for these high-tech machines?

"Nobody," he says. "We paid."

Why?

Fish ponders this a moment, looks up, then down, seems to draw a blank. "I must have been tired that day," he offers.

Sometimes that will happen. There are moments when it must seem so easy to get money, to receive freebies, to pick people's pockets for donations to the sports juggernaut, that Fish just flat-out forgets to ask. There are so many UW fans out there now who are in a frenzy to be part of this rare thing. Is there any better way to explain the auction at this year's Butch's Bologna Bash, in which the five pens Alvarez used to sign his fifteen-year coaching contract—in the manner of a world leader endorsing an important treaty—were sold to bidders for, in order, $2,000, $2,300, $2,600, $3,700, and $5,900?

The University of Wisconsin athletic department needs to keep doing well, because supporters now expect it to and because the till had better never run dry again. "I think back to those days of the sports cuts and being in the red," says Richter, "and I get sick to my stomach. It was the worst time ever. Nothing compares. But we always felt we wouldn't be alone for long, that no athletic department could escape some of the things we were going through. In a lot of ways we were just ahead of the curve."

Curve or no curve, sometimes Richter must ponder the department's new $25 million budget for 1994–95 and wonder how and why it got there. In 1990 the budget was $15 million, and that was *before* five sports were dropped and two capped. The axiom holds: There is no amount of money an athletic department can't spend. In truth, UW's woes were never really about money, anyway. They were about something less precise, less tidy, less easily understood than money. Money, and its absence or abundance, was just a simple concept to latch on to to make sense of events. As it is to rich entrepreneurs, money to the department was just a marker indicating something that had already happened.

The tumult was about pride fulfillment and ego-gratification, and about saving face and pursuing excellence and, yes, about kicking ass. UW did all those things, and now it must decide if it was worth it.

THE CHARACTERS IN THIS BOOK HAVE GONE THEIR SEPARATE WAYS SINCE THAT singular year bound them together. This is what they are doing as of late spring 1994.

Rick Aberman works for the University of Minnesota athletic department, counseling the men's hockey and baseball teams, and is in private practice at the Minneapolis Sports Medicine Center.

Barry Alvarez is the head football coach at the University of Wisconsin.

Jim Bakken is the Associate Athletic Director in charge of Special Events at the University of Wisconsin.

Amy Bauer graduated with distinction (above a 3.5 GPA) in December 1993, and is a certified preschool-through-kindergarten teacher living in Durand, Wisconsin. In April 1993, she lost the lawsuit she brought against coach Mary Murphy for invasion of privacy and defamation of character, believed to be the first suit of its kind brought against a college coach. Though Bauer lost her case, psychologists on both sides agreed she suffers from clinical depression because of her treatment by Murphy, and the jury foreman commented after the trial, "I'm glad I wasn't Amy Bauer."

Barry Baum is a freelance writer living in Los Angeles. He has had articles published in the *Chicago Sun-Times*, the *Detroit Free Press*, the *Los Angeles Times*, and the *Washington Post*, among other large papers. He has appeared as a featured contestant three times on the TV show *Love Connection*.

Keith Breneman is still suffering from the beating he received on Halloween night in 1991, with short-term memory, coordination, and balance problems. He has been unable to hold a job, having most recently been fired as a carpenter, because he could not swing a hammer properly. He lives at his parents' home in Rhinelander.

Matt Buss played a reserve role on the UW hockey team and graduated in May 1994 with a degree in mechanical engineering.

Meredith Chang transferred to the University of Iowa on a gymnastics scholarship in 1991 and recently completed her senior season there.

Duane Derksen is a goaltender for the Adirondack Red Wings in the American Hockey League.

Greg Elkin is the assistant sports information director at Indiana

University, acting as the liaison between head basketball coach Bobby Knight and the press.

Al Fish is still the administrative officer for the UW athletic department.

Margie Fitzpatrick was named head women's volleyball coach at Northwestern University in February 1994.

Jim Frueh is a product design engineer for the Amana Corporation in Cedar Rapids, Iowa, and will be enrolling at Princeton University in the fall on a scholarship to study for his Ph.D. in aerospace engineering.

Dave Gassman is a graduate student at the New York Law School in New York City.

Suzy Favor Hamilton lives in Oregon, where she is training for the 1996 Olympics in the 1500 meters.

Sean Hill played for the Montreal Canadiens on their 1993 Stanley Cup championship team and is currently a defenseman for the Anaheim Mighty Ducks.

Elroy Hirsch is a part-time consultant for the UW athletic department, earning $20,000 for his services. "He is a goodwill ambassador," says Pat Richter.

Tami Holmquist works as an accounting software consultant for Suby, Von Haden & Associates in Madison.

Katy Ishmael works as an assistant manager at a sporting goods store in Vail, Colorado.

Jason Kerstein is the manager of the Lone Star Barbecue Restaurant in Waukesha, Wisconsin, and serves on the board of directors of the United States Fencing Association.

Jenny Kraeger is a marketing officer for the Chicago Power of the National Professional Soccer League.

Tony Lowery earned his degree in rural sociology from Columbus (Ohio) State University in 1993, and is now an independent distributor for Omnitrition International, a nutritional supplement company. He has also signed to play quarterback with the Cleveland Thunderbolts of the Arena Football League.

Doug Macdonald is one of the top goal scorers for the AHL Rochester Americans, a farm club of the NHL Buffalo Sabres.

Jay Macias is a seldom-used quarterback behind twenty-four-year-old sophomore starter Darrell Bevell.

Thad McFadden was released from Waupun prison to a halfway house in 1992. In December 1993 he left, stole a car, and was rearrested in January 1994. He is currently serving a three-month sentence at the Drug Abuse Correctional Center in Winnebago.

Jason Maniecki is a backup noseguard entering his fourth year on the football team.

Tom Miller is a portfolio management assistant for Robert Baird & Company in Milwaukee and is studying for the Chartered Financial Analyst Test to become a registered financial analyst.

Don Morton says he is "in the process of leaving Madison" and is "looking at some different things in athletics," but cannot be more specific. "It is definitely time to move on."

Josh Morton is a sophomore walk-on quarterback on the football team at the University of North Dakota.

Brent Moss returns for his senior season at UW after winning the Big Ten Most Valuable Player Award and finishing as the third-leading rusher in the nation.

Mary Murphy resigned as the UW women's basketball coach in April after the UW athletic board recommended her contract not be renewed. Her poor relations with her players was cited as a main reason for the dismissal.

Steve Myrland is on leave from UW and is working as the strength and conditioning coach for the NHL San Jose Sharks.

Mike Peckham is a recreation specialist and head basketball coach at the Federal Correctional Institution in Estill, South Carolina.

Mark Pflughoeft teaches art at the Monona Grove Middle School and High School in Monona, Wisconsin.

Nick Polczinski is a sales representative for a wine wholesaler in the Fox River Valley area in Wisconsin. He has trimmed down to 310 pounds, but still wears a 20-36 dress shirt and a 56-XL sport coat.

Scott Raridon is an artificial joints salesman in Omaha. In August 1992, Raridon was charged with misconduct in public office and forgery in connection with turning in false time cards for his girlfriend. He later pled guilty to one count of misconduct in public office.

Barry Richter played on the 1994 United States Olympic hockey team and is now a defenseman for the Binghamton, New York, farm club of the NHL New York Rangers.

Pat Richter is in his fifth year as the athletic director for the University of Wisconsin, making him the longest-reigning AD in the Big Ten.

Greg Ryan resigned as women's soccer coach in March for religious reasons, stating in a letter to Pat Richter that "after many days of prayer God broke through my heart," and "simply asked me to follow Him, making it clear that I could not go back into the world."

Dick Schrock runs a Maid-Rite fast-food restaurant in Madison.

Donna Shalala is the United States Secretary of Health and Human Services, appointed by President Bill Clinton.

Paul Soglin, the mayor of Madison, had heart bypass surgery in February 1994, and while he was recovering at home, he and his family (including his mother, who was visiting) were awakened in the night by the smell of gasoline. An arsonist had soaked all the entrances to the house with gasoline, but the torch that was to ignite the fuel had gone out in the snow. The arsonist has not been apprehended. The reason for the crime is not known.

Butch Strickler is grinding meat and preparing for the next Butch's Bologna Bash.

Stall-Tactics, the Milwaukee-based advertising firm, continues to place advertising in restrooms throughout Wisconsin and, according to president John Mueller, will be expanding to Florida soon.

Heather Taggart is completing her second year of medical school studies at the University of Nebraska–Omaha.

Mike Verveer is a legislative aid for state representative Tammy Baldwin in Madison.

Steve Yoder lives in Indianapolis and is a partner in the National Scouting Report newsletter of Indiana and has done color commentary for college basketball games produced by Ray-Com.